Practical Audacity

Critical Human Rights

Scott Straus & Tyrell Haberkorn, Series Editors;
Steve J. Stern, Editor Emeritus

Books in the series Critical Human Rights emphasize research that opens new ways to think about and understand human rights. The series values in particular empirically grounded and intellectually open research that eschews simplified accounts of human rights events and processes.

Practical Audacity

*Black Women and International
Human Rights*

Stanlie M. James

The University of Wisconsin Press

The University of Wisconsin Press
728 State Street, Suite 443
Madison, Wisconsin 53706
uwpress.wisc.edu

Gray's Inn House, 127 Clerkenwell Road
London EC1R 5DB, United Kingdom
eurospanbookstore.com

Printed in the United States of America
This book may be available in a digital edition.

Library of Congress Cataloging-in-Publication Data

Names: James, Stanlie M. (Stanlie Myrise), author.
Title: Practical audacity : black women and international human rights / Stanlie James.
Other titles: Critical human rights.
Description: Madison, Wisconsin : The University of Wisconsin Press, [2021] |
    Series: Critical human rights | Includes bibliographical references and index.
Identifiers: LCCN 2020051975 | ISBN 9780299333706 (hardcover)
Subjects: LCSH: International law and human rights. | African Americans—Civil rights. |
    African American women civil rights workers—Biography. |
    African American women lawyers—Biography.
Classification: LCC KZ1266 .J36 2021 | DDC 341.4/8—dc23
LC record available at https://lccn.loc.gov/2020051975

ISBN 9780299333744 (paperback)

The cover photo is of *Brick House*, a stunning sixteen-foot-tall bronze bust of a Black woman created by artist Simone Leigh. It was the inaugural commission for the High Line Plinth, a landmark destination for public art in midtown New York City. A copy of the sculpture was installed in November 2020 at the entrance to the University of Pennsylvania in Philadelphia. Leigh is the first Black woman to exhibit her artwork at La Biennale di Venezia.

Dedicated to human rights
practitioners, especially

Adrien Wing

Lisa Crooms (Robinson)

Hope Lewis (1962–2016)

Catherine Powell

Judge Gabrielle Kirk McDonald

Patricia Viseur Sellers

Ayesha Imam

Loretta Ross

Linda Burnham

Dazon Dixon Diallo

Jaribu Hill

Filomina Chioma Steady

Barbara Phillips

Gay McDougall

Contents

Acknowledgments

I thank all the women who so graciously responded to my requests for interviews. The respondents were highly knowledgeable and deeply committed to transformative change through the development and application of human rights. Our conversations were most certainly enlightening but often punctuated with great gusts of laughter even as I listened and learned from the very serious information they so willingly shared with me about their work. Several of the women that I interviewed thanked me for the opportunity to be interviewed because it allowed them some precious time to reflect on the work that they were engaged in. They were so busy that they very rarely had time to take stock of how and what they were doing and why. One even mentioned that no one had really recognized the importance of their work aside from their colleagues. She appreciated the fact that I provided questions that helped them reflect on their work and that others outside their human rights cohort would be provided with an opportunity to recognize and appreciate their endeavors because of this book.

I am so grateful to my wonderful collegial friends who have traveled so patiently with me along the path of bringing this book to fruition. They include Nellie McKay, a literary scholar, who continues to be sorely missed although her absence has been softened by time. She read this manuscript in its very early stages and provided tough criticism in her direct and loving manner, impressing upon me the need to make it interesting and readable. I have tried to follow those instructions. Aili Tripp, another close friend and brilliant colleague, encouraged me every step of the way, and opened her home to me during one glorious fall when I returned to Madison on a writing sabbatical. Mary Margaret Fonow recruited me to Arizona State University, where we collaborated with our colleagues to imagine and then do the hard work of building the School of Social Transformation. Even though she was busy being a brilliant founding administrator, she always found time to read the chapters of this manuscript and provide important criticism and support. She, her partner, and another family share their pod with me during these difficult days of the COVID-19 pandemic. Craig Werner, another literary and cultural scholar, brought his superb talent for incisive editing to bear on this manuscript. Florencia Mallon, historian, feminist, mentor, and friend, shared her brilliance with me in so many critically important ways over my many years at the University of Wisconsin–Madison. Freida High Tesfagiorgus, artist, art historian, Black feminist, is the person I have relied upon for artistic expertise throughout my career. This is the third book for which she guided me toward beautiful and absolutely appropriate artwork to grace the covers. Not only does she find wonderful and uplifting art by Black/African women, but she makes sure that the editors display the art in the most attractive and effective way. Jualynne Dodson, Michigan State University, hosted me in her lovely home for six weeks to write, as did Kathy Sanders in Madison, Wisconsin. Those quiet periods of time were crucial to the progress of this project.

I received critical financial support from the Ford Foundation that enabled traveling to meet the respondents in the places where they worked and lived as well as with critical opportunities to write in supportive environments. Along the way, I received sabbatical and leave support from both the University of Wisconsin–Madison, where this project was conceived and initiated, and Arizona State University, where it matured and was completed. I was blessed with opportunities for writing: in Santa Fe at the wonderful Women's International Studies Center; in Newark, New Jersey, at the beautiful Easton's Nook, where the hospitality and the insistence on accountability provided by the two sisters, Jacqui and Nadine, were incredible. I so enjoyed that time with my colleagues Deborah Johnson and Beronda Montgomery as we worked on our respective projects and enjoyed the fabulous meals prepared by Nadine! I also stayed in Lynn Bolles's comfortable "tree house" with the lovely view on Martha's Vineyard where I wrote during the days but enjoyed evening meals and wine, early morning walks on the beach, and lively conversations with old and new friends, especially Carolyn Brown, Deborah Gray White, Sharon Harley, Charlene Hunter Gault, Evelyn Brooks Higgenbotham, and Tara Hunter.

Of course, I must acknowledge the incredible love and support that my family has always provided for me but especially for this project. My mother, Barbara James, was not an academic; however, she read parts of the book and insisted that I complete it because it was "so important!" Neither she nor my grandmother, Pauline Humphrey, are physically with us, but their indominable spirits along with all the spirits of my "dearly departed" ancestors are with me. My fierce and beautiful Black feminist daughter, Reagan Jackson, herself a wonderful writer, artist, and social justice warrior, has been an inspiration to me throughout her life! She makes me very proud and humble to be her mother. My sister, Julie James, is a critically important member of this family of Black feminists; and my brother, Lewis James, is quietly evolving into a wonderful Black male feminist.

I am certain that I have neglected to include everyone who has been a part of this journey, but please know that it was unintentional and that you are also deeply appreciated.

Practical Audacity

Introduction

Anything worth doing takes more than a single lifetime to accomplish.

Goler Teal Butcher, paraphrasing Reinhold Niebuhr

Law is relevant to the problem of hunger and securing food for hungry people with respect to both the short and long term approaches to the problem because it is *through law* that we structure both the various mechanisms to respond to hunger in a crisis and the means to assist people with pursuit of a development policy aimed at achieving food self-sufficiency. Moreover, it is through law that we implement our convictions: on the right of hungry people to food and on the duty of the well-endowed to assist in the alleviation of hunger.

Goler Teal Butcher, keynote address, World Food Day
Food and Law Conference, 1986

Following World War II, some three thousand delegates from around the world convened in San Francisco from April to June 1945. They were focused on establishing a new organization, the United Nations. Among the delegates was Mary McLeod Bethune (1875–1955), the only American Negro woman attending the conference in an official capacity. With Walter White, executive director of the National Association for the Advancement of Colored People (NAACP), serving as an official consultant, Bethune and W. E. B. Du Bois served as associate consultants. They represented the NAACP, the lone American Negro organization granted official status for the conference.

Born in 1875 in Mayesville, South Carolina, Mary Jane McLeod was the fifteenth of seventeen children born to formerly enslaved parents. Her parents and older siblings struggled to survive grinding poverty in the aftermath of slavery, so she was the only child allowed to attend school. Eventually she was awarded a scholarship to Scotia Seminary for Girls in Concord, North Carolina.

After graduating in 1893, she attended Dwight Moody's Institute for Home and Foreign Missions from 1893 to 1895 with the intention of becoming a foreign missionary. When she was not selected to be a missionary, she returned home to work as a teacher in various schools around the South, coming to the realization that her missionary work was right here in her own country. She married fellow teacher Albertus Bethune in 1908; they became the parents of one son but would later divorce.

In 1904 Bethune founded the Daytona Normal and Industrial Institute for Negro Girls in Daytona, Florida. The school, which was built on a garbage dump, started with four students. Under her leadership as principal, the school would grow to 250 girls. The school's campus included a hospital infirmary so that students who were in need of medical attention would not be subjected to the indignity of segregation in Daytona hospitals. The infirmary was also open to serving members of the Negro community that surrounded the school so that they too could avoid the physical and psychological dangers of segregated second-rate medical attention. The school merged with the Cookman Institute for Men in 1923 to become Bethune-Cookman College. Mary McLeod Bethune served as its first president.

Bethune was known as "the First Lady of the Struggle" for her staunch commitment to, and work for, civil rights and education. In addition to her vocation as an educator, she was very active in the NAACP and the Negro women's club movement, rising to national leadership positions. She served as president of the National Association of Colored Women, and later, in 1936, she founded the more political National Council of Negro Women. Her civic work at the local and national levels on behalf of the rights of Negroes captured the attention of Eleanor Roosevelt, and the two became good friends. Mrs. Roosevelt encouraged her husband, President Franklin Delano Roosevelt, to appoint Bethune to the position of director of the Division of Negro Affairs in the National Youth Administration. She served in that position from 1936 to 1943 and from that position became the unofficial president of President Roosevelt's "Black Cabinet." Roosevelt frequently consulted her on Negro affairs and interracial relations.

Bethune's core beliefs incorporated a profound religious faith, staunch racial pride, and a strong commitment to fostering opportunity for Negro women, children, and men in the United States. According to Audrey Thomas McClusky and Elaine M. Smith, as she assessed the existing conditions, Bethune became adept at deploying multiple strategies to advance an agenda for racial progress. Armed with numerous strategies despite her limited education, she was more than capable of pairing sophisticated political instincts with an orator's command of the language.[1]

Bethune petitioned the State Department for her organization, the National Council of Negro Women (NCNW), to be represented at the San Francisco conference but was informed that the NAACP had already been selected to represent American Negroes. Likewise, the General Federation of Women's Club, the National League of Women Voters, the American Association of University Women, and the International Council of Women had been chosen to represent women. It was therefore assumed that there would be no need to invite a separate Negro women's organization. Bethune, however, challenged the assumption that either a single Negro organization or segregated white women's organizations could adequately represent the specific concerns of Negro women.[2] This marginalization of Black women reflects an age-old problem that Black women (and other women of color) encounter: the assumption that identity is limited to one overarching characteristic, in this case, either Black or female. Such an erroneous assumption denies that our identities are robust, diverse, intersecting, and therefore complex. According to Bethune, the NCNW represented 6.5 million Negro women, a constituency that strongly supported the appointment of Bethune as the consultant most representative of their multiple concerns to what would surely be a historic conference. However, by the time the San Francisco conference was convened, Harry Truman was president of the United States, and Bethune did not enjoy the same rapport with him and his administration that she had cultivated with the Roosevelt administration.

Bethune was an official representative of the NAACP to the conference, but she was forced to be content with leading an unofficial delegation of four women from the NCNW to San Francisco to observe the conference. Sue Bailey Thurman, head of the International Relations Committee of the NCNW and founding editor in 1940 of the *Aframerican Woman's Journal*, served as the leader of the NCNW delegation observer team. Well-known medical doctor Dorothy Boulding Ferebee and attorney Eunice Hunton Carter were also team members. The highly qualified delegation worked closely with the National Council of Jewish Women and the National Council of Catholic Women to ensure that the Negro female perspectives and concerns were acknowledged and hopefully reflected in positions adopted by the US government. This embryonic alliance united around issues of international security, the conditions of poor people around the world, and the rights of women. The NCNW representatives also made overtures to others at the conference, including prominent women and men from Asia and South America.[3] Bethune, White, and Du Bois conferred with many of the delegates, experts, and other consultants, advocating principles that would be foreshadowed in the United Nations Charter and enshrined in the International Bill of Rights.[4] They also lobbied for including adequate education and cultural programs.

Bethune's endeavors at the San Francisco conference and her later unsuccessful attempts to attain consultative status with the UN Economic and Social Council (ECOSOC) between 1945 and 1947, after the UN was established, represented an important transition. Prior to the conference, many "race people" such as Bethune and Walter White had concentrated on the difficult but essentially domestic social justice task of "uplifting" the Negro race.[5] After the conference, some began to focus on a broader, more global vision of social justice that was emerging from the new perspectives and strategies incorporated in the modern international human rights movement. Indeed, Bethune had even come to envision Black women as international ambassadors for human justice.[6]

Although less well known than Bethune, Goler Teal Butcher (1925–93) certainly merits both recognition and acclaim as an important early contributor to the development of an emphasis on international human rights as a significant avenue toward social justice.[7] A Philadelphia native, Goler Teal graduated Phi Beta Kappa from the University of Pennsylvania in 1946. After moving to Washington, DC, she married George Hench Butcher, a math professor at Howard University, and they became the parents of four children. In an interview with the *Washington Post*, she recalled her fascination with the pre–Civil War era. She and her children brought home satchels full of books on the topic from a library in Washington, DC. She especially admired John Quincy Adams, a lawyer who served as president of the United States from 1825 to 1829 and as a member of the House of Representatives from 1831 to his death in 1848, where he fought valiantly against slavery. Finally, she came to the realization that she was fascinated by lawyers; she told her husband that she would like to attend law school when their children were older. He encouraged her not to wait but to start right away. So, while raising four children, she attended Howard University Law School, graduating summa cum laude. First in her class, she was also editor in chief of the *Law Review*. Her husband received a fellowship at the University of Pennsylvania, so the family moved to Pennsylvania for a year. While there, she attended the University of Pennsylvania Law School, where in 1958 she obtained an LLM. In 1959 she served as a clerk to Judge William H. Hasties of Philadelphia.

Butcher was highly trained in international law in the mid-twentieth century, and throughout the ensuing twenty-five years of her career (from the 1960s to the early 1990s), she worked in various capacities, including as public servant, activist, and law professor, advancing a plethora of causes for social justice. Hired as the first Black staff attorney in the Office of the Legal Adviser in the US Department of State in 1963, Butcher worked in a number of capacities, including in the Office of the Legal Adviser of the Bureau of Near Eastern and South Asian Affairs. From 1969 to 1971 she worked simultaneously in the Bureaus of Educational and Cultural Affairs and in African Affairs.[8] She served as a consultant to the US House Foreign Affairs Committee and counsel to the Subcommittee on Africa. An able strategist and advisor in the struggles to dismantle South African apartheid, she was also a strong advocate for developing a critical understanding of the vital interests of the United States in Africa. Intrigued in part by President Jimmy Carter's intention to embed his foreign policy initiatives within a context of human rights, Butcher accepted a position as assistant administrator for Africa in the United States Agency for International Development (USAID) with principal responsibility for Africa. Once again, she was a first—the first African American woman to hold such a position in the federal government.

Later, when President Ronald Reagan assumed office, Butcher left USAID to join the faculty of her alma mater, the Howard University Law School, where she was a professor from 1981 to 1992. There she taught a variety of international law courses, including the International Law of Human Rights. She was also the director of the graduate program in comparative jurisprudence. In the tradition of George Marion Johnson, the renowned Howard University Law School dean who had trained an earlier generation of law school graduates to become the "core of the nation's civil rights specialists," Goler Teal Butcher trained a new generation of Black law school students. She challenged those Howard graduates, as well as lawyers across the world, to broaden their perspectives beyond civil rights to form the core of the world's human rights specialists. While she was at Howard, in addition to her educational endeavors, she continued her advocacy work for African development and against apartheid in the face of Reagan's destructive policy of "constructive engagement" with South Africa. In addition to her focus on international human rights, she was also a human rights practitioner in her local community through serving as the chair of the DC Civilian Police Review Board from 1981 to 1987.[9]

One example of Butcher's impact on the task of conceptualizing expansive human rights was Howard Law School's World Food Day Food and Law Conference. In 1986 Butcher and her students (who, by the way, referred to themselves as "Butcherites") organized the conference, which was described by her colleague Henry J. Richardson as "no less than a bible on how to mount an interdisciplinary, multi-media, technology-friendly human rights conference on the cutting edge of both legal scholarship and public policy. She simply challenged, in her inescapable and impeccable manner, governments and food suppliers around the world to do what was within their current capabilities: to live up to their obligation to feed the people and conquer hunger."[10] In her keynote address, Butcher encouraged civil rights groups to "broaden their goals for individual liberties to better understand the 'interdependence' of food as a civil and political right." Promoting such an innovative approach to the critical problem of hunger was her method of challenging human rights theoreticians and practitioners to rethink arbitrary boundaries between civil and political rights and economic, social, and cultural rights. Insisting that hunger could indeed be eradicated despite its pervasiveness and intractability, she urged conference attendees and others committed to the development of human rights to define the right to food as a human right. Using the notion that the law should be an instrument to secure human rights, she argued that if it could be established that upholders of the law had an enforceable duty to obey it, the law could become a constructive tool in the struggle to eliminate hunger.[11]

Butcher's students, the Butcherites, deeply respected her intellectual proficiency in international law and human rights and were inspired by her unwavering commitment to the development of sophisticated analyses and creative strategic activism. She was at once a prototype, an inspiration, and a mentor for a new generation of human rights practitioners and legal scholars.

Butcher and Bethune were historic "firsts" who served as role models for the African American community not only of their eras but also into the twenty-first century. Indeed, they must be regarded as models for all Americans. As previously mentioned, in 1935 Mary McLeod Bethune was appointed director of the Division of Negro Affairs of the National Youth Administration, the first Negro woman appointed by a president to a high-level subcabinet position in the national government. Three decades later, Goler Teal Butcher would become the first Black woman to hold an important position in USAID. Their appointments to positions in the federal government meant that they were public servants in the traditional sense of the phrase; however, I propose that their commitment to social justice before, during, and after their official governmental appointments represented an even more profound form of public service.

Throughout their careers, Bethune and Butcher were innovative advocates for social justice. Prior to her appointment as an associate consultant to the San Francisco conference, Bethune's focus was generally on US civil rights and more specifically on the welfare of Negro women and children. Butcher's genre of advocacy emphasized anticolonial struggles specifically in, but not limited to, Africa. As Richardson noted, Butcher's career "spanned the axis from government to academia, from academia to activism, and from the rights of African Americans to the full sweep of international human rights."[12] Both women were clearly and deeply committed to education as a critical intervention into the lives of the dispossessed. Bethune concentrated her efforts on building an institution of higher education, Bethune-Cookman College, that brought poorly prepared southern rural Blacks to educational competency, while Butcher trained graduate students in the law. Both would come to understand and advocate for human rights as a crucial tool in the struggle to define and address wide-ranging forms of injustice.

Bethune and Butcher dedicated their lives to the creation and implementation of comprehensive and strategic agendas that would eradicate racism and secure the rights of Black women and men in the United States. However, their disappointment with the slow and disjointed progress toward equality and justice in the United States, along with their respective exposures to global debates around democracy and social justice, led them to refocus their attention beyond their essentially domestic struggles for racial and gender equality. They had come to understand that the strategies historically deployed to acquire civil and political rights were inadequate. This realization and their subsequent endeavors exemplify Black women's tradition of deploying ever more sophisticated analyses of, and challenges to, multiple oppressions from local to international venues. While the acquisition of civil and political rights was critical, that acquisition was also an integral aspect of a much more expansive vision of global justice as represented in the development of modern international human rights.

Butcher and Bethune are the critical precursors of the international human rights movement, and they provide a foundation for this project. That is, their stories are about more than the contributions of Black women to the American struggle for civil rights. Instead, they represent the comprehensive activism and scholarship within the contemporary political and social milieu of Black female human rights practitioners that informs the development of international human rights.

While this book is specifically about how Black women conceptualize, develop, and implement human rights, I would be remiss if I failed to acknowledge that the notion of rights for human beings has been a subject of yearning and discourse, and of legal and religious concern for centuries. As Paul Gordon Lauren observes, human rights "raise universal and controversial questions about the value of individual life, life lived with others, and what it means to be truly human." He reminds us that human rights "make us confront what we believe about the relationship between rights and duties, our responsibilities to those who suffer, and the ultimate value of people different from ourselves. . . . Human rights raise some of the most serious, painful, shocking, revolutionary, and hopeful features of the human condition itself, both in the past and in the contemporary world."[13]

Supporters of human rights envision a world in which abusive mistreatment, including but not necessarily limited to discrimination and oppression on the basis of one's race, ethnicity, gender, class, caste, religion, nationality, sexuality, abilities, or any combination of the above, is deemed to be morally wrong and/or ethically unacceptable. Human rights are in need of transformative social and political actions from the international community, from the global through the regional and all the way to the local community and individual levels. Human rights are an affirmation of how and why all women, men, and children are entitled to live their lives in freedom and with dignity. And these basic rights include a commitment to the formulation and protection of fundamental, universal, and inalienable rights despite such boundaries as national borders, religious affiliation, and political alignments.

International human rights must necessarily be acutely attentive to the complicated unfinished project of globalization. Indeed, the evolving human rights agenda is deeply committed to creatively exploring the challenges presented by globalization even as it envisions a global justice destined to serve as the foundation of just societies. Lee Ann Banaszak asserts, "Movement can only be understood by examining activism at multiple levels. Transnational, national and local activism all interact in the course of any social movement." There is, according to Banaszak, a complex world of multiple layers of activism. Each layer influences the others through serving as a source of ideas. Often those layers may also provide resources and relationships between levels that change over and are contingent upon the local context. Banaszak identifies a dramatic increase in concern about international issues and in international activism within the United States that corresponds with an increase in political constraints at home. She has observed a rise in the number of local organizations and groups that have developed relationships with groups in other countries without relying upon the US government or other national organizations to act as their intermediaries.[14]

In this book, I explore the stories of fourteen Black women who were, and in many cases still are, human rights practitioners engaged in various aspects of the multiple layers of activism in the field of international human rights at the end of the twentieth century and the beginning of the twenty-first century. Black women have an illustrious, often unsung history that includes participation in and leadership of a wide range of organizations and social movements. It became apparent to the subjects of this book, just as it had to Bethune and Butcher, that many of these endeavors were limited in their capacity to foster the transformative change these women so desperately desired. Frustrated by this slow progress, they chose to explore the promise of the global human rights agenda evolving in the international community. They questioned whether the vexing complexities of multiple and interrelated oppressions they were encountering at the local and national levels could be effectively challenged by the international human rights movement. And if that was indeed possible, in what ways could these women participate and assist in the development of a potent international human rights movement? All these women have worked at the local and national levels, frequently venturing into various venues in the global arena as well. Their stories reflect some of the diverse roads that one may travel to arrive at a definition of oneself as a scholar and/or a practitioner in the field of human rights. Likewise, their stories reveal the capacity of human rights to foster wide-ranging and innovative strategies to challenge the egregious abuses that impede the development and implementation of comprehensive human rights. As these women have searched for effective strategies to overcome multiple oppressions at the local and national levels within the global arena, their stories confirm that the evolution of human rights is necessarily a complex process.

Practical Audacity provides the contextualized stories of fourteen African American and African women engaged in a range of human rights activities that were designed to challenge the social realities of human abuses that these women observed and, in many cases, experienced. I conducted interviews of these women between 2002 and 2004. The interviews ranged from thirty minutes to five hours, with the majority of them lasting from two to four hours. Since then I have been in touch with some of the interviewees, asking them to respond to additional questions or to clarify some information that they had previously shared. I share their stories here.

Some women, like Loretta Ross, Dazon Dixon, Jaribu Hill, and Linda Burnham, were founders of their own organizations in various venues around the United States. Others, including Gabriel Kirk McDonald, Patricia Viseur Sellers, and Gay McDougall, conducted their human rights endeavors in UN agencies and organizations, including the International Court at The Hague. Adrien Wing, Lisa Crooms, Hope Lewis, and Catherine Powell were activists engaged in teaching and writing about human rights in law schools. Filomina Steady, Ayesha Imam, and Barbara Phillips have focused some of their expertise and energies on developing and managing nongovernmental organizations, as well as working on projects under the auspices of the UN. Although these women's endeavors were most often discrete and unconnected, their work sometimes overlapped, and they have been supportive of each other at various times when they deemed support necessary.

I asked them about the organizations they had founded or worked with and about their training, both formal and informal, for the work that they were engaged in. They answered questions about how they define social justice and whether that terminology was either an accurate or an appropriate description of their human rights endeavors. Did their involvement in human rights specifically focus on women's international human rights? Did they feel that they as Black women bring something unique to this work? Did they feel that their experiences, perspectives, and historical knowledge had an impact on the ways that they understand and perform or practice human rights? Did they engage in crafting human rights alliances or coalitions both domestically and across international boundaries, and if so, what challenges did they encounter in such endeavors? I also asked them to consider if feminist, particularly Black feminist, theorizing and activism were beneficial to the development of international human rights. Have international human rights theorizing and activism been beneficial to the development of Black feminisms?

Given the subject matter, it was not surprising that eleven of the original respondents had been trained as lawyers, one was a former international human rights judge, another served as an international human rights prosecutor, and four were law professors. Eight of the respondents were directors of organizations, one was a program officer in a large foundation, and two had worked in UN agencies. One was a freelance activist who worked extensively as a volunteer in several different capacities. Notably, only five of the respondents had previously been civil rights activists in the United States, while three had previously worked in the feminist movement, and, interestingly, one defined herself as a labor or workers' rights advocate. Four of the respondents had been educated in Historically Black Colleges and Universities (HBCU), while two had been educated in Ivy League women's colleges. All were continuing in the illustrious traditions forged by the endeavors of Goler Teal Butcher, Mary McLeod Bethune, and countless, often nameless others, in speaking out against injustices, crafting strategic alliances, and deploying ever more sophisticated, nuanced, and versatile strategies in the service of human rights and social justice.

The specific stories of Black women recounted in this book reveal that they are at once visionary, practical, flexible, audacious, and intellectually gifted scholars and activists. I found their human rights endeavors to be a reflection of their intrepid and astute resourcefulness, their innovative intellectual prowess, and their individual and collective commitment to imaginative pragmatic innovation. They are contributing ever more creative strategies to our historical struggles for racial and gender equality and economic equity. Their devotion to constructing just societies through the conceptualization and implementation of a full complement of international human rights requires the development of accessible theory and adroit strategy. As this book explores the innovative activities of these key human rights practitioners engaged in various aspects of multiple layers of influential activism, these women's skillful versatility clarifies not only the importance of their work but also its profound impact on the critical task of social transformation. What follows are some strategic and critical interventions representative of the stories of Black women committed to creating and implementing transformative visions of human rights that not only impact the lives of their specific constituencies but also have a profound effect on the lives of all people who are suffering the challenges of abuse, oppression, and social injustice.

1

A Global Feminist "Jurisprudence of Resistance"

Global critical race feminism moves beyond the boundaries of a narrower US focus on race, gender, and class to embrace a transnational perspective of evolving human rights. It dares to challenge both the particularized and globalized complexities of deeply embedded multidimensional oppression. It is intriguing to imagine global critical race feminism as a kaleidoscope of critical theory composed of a range of vivid and subdued colors representative of the flow between multiconnected yet often colliding aspects of oppression and critical theorizing around human rights. Each constituent dimension of multiple oppressions strains to retain its discrete properties even as it shape-shifts through shades of challenges presented by combinations of alliances and collaborations of critical theorizing. Thus, the law professors discussed in this chapter are committed to a colorful panoply of human rights supportive of the development of just societies.

Global critical race feminism may be characterized as an offspring of the Frankfurt school of critical theory, but, more specifically, it is also the progeny of several interrelated twentieth-century intellectual legal trends that traced their genesis to the legal realist movement of the 1920s and 1930s, a movement that set out to challenge customary notions of neutrality and objectivity in the law. Retrieved from obscurity, this early trend provided a basis for the development of the critical legal studies (CLS) movement in the 1970s. In a series of conferences that attracted the attention of hundreds of progressive law professors, students, and lawyers, the prevailing concepts of law as apolitical, settled, fixed, and determined were challenged. Instead, this radical left-wing and intellectually sophisticated movement, comprised predominantly of white male legal academics, argued that the law was neither apolitical nor neutral. Furthermore, they argued that power was embedded within the very social institutions that shaped lives, including law schools. Characterized as "workplaces," enterprises where knowledge is produced, law schools were designated by critical legal scholars as appropriate sites for political resistance. Indeed, scholars argued that organizing for political resistance must no longer be limited only to territory outside the walls of law schools. Politically, philosophically, and methodologically eclectic, the CLS movement was engaged in a project of law school transformation through critiquing liberalism and constructing unabashedly leftist legal scholarship.

Critical race theory (CRT) emerged during the 1980s as a result of two key incidents: the development of the Alternative Course at Harvard Law School in 1981 and critical legal studies conferences held during the 1980s.[1] The Alternative Course was developed after distinguished civil rights scholar Derrick Bell, who, along with Alan Freeman, was considered to be one of the forefathers of critical race theory, left Harvard to become dean of the law school at the University of Oregon. One of only two Black professors in the Harvard Law School at that time, Bell had developed and taught courses from a political, race-conscious perspective that challenged the prevailing notions of colorblind law, pedagogy, and scholarship.

Upon Bell's departure, students demanded that another professor of color with a similar intellectual legal perspective be hired to replace him, but the administration refused, arguing that there were no other "qualified" Black scholars who merited a position in the Harvard Law School. The dean of the law school even had the temerity to ask the students to consider why they would not prefer having an excellent white professor rather than a mediocre Black one. In a response that was insufficiently attentive to the broader concerns of students, the law school hired two distinguished civil rights litigators to teach a three-week minicourse on civil rights litigation. While acknowledging that the subject matter, limited though it was, merited serious attention, it was not deemed an appropriate response to the students' insistence on courses that engaged the new scholarship on constitutional law that clarifies the integral role of race and racism in its conceptualization, development, and implementation. In response, the students not only boycotted the minicourse but also conducted demonstrations, rallies, and sit-ins. Their most significant action, however, was to organize a yearlong alternative course designed to study American law through the prism of race. The students were able to acquire some outside funding along with the support of some sympathetic white Harvard professors, many of whom were active in CLS, to bring an array of highly respected scholars of color from other schools to teach a course loosely based on Bell's book *Race, Racism and American Law.*[2] This attempt to provide a space for scholars to address the subject of the law's treatment of race from a self-consciously critical perspective was one of the earliest expressions of what was to become critical race theory.

Prior to the rise of CRT, a few law schools (most notably, Howard University) played a crucial role in legal endeavors to challenge race and racism in the United States.[3] In those institutions, critical legal weapons were conceived and deployed in the "real world," where racism lived and contaminated the lives of people of color, mostly in the American South and the northern ghettos. Although that work has been accorded much deserved respect, CRT advances a different strategy through its recognition that racial power is wielded not only in spaces where people of color were concentrated but also in places like law schools where such perspectives and positions are legitimized and institutionalized.

Interestingly, the Alternative Course highlighted an approach shared by both CRT and CLS of the critical necessity of simultaneously contesting the terrain (law school as work space) and the terms of dominant legal discourse. Both CRT and CLS emerged from a perspective that views mainstream law school discourse as the place where certain topics and viewpoints have attained a privileged position within the curriculum and the understanding that knowledge and politics were deeply and inevitably intertwined. They insisted that law schools were influential sites for indoctrination and propagation. CRT expands the argument by insisting that the ideology of law schools in turn shapes and gives substance to broader legal and social ideologies about race and legitimacy precisely because law school workplaces were an integral aspect of the enterprise that produces crucial knowledge about race, racism, and law. Thus, the Alternative Course was seized as a significant opportunity to create a radical Left intervention into conventional race discourse even as it forged an oppositional community of leftist scholars of color within the mainstream legal academy.

Throughout the 1980s a small cadre of scholars who attended the CLS conferences began to argue that critical legal scholars had not addressed the notion that race and racism were also functioning as central pillars of hegemonic power; therefore, they had not developed and incorporated into their analysis a careful critique of racial power. As analyses of race began to migrate from the margins of critical legal studies scholarship, the central themes of CRT began to emerge.

A schism also began to appear at the 1986 CLS conference, which was organized by women working in feminist legal theory. Also an offspring of CLS, feminist legal theory placed feminism and its critique of patriarchy squarely within the discourse of and about CLS, thereby further problematizing and exploring conceptualizations of the workplace by drawing parallels to feminist critiques of "home." The feminist legal theory scholars invited scholars of color to facilitate concurrent discussions about race at the conference. Deploying the central tenets of CLS, including the notion that power is located not only "out there" but also within the very institutions and relationships that shape our lives, the scholars of color designed a workshop to uncover and discuss the various dimensions of racial power manifested within CLS itself. They posited the challenging question, What is it about the whiteness of CLS that discourages participation by people of color? This question elicited an immediate and often defensive response from many CLS scholars. An additional point of contention was the race theorists' critique of rights debates that failed to reflect the lived experiences of people of color. CRT observed that a critical dimension of Black empowerment during the civil rights movement was the customary, albeit innovative, notion of subordinated people exercising their rights. Not only were historically subordinated peoples garnering occasional legal victories in the arena of civil rights, but as they did so they were transformed by daring to simultaneously imagine themselves as full rights-bearing citizens within the American political arena. Such a transformation was the basis for another critical and integral theme of CRT: the absolute necessity to centralize history and context in any attempt to theorize the relationship between race and legal discourse.

The term "critical race theory" was coined by Kimberlé Williams Crenshaw, a former student of Bell, a principal organizer of the Alternative Course, a cofounder of the CRT workshops, and one of CRT's most eloquent and prolific critical thinkers. The 1987 CLS conference in Los Angeles was the site of the first formal meeting of the minority caucus within CLS. Crenshaw defines the "Sounds of Silence" conference as a watershed moment in which "a loose group of colored folks [had progressed from] the margins of CLS to an experienced group of insurgents who occupied center stage at a national CLS Conference."[4] In 1988 Crenshaw was a visiting fellow at the University of Wisconsin–Madison Law School. She and Stephanie Phillips, who was at the same time the law school's visiting Hastie Fellow, began to explore the idea of developing a venue where those who were interested in this issue could come together in a workshop that would foster more sustained conversations around the issues of concern. With then UW law professor Richard Delgado, they approached David Trubek, a founding member of CLS and then director of the Institute of Legal Studies, with a request for financial support for the project. Recognizing a need to create a term that captured the essence of the undertaking, Crenshaw and her colleagues eventually settled upon critical race theory: "We would signify the specific political and intellectual location of the project through 'critical,' the substantive focus through 'race.' And the desire to develop a coherent account of race and law through the term 'theory.'"[5] They developed a list of potential participants and invited them to apply to attend a workshop. On July 8, 1989, twenty-four participants assembled for the first critical race theory workshop in Madison, Wisconsin. The five-day critical race theory workshops would meet annually by invitation only from 1989 to 1997 for the sustained reflection of people who defined themselves as committed to "radical transformative politics."[6]

Offspring of critical legal studies, critical race theory, and feminist legal theory, the embryonic movement dubbed critical race feminism by Richard Delgado developed as yet another intervention in these self-described movements of radical transformative politics of law. Just as CRT adherents were expressing feelings of exclusion from CLS, there was an emerging feeling among some CRT legal scholars that too often CRT tended to emphasize male experiences of race and racism in a manner that overshadowed the possibility of variant female experiences. Likewise, traditional feminist jurisprudence seemed to distill female experiences into an essentialized white upper-middle-class woman. In both instances, some women of color who were advocates of CRT felt compelled to develop more nuanced critical theorizing that would simultaneously "race" our understandings of patriarchy while "genderizing" our conceptualizations of race.

Adrien Wing observed that it would be inaccurate to characterize this perspective as an organized or distinct movement. Instead, as proponents of critical race theory, these women also recognized that they too were a part of the evolving eclectic tradition of CLS.[7] They insisted that issues of multiple discrimination based on interrelated factors of race, gender, and class within institutionalized systems of white male patriarchy and racist oppression must be analyzed, critiqued, and dismantled. Multi- and interdisciplinary critical race feminists draw upon the scholarly endeavors of women and men both within and beyond the boundaries of legal studies. They too immerse themselves in both theory and practice and, like CRT, often rely upon the innovative methodology of storytelling and narrative analysis to expose ordinary and unfortunately unremarkable occurrences of everyday racism, sexism, and classism. They are called "to render the invisible visible and tangible, to move what is in the background to the foreground; to tell a different story that is neither known or familiar and indeed may be disturbing, annoying, and frightening."[8] Cheryl Harris, professor of civil rights and civil liberties at the UCLA School of Law, challenges legal scholars to concentrate on "the task of exposing the jurisprudence that oppresses in order to work toward articulating a jurisprudence that resists subordination and empowers."[9]

Law professors Adrien Wing, Lisa Crooms, Hope Lewis, and Catherine Powell are representative of the proponents of critical race theory, critical race feminism, and the more recently emergent global critical race feminism. They bring this amalgamation of critical theorizing to their teaching, research, and activism in the field of law, specializing in international human rights. In the tradition of the Frankfurt school, the pluralistic inquiry of their critically reflective scholarship is deeply informed by questions of justice and emancipation. The active thought of their jurisprudence represents the synergistic relationship of theory and practice. They are committed to the task of constructing a sturdy scaffold of international human rights jurisprudence that is supportive of global projects directed toward establishing just societies. Their law school teaching and research have been enhanced by their experiences of practicing law and their human rights activism. Likewise, their practice of law and human rights informs their teaching and research.

Adrien Wing

Human rights activist and proponent of CRT Adrien Wing is perhaps best characterized as the self-described mother of critical race feminism and global critical race feminism. She is the Bessie Dutton Murray Distinguished Professor of Law at the University of Iowa College of Law. She graduated magna cum laude with a bachelor of arts degree in American politics and Afro-American studies from Princeton, where she was also involved in the antiapartheid movement. The summer before her senior year she went to Kenya with Operation Crossroads Africa and decided that her career would have both an African and a human rights focus. To that end, she completed a master of arts degree in African studies at UCLA in 1979 before going on to law school. In 1982 she received the doctor of law degree from the Stanford Law School, where she also edited the *Stanford Journal of International Law* and was the director of the Southern Africa Task Force of the National Black Law Students Association. While in law school, she spent a semester working at the United Nations as an intern in the Department of Political Affairs, Trusteeship and Decolonization, performing legal and policy analysis with the Council for Namibia. This was a crucial position in Wing's professional development because through it she became knowledgeable about Namibia's history and its struggle for independence. While in New York, she also met many of the young men who were affiliated with different African liberation movements. The men—and she emphasizes that in those days the representatives of the African independence movements in New York were all men—were affiliated with the African National Congress (ANC) of South Africa, the Frente de Libertação de Moçambique (FRELIMO, Mozambique Liberation Front), the Movimento Popular de Libertação de Angola (MPLA, Popular Movement for the Liberation of Angola), the South West Africa People's Organization (SWAPO) of Namibia, and the Western Sahara's Polisario Front. She developed long-lasting friendships with many of these young men who were at that time attached to the UN. During an interview, she observed that today some of them are instrumental in running their countries. "That part of my human rights work was very important also because I became known as a student back in the era . . . when the Reagan administration was calling all these groups terrorists. . . . I was running around with all the terrorists," she laughingly exclaimed.[10]

After graduating from Stanford, Wing joined the international corporate law firm Curtis, Mallet-Prevost, Colt & Mosle in New York City in 1982. At the same time, she began working on a pro bono basis with the National Conference of Black Lawyers (NCBL), a group that she had affiliated with as a law student. In contrast to the National Bar Association, the more traditional professional organization for Black lawyers, the NCBL fostered a progressive African American global focus and agenda. It described itself, in the language of the 1960s, as the legal arm of the Black revolution. Wing worked with the NCBL for many years in a number of capacities. From 1985 to 1995 she was the chairperson of the NCBL's International Affairs and World Peace Section and from that position oversaw their committees, including the Middle East committee and the UN committee. She actually established their Middle East committee and eventually became their UN delegate when the NCBL became affiliated with the UN Department of Public Information. She represented the NCBL at conferences and other events across the United States and in a plethora of countries, including Angola, China, Cuba, Egypt, England, Grenada, Israel, Ghana, Jordan, Namibia, Nicaragua, the Occupied Territories, South Africa, Sudan, Tanzania, and Zimbabwe. On some trips she attended conferences, while on others she led delegations of lawyers to discuss constitutional reform or establish reciprocal relationships with schools, and on still other trips she was a member of a congressional fact-finding delegation.

Although Wing had no academic training in the Middle East, she was thrust into the area in 1982. While she was traveling in Europe with her mother after graduating from law school, her husband, Dr. Enrico Melson, heard a lecture at Riverside Church in New York City about the war in Lebanon and the desperate need for doctors and nurses to go to Beirut. Although her husband also had no background in Middle Eastern politics, he too was an activist, first in the Black Panthers while in high school and later in the anti-apartheid movement, so it was not surprising that he would feel compelled to volunteer. Although he had planned to meet her in Portugal, and then the two were to go on to Mozambique to meet Albie Sachs, the white South African freedom fighter affiliated with the ANC, Wing's husband told her that he was going to go to Beirut instead. Wing reasoned that because Ruth First, the white South African writer and Communist, had recently been assassinated, it was perhaps too dangerous to go to South Africa at that time, so, young and in love, she agreed to go with him to Beirut, where, ironically, there was open warfare.

Based on his compulsion to go (and, Wing admits, influenced by the movie *Reds*), they flew from Portugal to Cypress and then took an oil freighter to Beirut, because by that time the airport had been bombed. Eventually, they made their way to West Beirut to the American hospital. They were told that they were not needed there but that they were needed at the Palestinian hospital. She recalled that they knew nothing about the Palestinians at that time, although they had heard about a group called the Palestine Liberation Organization (PLO) that many Americans described as terrorists. However, Wing and her husband were not alarmed by such a designation because they were aware that many Americans had also designated South Africa's ANC and Namibia's SWAPO as terrorist organizations. They were sent to the Palestinian hospital in Gaza, where they worked for a month. Wing met with the woman who was administering the Palestinian Red Crescent Society and who was also a lawyer, and that meeting led to Wing taking on the position of hospital administrator, even though she had no medical training. She found a Lebanese and Palestinian staff overwhelmed by the war and its attendant shortages. She recalled:

> Meanwhile, there were foreigners from Europe, America, from Egypt, all these foreign doctors and nurses were descending on these hospitals, and there was no one organizing it, and so there was also no one to really deal with the people who were primarily English speakers. . . . So I basically inserted myself in it and helped run things in this hospital. We were there for a month, and I experienced all kinds of things where to this day I go into like what I feel is a post-traumatic stress kind of period whenever I see collapsed buildings like the World Trade Center, or the embassies in Tanzania or Kenya, or the Federal Building. I have a very bad reaction, because in Beirut the buildings were bombed like that, and people were killed in those buildings . . . and the odor—I can't even tell you what the odor was like.

Wing and her husband survived the experience, and then it was time to return home to begin their professional careers as a doctor and a lawyer. They left on a Sunday, the day the president of Lebanon was assassinated. They returned to Cypress, where they remained for a few days until they could secure plane reservations. By the time they reached London, they learned that a massacre was taking place in the area where they had been working—people they knew were killed, and places they were familiar with were destroyed: "Nobody knows today how many thousands of Palestinians were massacred. And we would have been massacred with them because we looked just how we look, exactly like the people there. No one would have looked at us and said, 'Oh, those are clearly foreigners or Americans.'"

When Wing and her husband returned to the United States, the NCBL and other groups were beginning to ask them to speak about their experiences. They decided after that experience that they would devote a portion of their political efforts and their pro bono work to the Middle East, and it was then that Wing established the Middle East committee for the NCBL.

As previously mentioned, Wing went to work for a large corporate law firm in New York. Like the other employees, she was working eighty to one hundred hours a week, so her pro bono activities were mostly confined to evenings and weekends or during her annual vacation time of four weeks. She hired a secretary and befriended many of the Black and Latino people work-ing in the Xerox room, so in lieu of an "old boy network" she cultivated what she termed a "people of color network" to "liberate" or facilitate her access to the necessary resources for her pro bono endeavors.

In 1984, over the Thanksgiving break, Wing attended a meeting of the Palestinian National Council in Amman, Jordan, and was asked to give a five-minute speech acknowledging that she was there to observe their conference. She returned to work the following Monday only to discover that her remarks were the subject of a front-page story in the *New York Post* with a headline that read "Black Lawyer Beats the Drum for the PLO." The article concluded by mentioning that she worked for the Curtis law firm. A conservative former classmate from Stanford who was working at the same law firm made copies of the article and then made sure to circulate it to everyone who worked in the firm in case they had missed it in the newspaper. As a result, the NCBL, which was also mentioned in the story, and the law firm became the recipients of bomb threats. Wing recalled this as an extremely stressful time for her because she was under pressure at work—there was a strong move to fire her, and she was also fearful of the threat of physical violence at home. Fortunately, she and her husband were not the recipients of specific threats at their home, although the couple and their six-month-old baby moved out of their home for a week as a precaution. Wing speculated that their home was not threatened because her husband's surname was Melson, and the couple had an unlisted phone number. She described herself as kind of "an invisible person" because diligent sleuthing would have been required to discover whom she was married to and where they were living.

In the meantime, the NCBL had planned a fund-raiser at which three Black judges, including Judge Constance Baker Motley, would be honored.[11] Some of Motley's Jewish friends had planned to attend the luncheon but withdrew both their acceptance of the invitation and their contributions to the NCBL. They also insisted that the organization denounce Wing's support of the PLO. This in turn led to debates within the NCBL as to whether it should or should not support Wing and her work.

Despite the controversy and the pressure to force her to resign, Wing remained in her position at Curtis until June 1986. She speculates that the firm, cognizant of its representation of Middle Eastern clients, including Muammar Khadafy, the government of Libya, and its national oil company, would have found it difficult to publicly castigate her Middle Eastern political activities, especially since they were done on her personal time. She also had support within the firm, including the support of her two powerful male mentors, Keith Highet, who encouraged her to become a member of the American Society of International Law, and Manuel Angulo, a Cuban American who was in charge of the firm's International Department. Despite their support, she was working in a hostile environment in which her salary was frozen and she was denied opportunities to work on certain projects. Finally, in July 1986 she left and went to work with a small progressive Jewish firm, Rabinowitz, Boudin, Standard, Krinsky & Lieberman, that specialized in international law issues regarding Africa, the Middle East, and Latin America.

Throughout the controversy Wing continued her international activism in support of human rights. In 1985 she visited Egypt, and later that year she organized her first fact-finding delegation. Under the auspices of the NCBL she took a group of twelve people to the West Bank and Gaza to investigate human rights violations. In 1986 the Arab Lawyers Union of Sudan invited the NCBL to engage in what Wing referred to as "unsung shuttle diplomacy" between the interim government established after the fall of Gaafar Nimeiry's dictatorship and the Sudan People's Liberation Army (SPLA). The delegation traveled to England to meet with the SPLA and then to Khartoum to meet with the Sudanese government and back again to report on their discussions. Although they had hoped to travel to the Ethiopian headquarters of SPLA to meet with the leader, John Garang, that meeting never came to fruition, most likely because, Wing speculated, the new government had little interest in pursuing a diplomatic course.

In 1987 Wing and her husband, Rico, moved to Iowa. He had been educated through a US public health service program that paid for medical school and then sent the graduates to places that were underserved by private doctors. The idea had been to educate more minority doctors and then send them to urban centers, but the guidelines were changed under President Reagan so that graduates could instead be sent to rural areas such as Appalachia, to Indian reservations, or to prisons. Wing's husband was sent to Tama, Iowa, to work on the Meskwaki Indian Reservation. Serendipitously, Wing had been invited by the renowned international law professor Burns Weston to give a speech on Namibia at the same time that her husband was being assigned to the Iowa Indian reservation. She and Weston had met five years earlier when she became a member of the American Society of International Law. While in Iowa, she mentioned to Weston that she would soon be moving to the state with her husband and that she was wondering what an international lawyer could do there. It happened that the University of Iowa had been attempting to hire people of color for the faculty, but three Black men who had been offered positions had all declined. Weston asked if she would be interested in teaching, and although she had not considered a career in teaching, she happily accepted a position at the University of Iowa Law School in 1987.

At the University of Iowa with the support of her mentor, Wing found that she was able to pursue her tenure by writing about the Palestinian situation, something that deeply mattered to her. Although her husband would only remain in Iowa for about a year before eventually moving on to Alaska to head the government hospital at Point Barrow inside the Arctic Circle, Wing decided that she would not follow him to his next post. Then pregnant with their second child, she actually discovered that she liked Iowa and felt that it was a great place to raise children. She was also learning to appreciate the life of an academic, which included extensive time away from the classroom. She could devote this time to research and writing and pursue her own human rights activities as she trained students in not only the theoretical but also the practical activist aspects of human rights. She marveled: "We can reschedule our courses, and I can be me. I can be me. These people know whom they hired. They knew what they were getting." Further, she observed: "I lucked out, coming to a state where it's not a big issue, where the forces against the Palestinians are not in ascendance at either the university, the law school, or the state. So that has enabled me to operate here in a way that I couldn't in most states where the law schools are so heavily dominated by people who are anti-Palestinian. I couldn't be hired, or else the state is a place where whatever my activities were I can get negative press, etcetera."

As previously mentioned, Wing's interests also included Africa. In 1991 she led a delegation of thirty African American lawyers to Namibia and South Africa. Apartheid was still legally in effect in South Africa, although Nelson

Mandela had been released from prison, and the government was negotiating a transition with the ANC. The delegation went to Johannesburg and also participated in a conference in Cape Town on constitutional options for South Africa. From there they traveled to Namibia to participate in the celebration of the first anniversary of independence. This trip to South Africa was a part of a three-year process in which Wing served as an advisor to the ANC constitutional committee.

In 1996 Wing returned to the West Bank and Gaza with a delegation of law students (an activity that was not sponsored by the NCBL). At that point the Palestinians were also in the process of writing a constitution. Under the 1993 Oslo Accords the PLO was to take control over some parts of the West Bank and Gaza, conduct an internationally supervised election, and produce a constitution between 1996 and 1999. In 1999 there was to be some form of final status talks that would lead to an independent situation for Palestine. The United States, which was funding aspects of this democratization initiative through USAID, asked the Palestinians for suggestions of people who could work on this process. Because of her prior experiences with them and because the PLO and the ANC had a very close relationship, the Palestinians insisted that Wing be hired to work with the Palestinian National Council. They were quite interested in her experiences with constitution building in South Africa and most specifically interested in the human rights provisions of the South African constitution. Hired to go to the Middle East to work with the legislative drafting committee for what was supposed to be two weeks, Wing actually remained for six weeks in what she describes as a very "formative experience" for her. She had progressed beyond participating in fact-finding trips to investigate allegations of human rights abuses. Instead, she stated, "Here I was helping the founding fathers and mothers of a future state of Palestine."

Wing left the Middle East to travel to Cape Town, South Africa, to teach in a six-week summer program for Howard University, a program she was affiliated with between 1996 and 2001. In 1996 she told her students about her work on the constitutional project, and at the completion of the course nine of those students (all of whom were African Americans) returned with her to Palestine, where she continued to work for two additional weeks in what she termed "a pedagogically incredible" experience for them. The Palestinian constitution was completed by the legislature in 1997; however, for five years Yasser Arafat refused to sign it. Wing speculated that he refused to sign the constitution because of its checks and balances; "It would have limited his power," she stated. He finally signed the constitution in 2002, but according to Wing, by that point it was irrelevant, because by then the Oslo process had disintegrated, and Arafat, effectively disempowered, was living in rubble in Ramallah on the West Bank.

Wing was approached by the US State Department for another democratization project in 2001, and that led to her third constitution-building experience, in postgenocide Rwanda. She, along with Henry Richardson from Temple University, three other Americans, and sixteen Africans from various countries, went to Rwanda for two weeks. They met in a rural area on the Congo border with the Constitutional Commission of Rwanda, which was preparing to draft a new constitution. The constitution they helped draft in 2001 was finalized and approved in 2003.

Because of the prior incident in New York, Wing attempted to maintain a careful and fairly distant relationship with the press. That protective stance was pierced by another unpleasant incident after she moved to Iowa. An article that appeared in a local newspaper, the *Daily Iowan*, described her plans to advise the Palestinians, and while she was in the Middle East, the *Weekly Standard*, a conservative newspaper, published an article on her titled "Wing Nut." The article, by David M. Mastio, not only referred to her as a wing nut but also included a cartoon with Arafat's head and a woman's body in a skirt with a little lace on it with the caption "wing nut." Denigrating both her scholarship and her human rights activities, the article described her as "an obscure law professor who shills for leftist causes and changes here [*sic*] 'expertise' like a suit of clothes."[12] The article did not elicit a reaction from the university similar to what happened in New York; indeed, she was relieved to realize that her job had not been jeopardized by the article's appearance. She noted that her only fear was that forces in the US government would misuse the article in a manner similar to the Lani Guinier case.[13] Fortunately, while that did not happen, the article did serve to reaffirm Wing's long-standing mistrust of the press.

Although Wing was deeply engaged in the practice of international human rights through helping to construct constitutions that sought to incorporate human rights, she also has a deep interest in African America. She has taught courses such as Constitutional Law and Critical Race Theory, and she has based a course on Derrick Bell's book *Race, Racism and American Law*, but she has also become involved in working with US gangs, which, oddly enough, had an obscure relationship to her work in the Middle East.

Wing had read an article in a magazine published in the Middle East in the early 1990s about a truce between gangs in Los Angeles based on an Arab-Israeli peace accord. "How could some gangsters get a hold of a Middle East document? And since it represented the intersection of my international and domestic interests, I said, 'I'm going to find those people.'" So off she and her children went to Los Angeles (she had family and friends there) to find the people who had written the gang truce. They were members of the Bloods and the Crips gangs, and their truce was based on a peace accord written by Ralph Bunche in 1948.[14] The author of the truce was a young man named Tony who was from Los Angeles but who had played basketball for Iowa State University. Although he was a gang member in LA, he had also matriculated in a small-town midwestern college for a year, and he was also a Muslim. Tony and his friends worked for Jim Brown, the former football player and actor, in an organization Brown had founded called Amer-I-Can.

Amer-I-Can was originally designed as a gang intervention tool; however, the curriculum, consisting of eight components, was designed to encourage participants "to examine their motivations and prejudices, gain control of their emotions, solve everyday problems and build family ties."[15] The course also helps students find and keep jobs as well as maintain financial stability.[16] The curriculum is sold to various organizations, including prisons, and to local and state government organizations, and the skills are then taught to groups such as former gangsters, prisoners and ex-cons, and students. After meeting Wing, Tony and his friends insisted that she meet Brown. She met with Brown in 1992 and was so impressed that she became affiliated with the program. She trained to become a program facilitator and later traveled around the country to speak about the program and actually sold the program to organizations in places as diverse as Des Moines, Iowa, and New Orleans. This enabled her to participate in what she terms "critical race practice," the capacity to develop theory (in this case, about gangsterism) while also becoming grounded in the realities of gangster life.

When asked to describe the mission of the Amer-I-Can program, Wing acknowledged that "there are a number of particular skills that people like this [members of gangs] have never mastered . . . things like emotional control, problem solving, role setting, family relationships." In prisons, the program also concentrates on helping prisoners to think about and begin taking responsibility for their own behavior. Because gang members have not acquired these kinds of skills, it is extremely difficult to transition from the gangster lifestyle into something more productive, such as education and/or employment. Wing states emphatically, "They'll fail if you don't teach them these building block skills." Much of her work was with people who were in the program or were interested in trying to get into the program.

Wing was especially committed to working with young men because she was the mother of five sons—two biological sons and three orphaned boys. She became involved in the lives of the three foster sons through her former husband, Rico. After their divorce, he lived for a time in Cedar Falls, Iowa, near where the three boys lived. Although their Caucasian mother was from a rural town in Iowa, she had cultivated sexual relationships with different drug-addicted Black male criminals. Two of them fathered her children. The mother was diagnosed with full-blown AIDS and died in 1992 at a time when, as Wing put it, "there were no heterosexual white women dying of AIDS in Iowa." Her relatives refused to take custody of the three biracial boys. Although Rico was never involved with them, Wing had become aware of them when she took her own sons to visit their father. She undertook the responsibility of being a surrogate mother to the three boys and brought them to live with her, her two sons, and her partner, James. Wing was aware that she would need guidance in her efforts to parent boys with such widely divergent needs and experiences, and she was cognizant of their need for additional positive male role models, so her involvement in the Amer-I-Can project seemed serendipitous.

As she and her partner navigated the complexities of parenting the five boys, she came to realize that her concern about the future of Black males in America was necessarily linked to the survival of Black females. Her scholarship began to reflect this newly developing concern about the growing surplus of Black females and the impact of that imbalance on the Black community. Once she realized that her work on gangs was focused only on men, in 1994–95 she began to talk to women affiliated with gangs. She learned that there are several roles that women play in relation to gangs, including as members and as relatives or lovers of gang members, and that much of the fighting in gangs is over women.[17]

Contemplating this broader context meant Wing had to acknowledge how much of her own behavior in terms of her relationships with men was linked to the loss of her father, who had committed suicide when she was nine years old. As she worked with Amer-I-Can, she developed a close relationship with Brown, who assumed the role of a father figure in her life. That in turn led her to realize that, in general, the need for Black women to have positive male figures in their own lives has an impact on how they relate not only to Black men but also to other Black women. From this epiphany she began to contemplate the existence of what she recognized as a form of "de facto polygamy" in the African American community similar to the forms of legal polygamy found in Africa and the Middle East.[18]

> We have the conditions of war that have led to a reduction in the men. So we have a surplus of women, and we have this polygamy, but it is not legal, of course. I am not saying it should be legal, but it makes for very bad Black male/female relations—exploitative black male/female relations where there is a surplus of women. They are each fighting. I've seen it with my students and with women interested in my sons. They are each fighting over a piece of a man, which makes even law school–educated women

do very stupid things. . . . We've got to get a better control on these men, right?

Wing went on to suggest that she felt she could be of some help at least on an individual level if she were successful in raising some of her sons to be "stable, productive men who are in a family structure." That would be positive for the Black race and its future; furthermore, she observed, this concern is interwoven into her US human rights interests. Thus, she views her human rights work as both theoretical and personal. "I have to do it on all levels. Not just write about AIDS or write about [the] need to help Black children, but I have to do it myself physically, with my time and my money. . . . So having taken on those children, those boys . . . that's part of my kind of domestic focus, activism that I feel committed to do."

Previously she had not identified with feminist issues; however, as she evolved intellectually, she was also deeply influenced by two events. The *Berkeley Women's Law Journal* happened to be doing a special issue on the experiences of Black women law professors, and she was invited to contribute to the issue. Reading the issue brought her to tears, because for the first time she understood that her experiences were very similar to those of other Black women teaching law. Prior to that special issue she had been under the impression that any discrimination she was experiencing was due to race and racism, although as the first woman in the International Department of her law firm she had an inkling that gender discrimination was an important issue. The eruption of the Clarence Thomas / Anita Hill debacle also had a profound impact upon her. Together, the Berkeley law journal issue and the Hill/Thomas hearings compelled Wing to focus on both gender and race. Others, including Kimberlé Crenshaw and Angela Harris, were already writing about the intersections between race and gender, and their efforts influenced Wing's determination to devote some of her own scholarly endeavors toward this issue. To that end she gathered material for an anthology from 1994 to 1996 and published *Critical Race Feminism: A Reader* in 1997. By that time, a substantial number of women of color law professors were writing about the intersection of gender, race, and the law, much like their counterparts in liberal arts and social sciences who were producing scholarship on the intersectionality of gender, race, class, and sexuality.

Wing does not necessarily define herself as a Black feminist; rather, she is more comfortable with the terms "critical race feminism" and "global critical race feminism." She finds that these terms—Black feminist, critical race feminism, and global critical race feminism—all refer to a Black woman's worldview, a perspective that can and must be brought to bear on a variety of interconnected issues. Such an expansive conceptualization asserts a perspective that is not limited, for example, only to the survival of Black males and gangsters. Instead, because this conceptualization seeks to be an open approach, its focus can as easily be foreign policy in the Middle East—something that on the surface may appear not to have a direct impact on Black people or Black feminists.

Wing is more comfortable with critical race feminism for two reasons: first, it has a legal angle, since it emerges from the law, and second, it attempts to incorporate all women of color. She views Black feminism as too narrow, while critical race feminism seeks to embrace all the different groups, including but not limited to African Americans.

Wing posits the notion of a position of simultaneous privileging and discrimination for women of color, particularly Black women, in America. "Globally speaking," she argues, "on the one hand, we are discriminated against in this superpower [or hyperpower] on the basis of our race and gender and other identities. And yet within the global privileged American society, we who are lawyers and law professors are leading unbelievably privileged lives." She insists, "This is the only country in the world where I, as a minority group female, could have achieved the education that I have." She continues, "We're in this unique global position, and because of this I feel it is my responsibility and our responsibility, who are in this privileged set of Black women, human rights organizations, to use that privilege on behalf of other people in the US and abroad who will never have any of these privileges."

Professor Wing is embedded in a network of colleagues who are legal scholars and human rights activists. While their teaching and research are conducted in law schools around the country, they have collaborated on and contributed to projects such as the second edition of *Critical Race Feminism: A Reader* (2003) and *Global Critical Race Feminism: An International Reader* (2000), both of which were edited by Wing. It is not possible to include here all Black women teaching international human rights in law schools while simultaneously engaging in human rights activism; however, the human rights activism and scholarship of Lisa Crooms, Hope Lewis, and Catherine Powell are representative, and some of their most interesting work is reviewed below.

The Praxis of Human Rights Scholarship

The mid-twentieth-century white middle-class feminist movement adopted the slogan "the personal is political" to encourage women to give voice to their experiences and to emphasize a belief that their everyday reality not only was formed and shaped by politics but also was political. While this was certainly a significant step toward social change, it was not sufficient. Indeed, as bell hooks has urgently reminded us, "When women internalized the idea that describing their own woe was synonymous with developing a critical political consciousness, the progress of feminist movement was stalled. Starting from such incomplete perspectives, it is not surprising that theories and strategies were developed that were collectively inadequate and misguided. To correct this inadequacy . . . we must now encourage women to develop a keen, comprehensive understanding of women's political reality. Broader perspectives can only emerge as we examine both the personal that is political, the politics of society as a whole, and global revolutionary politics."[19]

In addition to Adrien Wing, the intellectual endeavors of Lisa Crooms, Hope Lewis, and Catherine Powell are responsive to hook's broad admonition to craft a multilayered and nuanced feminist politics that is personal and societal, global and revolutionary.

Lisa Crooms

Howard University law professor Lisa Crooms has a bachelor of arts degree in economics from Howard and a doctor of law degree from the University of Michigan Law School.[20] After graduating from Howard and before matriculating at the University of Michigan Law School, Crooms engaged in human rights activism, working with two American NGOs. She first worked for two years (1984–86) at the Washington Office on Africa (WOA) and the WOA Educational Fund in DC as project coordinator. Crooms credits Jean Sindab, the executive director of the WOA, with making sure that she recognized the connection between domestic struggles for civil rights and the contemporary international human rights movement. Indeed, Crooms declares that she "never got that human rights work was supposed to be only internationalized." Under Sindab's guidance Crooms not only became deeply cognizant of the connections but also recognized that there was and continues to be a necessity to acknowledge the fact that the limited traditional vision of US civil rights is, along with the often snubbed economic rights, integral to the broader vision of human rights. Furthermore, Crooms observed that while we are focused on contemporary globalization, it is important to acknowledge that it is only the most recent iteration of globalization: "If you want to go back to [historical] globalization, let's start with the Middle Passage and move from there . . . because the triangle was nothing more than the globalized economy . . . just operating with a little less technological sophistication."

Two years later, in 1986, Crooms moved to New York to work for another two years at the American Committee on Africa as the research director. During her time in New York, she was also involved in the formation of the National African Youth Student Alliance (NAYSA). One of its first actions was in response to the notorious Tawana Brawley case.[21] The group organized a march in support of Brawley that disrupted traffic from about Fifth Avenue to then mayor Ed Koch's apartment in the Village. NAYSA later went on to develop a relationship with Ben Chavis, one of the Wilmington Ten and later executive director of the United Church of Christ (UCC) Commission for Racial Justice.[22] Under the auspices of the UCC commission, members of NAYSA went to Alabama to work on voter education, another turning point in Crooms's development. It was there that Crooms trained in strategies for effective community organizing, and it was from that work with NAYSA and the NGOs that she honed her commitment to creating and maintaining a crucial interrelationship between academic and activist endeavors. During our interviews, she argued that her experiences led her to believe that the relationships "feed each other. You either try it out as an activist, and then as an academic you look at it and analyze it and then try and assess what worked, what didn't work, and then you try and have it feed back into the activism, or it goes the other way." She went on to observe, "I find a lot of folks on either side don't value. The academics don't value the activists, and the activists really don't value the academics, and particularly if you are both a lawyer and an academic, then you come up for special ridicule. Because not only are you abstract and useless, you are accommodationist."

After graduating from the University of Michigan Law School in 1991, Crooms joined the law firm Crosby, Heafey, Roach & May PC in Oakland as an associate in the aftermath of the Rodney King trial. Her plan was to practice law for no more than two years, but along the way she would "liberate as many of my firm's resources by way of pro bono work." Her pro bono work included membership on the board of the Berkeley Community Law Center, representing the National Black Women's Health Project, and working with Eva Patterson, who was the director of the San Francisco branch of the Lawyers' Committee for Civil Rights under Law.

Crooms use of the firm's resources in her pro bono work was mutually beneficial. Because they were the largest firm in the East Bay area, they were also very interested in developing a business relationship with the city of Oakland. As Crooms put it, "You got to have faces." That is, the firm recognized that the then mayor of Oakland, Elihu Harris, wanted to see certain faces (presumably of color), and they reasoned that Crooms was "a good gamble" because she carried credibility as a graduate of the University of Michigan Law

School. As Crooms laughingly stated, she had the credentials, and she could be dressed up. So although her hair was in locks and her nose was pierced, members of the firm were reasonably certain that she would not be an embarrassment to them. Crooms pointed out that she was also beneficial to them when the firm was asked about the number of women and people of color they employed. She made a personal decision to restrict her practice of law in a firm to two years, and for that reason she felt free to request resources that most associates who were intent upon building a career with a firm would refrain from requesting. In addition to her insistence on engaging in pro bono work, she also reserved the right to refuse to work on cases that were personally repugnant to her. Any pro bono work was, of course, in addition to the thousands of annual billable hours she also undertook for her firm.

Asked if there were other reasons for her decision to practice law in a law firm, Crooms commented that she felt her professors in law school really had "a very unrealistic view of the law. Very theoretical and abstract." She felt that she could bring her exposure to, and knowledge of, how law was actually practiced into the legal academy. Thus, because of this background, she would be able to provide her law students with very practical information about, for example, the precise steps in filing a motion for summary judgment.

Through her own scholarly endeavors, Lisa Crooms joins the others in testing the limits of the framework of international human rights. One of her innovative contributions to this sweeping venture unfolds through her contemplation of a more nuanced heuristic of the concepts of intersectionality and oppression in order to re(de)fine the concept of violence against women. In her article "Using a Multi-tiered Analysis to Reconceptualize Gender-Based Violence against Women as a Matter of International Human Rights," she applies her critical race feminist theorizing to the predominant conceptualization of violence against women evident in the 1993 UN Declaration on the Elimination of Violence Against Women (DEVAW). Violence against women is defined as "any act of gender-based violence that results in, or is likely to result in, physical, sexual or psychological harm or suffering to women, including threats of such acts, coercion or arbitrary deprivation of liberty, whether occurring in public or in private life."[23] While DEVAW has offered a long-overdue and much-needed definition of violence against women that is both concise and comprehensive, Crooms argues that its expansive view of gender-based violence is at the same time limited. She identifies three critical limitations. First, DEVAW, despite its gender-neutral language, "lends itself more readily to a paradigm involving violent men and violated women . . . [thereby robbing] violent women of direct responsibility for violent conduct." Second, arguing from the context of an intersectionality framework, Crooms emphasizes that DEVAW "fails to recognize explicitly economic exploitation and racial supremacy as parts of the violence it seeks to eliminate." And third, she insists, the declaration "focuses primarily on positive violent acts, paying little attention to omissions which contribute not only to physical, sexual and psychological injuries suffered by women but also to the economic, racial and other harms experienced as gender-based violence."[24]

Foundational to these limitations are Crooms's challenges to a mainstream feminist paradigm on violence at both the domestic and the international levels. She begins to build her case with the premise that the relationship between child abuse or neglect and motherhood is complicated. Because women are most often primarily responsible for the care of children, they are, regardless of the degree of their direct responsibility, held accountable for abuse and neglect. The law, according to Crooms, "negotiates a disconnect between idealized motherhood and maternal culpability for child abuse and neglect and it does so based on a belief system that has masculinized violence." She argues that "the value society assigns to women and mothering means that the least valued women are more likely to be severely punished for their maternal lapses than those women with higher societal value. In order for the story about bad mothering to make sense, it helps if the woman is of the type who could credibly be a bad mother, who would resort to violence, a male behavior. Absent this, women who abuse and neglect their children are likely to be excused, adjudged not guilty, or spared the most severe punishment for their conduct." Crooms suggests that "women who abuse or neglect their children prove troublesome for most violence against women advocates." The predominant paradigm of gender-based violence is comprised of violent men, violated women, and a patriarchal premise that allows women to be violent only in two situations. They can violently "strike back" sometimes to the point of killing if men are found to have been abusive to them. They can also be violent if they are compelled to do so by violent men and/or if they themselves are under a constant threat of violence. She points out "violent women, especially those who abuse and neglect their children, remain conspicuously absent from the discourse of violence against women even when they abuse and neglect their daughters."[25]

Crooms provides two horrifying examples of poverty-stricken US Black women who felt compelled to abuse and prostitute their own daughters out of economic desperation. Their stories assist in the elaboration of a more extensive analysis of the relationship between women and violence. She argues that incorporating an acknowledgment that women not only experience violence but also perpetrate violence complicates and problematizes the prevailing model of gender-based violence. Further, this undertheorized aspect of violence, she insists, must be explored within the context of a matrix of patriarchy, white supremacy, and capitalist exploitation that represents the status quo. In other words, she is engaged in reconsidering "both harm and responsibility as connected to the basic human rights and fundamental freedoms to which human dignity and full and free development of human personality is central. It analyzes violence as a matter of micro- and macro-aggressions at work in both the mother-daughter relationship and the relationship between individuals, the families to which they belong and the society of which they are a part."[26]

Crooms contends that DEVAW suffers from a conceptual shortcoming in what she describes as the "partial embrace of intersectional identity analysis." Although intersectionality theorizes that identity forms at the intersections of such axes as race, gender, ethnicity, class, and sexuality, Crooms correctly asserts that inaccurate or incomplete intersectional identity analysis could result in some gender-based violence against women being misunderstood as primarily a function of patriarchy. While she certainly recognizes that the role of patriarchy must not be dismissed from our understandings of gender-based violence, the danger arises when we fail to factor in other socially constructed characteristics of group membership beyond the usual suspects of gender, race, ethnicity, class, and sexuality that are used to allocate power in highly complex and competitive industrialized societies: "The danger of deploying partial intersectionality with sex at the center of the analysis is that what is experienced as gender-based violence by women whose identities are only partially represented, risks being simplistically and erroneously a matter of patriarchy." Recognizing how "institutionalized oppressions such as racial supremacy, ethnocentrism and heterosexism, work in concert with patriarchy to construct the ways that violence against women is both experienced and perpetrated" advances our understanding of gender-based violence.[27] Thus, complexity is introduced to those analyses that include scrutiny of the positioning of social groups within unjust power relations, and this, in turn, supports multidimensional endeavors to address all forms of oppressions.

Bowing to Patricia Hill Collins's admonishment regarding the "myth of equivalent oppressions," Crooms utilizes the concept of oppressions only as a way to "discuss the connections between the different identity-based injuries experienced by those as disparate as heterosexual, poor, single, United States born women of African descent with dependent children, on the one hand, and gay, middle-class, white, Anglo men, on the other hand." Such a conceptualization of oppression is designed "to explore the ways in which intersectionality and identity-based oppressions operate both to penalize and to privilege individuals and groups within a system in which the degree of oppression, most of which is historically constituted and bound, is at all times relevant.

It reflects the fact that 'the categories for subordination . . . are not equal; they have different historical bases and consequences, which are an integral part of how they are used to dominate.'" Crooms also explores arguments regarding relationship between poverty and physical violence and insists that the "violence of economic exploitation experienced as gender-based violence" must not be ignored. Thus, her redefinition of violence "alters the ideas of causation and responsibility to reach those omissions responsible for otherwise preventable harms caused by violence, particularly those committed against women which had been naturalized as part of the *status quo*."[28]

Hope Lewis (1962–2016)

Professor Hope Lewis, the child of a Jamaican immigrant family, was born during the 1960s, a period of great social unrest in both the United States and Jamaica.[29] Although visually impaired, she matriculated at Harvard University, where she received a bachelor of arts degree in 1983 and a doctor of law degree from the Harvard Law School in 1986. Though she was not trained in human rights, as an undergraduate she was always interested in similarities across cultures, and that long-standing interest stimulated her campus activism in the South African antiapartheid movement. In law school she began to take courses in international law and was one of the first three students to participate in the revitalized human rights program at the law school. Her research at that time focused on Haiti. After completing law school, she was the recipient of two fellowships that funded her work at TransAfrica, one from Harvard and one from the Women's Law & Public Policy Fellowship Program (WLPPFP) at the Georgetown University Law Center in Washington, DC. She worked at TransAfrica for two years as a research fellow primarily focused on women's issues in Africa and the Caribbean. While there she helped to organize a seminar and a symposium on Black women's approaches to development, and she also worked on the issue of Black women's involvement in trade unions in South Africa, as well as in the general antiapartheid work that TransAfrica was engaged in at that time.

From TransAfrica, Lewis, who wanted to continue living in the Washington, DC, area, went to work for the Securities and Exchange Commission (SEC). She observed that this "odd transition" between two such diverse organizations occurred as a result of her following the advice of her mentor Randall Robinson, founder of TransAfrica. He always advocated the need for Black people to be on both sides of the table. Many of TransAfrica's endeavors were then focused on a campaign that encouraged economic divestment from apartheid South Africa. When her fellowships were completed, Lewis learned that the SEC was hiring, and this, along with her intellectual interest in the regulation of financing, led to her application for the position. For three years she worked in the division of the SEC that regulates both domestic and international mutual funds while continuing to volunteer with TransAfrica. In 1991, at the invitation of her friend and former classmate David Hall, she began teaching at Northeastern University School of Law in Boston.[30] She founded the Northeastern Law School's Program on Human Rights and the Global Economy.

Hope Lewis observed that one of the essential challenges facing critical race feminist scholars is "to reinterrogate both the essentialization and the false dichotomization of Black women. One useful means of doing so is to test the limits of the international human rights framework by taking it places where it has, so far, been reluctant to go—simultaneously toward identifying violations of human rights within the United States and beyond, and beyond state-centered geographic and political boundaries."[31]

In her article "Lionheart Gals Facing the Dragon: The Human Rights of Inter/national Black Women in the United States," Hope Lewis relies upon her Jamaican American heritage and her vision-impaired status to enrich her critical theorizing about human rights. She coined the term "inter/national" to explore the complications of identity. Inter/national illustrates some women's often dual national and cultural identities and, further, recognizes that their identities are also transnational and beyond nationality. She observes that "although most Jamaican women identify themselves as Black, they are still regarded as 'other' by some Americans, including some African Americans. Conversely, the particularity of their experience is often subsumed under an externally imposed essential definition of 'Black.' Moreover, while many refugees, migrants, displaced persons, and 'voluntary' immigrants are female, the gender-specific aspects of their experiences remain largely invisible." She observes that the rights of multiply identified inter/national Black women "slip through the cracks of human rights law and domestic critical race theory." Nor are these women easily confined to either side of the division between the West and the Third World. The specificity of their lives is routinely overlooked when they are categorized as universal "woman" or when "their multiple identities as geographic and cultural travelers are essentialized as 'alien' or 'exotic other.'" She insists that "the failure to focus on inter/national Black women robs legal scholarship of rich veins of material for progressive analysis, . . . [analysis that] could contribute to the building of stronger coalitions for inter/national social justice."[32]

Likewise, international human rights suffers from its reliance on conventional narratives around women's rights. To that point, Lewis provides an interesting deconstruction of what she refers to as the "Beijing Narratives," her reference to the Fourth World Conference on Women and the accompanying nongovernmental forum in 1995. She observes that two overarching yet contradictory narratives were present at the conference. There was at once an apparently unified global call for the recognition and implementation of gender-specific human rights. This was exemplified by the mantra within Hillary Clinton's speech of "women's rights as human rights," which, in turn, elucidated efforts to blur the traditional public/private distinction in the formulation and application of international human rights law. This perspective was especially apparent in the expansive definitions of governmental responsibility to assign appropriate measures that would deter and punish domestic violence as a crucial component in the protection of the internationally codified human rights of women. At the same time, Lewis argues that a "counternarrative of discord arose from differences in culture, race, ethnicity and economic status among women." The discord illustrated differences that have often been characterized as the dichotomy between universalist and cultural relativist approaches to human rights. Many Third World feminists objected to Western feminists' characterization of Third World culture as "uniquely abusive to the interests of women." Rather, they insisted, "human rights norms should be elaborated and implemented in a cultural context, stressing that pretenses of universalism in the human rights system may mask Western parochialism and imperialism." Lewis observed that there were other examples of discordant clashes, such as charges of exclusion, particularly of feminists of color at all levels of the human rights agenda from the national, through the regional, to the global. The ongoing conflict over the relative prioritization of civil and political rights over economic, social, and cultural rights was also revisited at the conference. Often those conflicts were represented as the women of the North versus the women of the South.[33]

Lewis brings nuance to the positioning of such discord in her description of the third story that she argues emerged from Beijing, that of "South in North and East in West. This story involves women who cross geographic and cultural borders, carry those borders with them and recreate their meanings . . . a less noticed story . . . of women with a transnational or inter/national perspective." She goes on to observe that "female refugees, displaced persons, migrants, and asylum seekers often are not full or exclusive members of a single national community. They constantly negotiate borders associated with geography, legal citizenship, racial or ethnic identity, culture, gender roles or class."[34]

Lewis's theorizing builds upon her background to enhance our understanding of the processes of negotiating borders. She argues that the experiences of female Jamaican migrants have been shaped by interactions between the somewhat simplistic notion of "Jamaican culture" (i.e., reggae, Rastafarians, and dreads) and the equally homogeneous notion of "American culture." Lewis insists that such an understanding is complicated and problematized by the innumerable ways in which African, American, and British cultures (including African American and Afro-British culture) interact not only with each other but also with such institutions as tourism, transnational corporations, militarism, the global drug trade, and international trade and aid policies. She makes the crucial point that while there are certainly times when Black Jamaican women's identities are related to their political citizenship, more often than not their identities have to do with relationships of power that can either exceed or even mask state boundaries. She concludes that "neither an uncritical universalism nor an insular or exoticized relativism would protect the human rights of women in this context!"[35]

According to Lewis, both women's international human rights and critical race theory have been deficient in their analyses because they have not focused sufficient attention on the plight of Jamaican and Jamaican American women in either Jamaica or the United States. She notes that these women are all but invisible as the explicit focus of international human rights. She suggests that nationally Jamaica's invisibility emerges from its dubious designation as "a stable parliamentary democracy," while the duplicitous nature of the United States' relationships to international human rights has hampered its efforts to address human rights violations. Indeed, as Lewis notes, while the United States has made significant contributions to the conceptualization of contemporary international human rights norms, it fails to apply those norms to its domestic affairs in any significant way.

The US focus on civil and political rights with an attendant lack of attention to economic, social, and cultural violations of rights informs the manner in which human rights are generally addressed in the United States, Jamaica, and elsewhere. For example, Jamaica suffers from a high crime rate, including murder and domestic violence. Many of the female victims of domestic violence are reluctant to report it to the authorities, and that has, in turn, resulted in a lack of credible statistics on its prevalence. Furthermore, Jamaica's dependence upon a strong tourist trade has led police officials to blame the high rates of murder on domestic violence as a way of deflecting the fears of potential tourists.[36]

Jamaican women have often been forced to sell the land where they had engaged in subsistence farming and move to overcrowded urban areas, first in Jamaica and often later in the United States, in search of low-wage employment. Thus, the majority of Jamaican women who immigrate to the United States are not usually seeking asylum or refuge. They immigrate for economic reasons. While the conditions may be incrementally better for them in the United States, many find themselves in immigrant limbo awaiting permanent residency status. Lewis notes that the labels attached to their status range from "undocumented aliens" or visa "overstays" to "permanent residents" or "naturalized" citizens.[37] They are often relegated to low-wage work that sometimes could also be dangerous, especially if their status is precarious. Some who have experienced sexual violence or other abuses while engaged in low-wage domestic work in homes are fearful of reporting it because of their precarious status. Others who have married Americans either for love or as a strategy against deportation may find themselves in an abusive relationship that they are fearful of reporting. Additionally, according to Lewis, because of their immigration status, many women are denied access to everything from health care to bank loans.

Given the variety of abuses and harms that challenge Jamaican and Jamaican American women, Lewis questions whether CEDAW could begin to provide them with adequate protection. Jamaica has ratified CEDAW, while the United States has, of course, failed to do so. Since her article was first published in 1997, an Optional Protocol to CEDAW with an individual complaint procedure has also been ratified. However, Lewis's argument about where to place the blame for the lack of human rights implementation remains applicable. Sadly, the questions she posed at that time remain relevant today: "Who should be accountable . . . when a woman is driven to work in the informal sector for her subsistence?" Further, "which nation state—the host country or the sending country—bears responsibility when women are forced to migrate to survive? Of which article is it a violation to be forced to leave children behind in search of a living wage? Does 'domestic violence as a human rights violation' include violence against the 'domestic'?" And perhaps most telling, can an instrument intended to protect women against discrimination on the basis of sex adequately address discrimination on the basis of both race and gender?[38]

Critical race scholarship has focused on the implications of immigration policies; however; it has paid scant attention to implications of Black immigration from other parts of the African diaspora and to acknowledging that while the experiences of Black immigrants from Brazil, Cuba, Nigeria, Jamaica, and Haiti may share some similarities, differences will also most certainly be apparent. Meanwhile, critical race feminist scholarship, in an effort to thwart essentialism, pays particular attention to the combination of race-based and gender-based discrimination. Furthermore, in addition to examining issues of discrimination against immigrants, some scholars are also exploring the intersections of discriminations against sexual minorities and people with disabilities to understand how they work to intensify race-based and gender-based oppression and discrimination.

Black women immigrants are encountering multiple forms of identity discrimination. Lewis observes that "critical race feminist scholarship challenges the notion that US citizenship immunizes Black women from the violation of their human rights. It also challenges negative images and stereotypes of Black women." Lewis alludes to the harmful stereotypes deployed against various groups throughout American history as part of this country's efforts to deny the privileges of full citizenship to such groups as African Americans, Native Americans, Asian Americans, and other religious and ethnic groups. Even though African Americans and Jamaicans share a legacy of slavery, the peculiar forms of racial and gender oppression prevalent in America present new forms of discrimination to the immigrant. Ghanaian feminist Abena Busia once declared that while she always knew that she was African, it was only when she came to America that she realized that she was Black. At the same time, Black Caribbean immigrants may find themselves characterized as successful model minorities in comparison to native-born Blacks: "In both domestic and international popular media, native-born American Black women are portrayed as lazy, overly reliant on welfare, baby factories, and criminals." If both native-born and Caribbean-born Blacks internalize such stereotypes and fail to deconstruct and challenge them, they can hinder the development of alliances and, Lewis argues, "undermine projects of social change, including efforts to apply international human rights strategies to the United States." Lewis insists that "an important task facing critical race feminist scholarship . . . is to reveal how the images of native-born and immigrant women of color are manipulated and how the women themselves are moved around like chess pieces to suit hidden political agendas."[39]

Catherine Powell

Catherine Powell grew up in Washington, DC, the daughter of a civil rights lawyer and an educator. During our interview she observed, "It is perhaps no coincidence I ended up combining those two."[40] In college and graduate school she "wondered why there seemed to be a dichotomy between careers in international affairs, on the one hand, and careers in civil rights or other domestic social justice work, on the other." Powell received a bachelor of arts degree from Yale College in 1987, where she was an activist in both the antiapartheid and antinuclear movements. She went on to pursue a master of public administration degree from the Woodrow Wilson School of Public and

International Affairs at Princeton University. There she was required to choose a field, either domestic, or international development, or international relations, or economics. Despite feelings of intellectual schizophrenia because of her interest in both the domestic and international fields, she was, nevertheless, compelled to make a choice, so she chose international development. After completing her degree in 1991, she faced a similar dilemma when she pursued the doctor of law degree at Yale Law School, where she was again required to choose between international law courses and domestic civil rights courses. Recognizing that the United States was embedded in the international arena, she realized that the field of human rights provided a globalized framework that encompassed her interest in human rights both at home and internationally.

She found law school to be a transformative experience because she had a cohort of classmates who were also questioning how to combine social justice with a career in law. Her classmates included James Foreman, the son and namesake of the former executive director of the Student Nonviolent Coordinating Committee (SNCC), and Lisa Duguard, a white woman who strongly advocated that other white students embrace the idea that racial justice was as much in their interest as it was in the interest of communities of color. They, together with other students, prodded the law school toward a deeper commitment to social justice. Harold Koh, who would later become the dean of the Yale Law School and who served as President Clinton's assistant secretary of state for human rights, initiated a human rights clinic at Yale during their last year of law school. One of the cases that they worked on was a lawsuit against the US government for detaining Haitian refugees at Guantánamo Bay, Cuba. They won their case at the district court in New York and at the court of appeals but eventually lost it at the Supreme Court. Powell recalled that in addition to the lawsuit, the Haitians themselves galvanized a grassroots movement around the country to pressure the government to release the detained refugees.

After graduating from law school in 1992, Powell went to Guantánamo to do a one-year postgraduate fellowship funded by the Ford Foundation in public international law.[41] Days before her arrival, the Haitian detainees had initiated a hunger strike. The detainees had been imprisoned in Guantánamo as a result of a policy devised by the George H. W. Bush administration to capture them on the high seas as they tried to escape from their country. The intention was to detain them and eventually repatriate them back to Haiti. According to Powell, this was in violation of both international law and US refugee law. The policy allowed the Bush administration not to provide the Haitians with the protection they would have received once they reached US soil. In their lawsuit, the students had tried to argue that those protections should attach to people even when they were captured on the high seas or when they were brought to Guantánamo for detention. The students encouraged the Haitians to wait, because President-Elect Bill Clinton had promised that they would be released. However, by the time he was in office, he actually reversed this promise. Furthermore, because of the Zoë Baird scandal there was a lengthy delay before Janet Reno was finally appointed and confirmed as attorney general.[42] Concluding that they could no longer wait for the wheels of justice to turn, the Haitians determined to take matters into their own hands. They decided to stage a hunger strike in hopes that this would bring attention to their plight and accelerate the process of justice.

Powell returned to the United States, landing in Newark, New Jersey, in the midst of a blizzard. She called her former classmate Lisa Duguard, who was at that time working for the American Civil Liberties Union (ACLU). Duguard told her to go straight to the UN, where she was to meet Jesse Jackson to explain the case and seek his support. Upon arrival at the UN, Powell encountered a massive demonstration of Haitian Americans and their supporters, who were also waiting to seek Jackson's support. When he arrived, she got into his limousine and explained that he should "keep hope alive" by going to Guantánamo to support the Haitian cause. While she was still in the car, he taped a message to the Haitian detainees telling them they must eat, that they were needed back in Haiti to participate in rebuilding the country once the democratically elected government was restored to power. Furthermore, he promised that he would come, in love, the following week on Valentine's Day to support their cause. Although he encouraged the detainees to eat to stay strong, when he arrived in Guantánamo Jackson announced that he would join them in their hunger strike.

Following his highly publicized example, students on a number of college campuses, beginning at Yale, supported the Haitian cause by joining the fast. The Yale students brought the hunger strike to Harvard, where Powell was spending the year. Although that fast was to last a week, Powell had to take twenty-four hours out of her fast so that she could complete her preparation to take one of the exams for the bar. The hunger strike moved on to other college campuses around the country, and then some celebrities, including a professional basketball player, eventually joined the Haitians in fasting. Randall Robinson also joined the hunger strike to the point where he had to be hospitalized. The hunger strike received so much media coverage that President Clinton finally announced that he would bring the Haitians from Guantánamo to the United States as a humanitarian gesture, albeit not as a legal obligation. Powell commented that "even though we eventually did lose at the Supreme Court level in terms of the part of the lawsuit that was challenging their catching

Haitians on the high seas and repatriating them forcibly back, we were able to get the release at least of Haitians that were detained at Guantánamo."

Following that experience, Powell clerked for a judge in New York, and then over the next four years she worked at the National Association for the Advancement of Colored People (NAACP) Legal Defense and Educational Fund (LDF), staffing the Black Women's Employment Project, which sought to address discrimination at the intersection of race and gender. Because her interest in international human rights continued, she tried to apply that framework to her work at the NAACP, and in fact she was even able to attend the Fourth World Conference on Women: Action for Equality, Development and Peace in Beijing in 1995 on behalf of the LDF.

Powell identified her work representing Kemba Smith as another important aspect of her informal education. Smith was a young Hampton College student who was arrested, tried, and convicted as a result of her boyfriend's drug activities. Even though federal authorities acknowledged that she never used, touched, or sold crack cocaine, she was eventually convicted for her boyfriend's distribution of 250 tons of cocaine. At the age of twenty-three, she was given a twenty-five-year sentence. Powell pursued the case for clemency through the courts, but Kemba would eventually be granted clemency by President Clinton.

The UN special rapporteur on violence against women, Rhadika Coomaraswamy, visited the United States to study the conditions of women prisoners. She held a roundtable in Washington, DC, and invited a number of academics and advocates to attend. She asked about the issues that specifically confronted women of color and was particularly interested in how gender issues intersect with racial discrimination. Powell participated in the roundtable and spoke about some of the issues confronting women of color, mentioning the Kemba Smith case as an example. Although the UN special rapporteur was from Sri Lanka, she had heard about this case and asked to meet with Kemba while she was in the country. A meeting was arranged, and Coomaraswamy included Kemba's case in her report. In addition, Coomaraswamy wrote a letter to President Clinton seeking clemency for Kemba. Along with other written pleas, this letter may have had some impact on his decision to finally grant clemency.

In 1998, as Powell was completing four years at the LDF, she applied for a position as founding executive director in the newly created Human Rights Institute in the Columbia Law School: "One of its primary goals is to look at the connection between the international law of human rights and the domestic law of constitutional rights in the US and in other countries. So, I thought, finally here is a job that can bring together these two sets of interests I have in US social justice and US constitutionalism with international human rights laws." In addition to administering the institute program, Powell also taught a human rights class with the renowned international law professor Louis Henkin and discovered that she so enjoyed teaching that she wanted to teach full time. In 2002 she embarked upon a full-time position as a tenure-track professor at the Fordham Law School.

In an article titled "Dialogic Federalism: Constitutional Possibilities for Incorporation of Human Rights Law in the United States," Catherine Powell deploys her expertise in international human rights, US constitutionalism, and effective activism to intervene in the difficult processes of converting the principles of abstract international human rights into practical laws and policies at the national and subnational levels. Although she recognizes that it is not possible for state and local governments to "adopt" or ratify international treaties in the same way that national governments can, she argues that it is possible for them to incorporate international standards by enacting legislation that reflects international norms.[43] Her approach to this task is premised on developing cooperative intergovernmental relations through dialogue. She insists that dialogue among the various levels of government is absolutely essential to the meaningful implementation of international human rights law in the United States. Such dialogues link national and subnational governments in conversation about rights through the creation of "areas of overlap in which neither system can claim total sovereignty."[44]

Dialogic federalism, according to Powell, moves beyond the mere transmission of international human rights to envision a process of translation from the international to the domestic: "Just as we know that translation from one language to another requires more than literalness, we must recognize the creativity, and therefore the uncertainty, involved in domestic interpretation [of international law]."[45] Powell further explores the metaphor by observing that while translation owes fidelity to the other's language and text (with the "other" being international human rights law), it also requires the assertion of one's own language as well, the analogy to "one's own" being domestic law: "The negotiation between international and domestic legal regimes and the hybridity which results, are the driving forces behind translation of broad international principles into concrete articulation of rights reflected domestically in law and practice."[46]

Powell argues that the translation metaphor is central because it underscores the sense of foreignness or alienation that many Americans associate with international law. The institutions of our national government, including the executive, the Senate, and the Supreme Court, were mandated to speak "with one voice" on the foreign affairs of treaties and international customary law even as direct broad-based participation of Americans in foreign policy was discouraged. Although according to the US Constitution international treaties that have been ratified along with international customary law are the law of the land in the United States, practically speaking, they are often viewed as an alien source of law that lacks democratic legitimacy. This is especially apparent in Supreme Court jurisprudence, which almost always chooses either to ignore international law or to privilege US law over international law. (I once questioned Justice Sonia Sotomayor about this very point, and she confirmed that the Supreme Court routinely ignored international law.) Americans may also feel alienated by the lack of transparency in the manner in which treaties are negotiated at the international level and then, unlike purely domestic legislation, ratified only in the Senate without any input from the House of Representatives. Powell argues that this relative absence of public engagement in international law contributes to the failure of our national institutions to translate international law into domestic law. The problem is that a "transmittal of the international" is occurring rather than the "process of translation from international to national."[47]

The United States has a disappointing record on UN treaty ratification, and to that point Powell provides a cogent criticism of some NGOs based in Washington, DC, that assists in explaining such a dismal record.[48] Rather than mobilizing support for the ratification of treaties that could make a difference in the lives of the American people, they have concentrated on strategies that attempt to reassure lawmakers that adopting international human rights treaties would not disturb existing domestic laws. She observes that such reassurances become self-fulfilling as the reservations, understandings, and declarations (RUDs) negotiated and attached to the treaties to ensure passage limit the domestic impact of the treaties. Referring to them as "stealth treaties," she argues that human rights treaties cluttered with RUDs ensure governmental noncompliance to international standards of human rights by limiting the incorporation of the available international protections into domestic laws and policies.[49] Furthermore, because of the lack of media attention to these treaties, the average person has little to no knowledge of either the international treaties or the protection that they might offer to human rights.

Powell posits the notion that the processes of "localizing human rights law creates opportunities for standard setting that supplement, solidify and deepen opportunities at the federal level." She goes on to suggest that "by enabling democratic deliberation at multiple levels, dialogic federalism facilitates a broader and deeper consensus over human rights commitments." She advocates the need to develop a "more participatory mechanism through which Americans can foster a deeper human rights culture." To that end, the voices of state and local governments must be cultivated and amplified in the struggle to adopt and implement human rights in this country.[50]

Powell suggests that dialogic federalism offers a normative framework for negotiating conflict. Indeed, it seeks to embrace rather than avoid the conflict that is inherent in overlapping jurisdiction between national and subnational governments. Conflict is used in a productive manner through its reliance on dialogue, coordination, and negotiation to construct a consensus-based process. She argues that this approach, based on multiple and concurrent levels of deliberation, seeks to address both federally imposed mandates, which often fail to gain support at the state and local levels, and fragmented state and local initiatives, which often result in the failure to ensure full-scale national compliance with international human rights laws.[51]

Dialogic federalism usually proceeds along three different tracks, depending upon the linkages between the national and subnational governments. The first and most active approach is when state and local governments adopt international human rights standards when the federal government fails to ratify a treaty.[52] Powell briefly describes efforts in San Francisco to make the Convention on the Elimination of All Forms of Discrimination Against Women (CEDAW) part of its local law three years after the UN Conference on Women in Beijing. In 1998, in compliance with a new city ordinance signed by Mayor Willie Brown Jr., the city of San Francisco's Juvenile Probation Department and the Department of Public Works filed reports containing a gender analysis of their delivery of service, employment practices, and budget allocation.[53] The primary goal of the San Francisco CEDAW task force was to raise awareness about how every decision could affect women. While the task force was not a regulatory board, it was committed to educating, prodding, and cajoling rather than punishing. It has collected data on the advantages of allowing employees in the Adult Probation Department to telecommute, which was especially useful for busy mothers. It also encouraged the Rent Board to keep statistics on whom it served, and in the area of juvenile justice it focused attention on and supported plans to hire caseworkers to deal exclusively with girls. It even addressed such a subtle issue as the spacing of street lamps as a way to make neighborhoods safer for women. Krishanti Dharmaraj, a cofounder of WILD for Human Rights (Women's Institute for Leadership Development) and a member of the task force, stated, "What CEDAW does exquisitely is that it unveils gaps that we thought were normal—where the norm is men."[54]

The symbolic value of San Francisco's actions cannot be underestimated, according to Powell. Following San Francisco's example, the Los Angeles City Council adopted a resolution in support of CEDAW, and by August 2000 thirty-nine cities, seventeen counties, sixteen states, and Guam had adopted nonbinding resolutions that called for the United States to ratify CEDAW.[55]

In 2002 the New York City Human Rights Initiative was launched. A model ordinance, the initiative is designed to enable New York to implement two human rights treaties: CEDAW and the Convention on the Elimination of All Forms of Racial Discrimination (CERD). The model ordinance includes five sections: "Legislative Findings and Intent," "Definitions," "Local Human Rights Principles Based on CEDAW and CERD," "Implementation of Local Human Rights Principles in New York City," and "Implementation Bodies and Task Force." The intention of the initiative is to "positively promote equality and human rights" by setting forth local principles drawn from CEDAW and CERD as aspirational goals for the city to achieve. The city is mandated to undertake a series of procedures to study, evaluate, and create plans to achieve its human rights goals and to provide a forum for public participation in and comment on the process. An advisory committee and a task force established under the ordinance will help the city follow the procedures and oversee and enforce the implementation process.[56]

In addition to writing about dialogic federalism, Powell includes working, from the beginning, with the New York City Human Rights Initiative as an important part of her portfolio of human rights activism. She became involved at the project's inception at an event sponsored by the NOW Legal Defense Fund. Madeleine Albright had been invited to be the guest speaker at the event honoring Ruth Bader Ginsburg at the New York City Bar Association. The theme was human rights, and Powell was invited to speak on the panel that followed the speech. In her remarks, she discussed state and local efforts that were attempting to mount local responses to international human rights. Someone in the audience wondered why CEDAW couldn't also be adopted in New York City. In response to that question, the NOW Legal Defense Fund decided to call a meeting of civil rights and women's rights organizations to explore the possibility of the New York City Council adopting CEDAW and CERD. At the first meeting, Powell helped explain the issue of treaty obligations, while someone from the UN spoke about the UN's oversight of treaties. Over time, the coalition expanded to include a fairly broad range of local grassroots organizations, including the NAACP LDF and international organizations such as Amnesty International.

During our interview, Powell pointed out an important difference between treaty ratification at the national level in comparison to subnational responses. At the national level, she observed, "there is no real attempt to do public education, get community groups organized."

> What the coalition sees as very critical is not just getting this law passed but doing very participatory popular education along the lines of what

Loretta Ross and others have tried to do to get women involved at a very grassroots level and understanding what the norms are, but also in talking about how they can make these norms meaningful to their needs. So we have been thinking about models like Women Living under Muslim Law . . . that have created these really participatory, creative models of education. . . . I almost hesitate to call it "education" because it seems like it's not even so much a hierarchical model teacher/student but more like a community deliberation talk about what the norms are and how they mesh with feminist interpretations of the Koran and the context of women living under Muslim law. So we've been looking at those kinds of really innovative models and trying to think about how we can develop various participatory models of community deliberation and education here in New York.

Ultimately, Powell aims, in the words of Crooms, to "expand the cramped boundaries of domestic law."[57] Powell and her colleagues are cultivating a synergistic force of intellectual and activist innovation in their human rights endeavors. This synergy is a product not only of Powell's particular scholarly writing and teaching but also of her collegial relationships to other critical feminist human rights scholars (including the other subjects of this chapter) and the strength of her coalitional ties to activists engaged in doing human rights.

Conclusion

Deeply committed to testing the bricolage of international human rights and a critical practice intent upon expanding its "cramped boundaries," these professors are deploying sophisticated, cutting-edge strategies of activist scholarship to challenge the complexities of multidimensional abuses. Hope Lewis's conceptualization of the inter/national emerges from her intimate knowledge of the Jamaican American experience. She too is deeply engaged in bridging the fault lines that have traditionally separated the transnational community from national and subnational spaces. She skillfully commands usage of the particular to foster deeper understandings of the global, and that in turn encourages the deployment of a more precise and grounded application of global human rights to the task of ameliorating abuses in specific locations.

Catherine Powell's thesis of dialogic federalism presages the thesis of Sally Engle Merry's book *Human Rights and Gender Violence*. Merry observes that the effectiveness of human rights is dependent upon its capacity for translation, "to be remade in the vernacular," and argues that activists serve as the intermediaries engaged in translating the vernacular of "cultural understandings of gender, violence and justice."[58] Powell's endeavors as an intermediary also serve to bridge the scholarly activist divide. Her research on international human rights as exemplified by her work on dialogic federalism and her contributions to activist causes, including the New York City Human Rights Initiative, the Haitian detainee cases, and the Kemba Smith clemency case, exemplify the significant component in the translation and implementation of international human rights at the national and subnational levels.

Meanwhile, Lisa Crooms applauds the progress of the international community in finally addressing the crisis of pervasive gender-based violence while simultaneously prodding it into deeper multidimensional analyses. Her work, too, exemplifies her commitment to valuing scholarship and activism, as well as valuing the results of their mutual reciprocity.

Finally, Adrien Wing not only participates in the construction of new constitutions that reflect global progress in international human rights but also makes certain that her students have access to these rich pedagogical opportunities of participation. Further, her critical practice of human rights is deeply embedded in an African American context and ranges from the personal, which includes the manner in which her family was configured, to the subnational level, as expressed in her work with gangs, to the global, where she also makes certain to ensure African American participation in the practice of international human rights law.

With the tools afforded by critical race theory, critical race feminism, and global critical race feminism, these women are constructing a scholarly body of work that explores the articulation of contemporary human rights and its reciprocity with activism. This work is both critical and visionary, as it confronts the multidimensional nature of late twentieth-century and early twenty-first-century oppression and discrimination on both local and global levels. The sophisticated interplay of their critical theorizing informs and is informed by other theorists, including those of critical race theory, human rights, and feminism. Although it was not possible to review the entire catalog of their impressive scholarship, this chapter explored some of their most innovative contributions to the evolving corpus of human rights, and in doing so sought to invite readers to further examine their scholarly endeavors.

2

Humanitarian
Human Rights

Justice can be found at the end of a trial rather than the end of a gun barrel
or machete.

Judge Gabrielle Kirk McDonald

We can accept atrocities as inevitable, or we can strive for a higher standard.
We can presume to forget what only God and the victims have standing to
forgive, or we can heed the most searing lesson of this century, which is that
evil—when unopposed—will spawn more evil.

Former Secretary of State Madeleine Albright

Just as the law professors in the previous chapter have contributed to the development of the international jurisprudence of human rights, other Black women are also deeply involved with the
evolution and application of international humanitarian law. Judge Gabrielle
Kirk McDonald and attorney Patricia Viseur Sellers are profoundly immersed
in both the implementation of humanitarian law and the practice of human
rights. Both were vitally involved, though in different capacities, in the work
of the International Criminal Tribunal for the former Yugoslavia (ICTY) in The
Hague, the Netherlands, and to a somewhat lesser extent in the International
Criminal Tribunal for Rwanda (ICTR) in Arusha, Tanzania. Both were also
participants in the Women's International War Crimes Tribunal on Japan's
Military Sexual Slavery in Tokyo from December 7 to 12, 2000.

The terms "human rights" and "humanitarian law" have often been used
as if they were interchangeable; however, the two are distinct aspects of international law. Human rights are concerned with the development and protection
of individual rights at all times, including first-generation civil and political

rights; second-generation economic, social, and cultural rights; and third-generation rights, including rights to peace and development.[1] The subject of international humanitarian law is armed conflict, *jus in bello* (laws governing hostility), and its goal is to limit the dreadful effects of war on people and property. Historically, humanitarian law was limited to international wars and the manner of (limited) restraints that could be applied to the conduct of war through, for example, national laws or bilateral treaties. It was not until the nineteenth century that the international community began significant movement toward the creation of internationally recognized laws that sought to regulate how wars should be carried out and how people should be treated during the course of a war.

Humans have engaged in warfare throughout history and, no doubt, prior to recorded history; however, the growth of a body of humanitarian law received impetus from technological advances of the nineteenth-century industrial revolution. The development of railroads and steamships, for example, made it feasible to transport large numbers of soldiers and sailors to theaters of war, while the mechanization of more accurate and deadly armaments produced the devastating results of ever-escalating numbers of the seriously wounded and dead. With the development of photography, civilians were compelled to confront the gruesome reality of battlefield carnage as photographs of mutilated bodies and body parts strewn across the battlefields of war fought their way into the public awareness through newspapers and other publications. A few audacious women, such as the Grand Duchess Elena Pavlovna of Russia, organized nurses to aid the wounded in the Crimean War. Clara Barton provided similar service during the American Civil War, and nurse Florence Nightingale traveled to Crimea to aid British soldiers and worked tirelessly to care for the wounded.[2] A forgotten heroine of that same war was nurse Mary Seacole of Scottish and Jamaican descent, who at her own expense moved close to the front lines of the Crimean War to nurse wounded and dying soldiers.

Henry Dunant was traveling in northern Italy in 1859 when he unexpectedly happened upon the Battle of Solferino. Thousands of Italian, French, and Austrian troops, using the weapons of the industrial revolution, battled ferociously for some fifteen hours in suffocating heat. Once the battle was over, Dunant witnessed the awful carnage wreaked by war even as he confronted the unfathomable—the fact that the "armies of the time had four veterinarians for every thousand horses but less than one physician for the same number of men." In his searing memoir, *A Memory of Solferino*, Dunant recounted the atrocities of war that he had witnessed and shared his epiphany that soldiers did not give up their basic rights as human beings simply because they were participating in war. Deeply motivated and inspired by the work of Florence

Nightingale, he proposed the development of an international principle codified within an international convention (a multiparty treaty) of some sort that would provide relief for wounded combatants regardless of their nationality, class, race, or any other distinctions. Dunant's vision managed to capture public attention, resulting eventually in the Geneva International Conference in 1863. Although not formally authorized by their specific countries, representatives of fourteen nations and four philanthropic organizations agreed to establish auxiliary medical societies in their countries to address the issue of wounded combatants. They adopted as their emblem the Swiss flag in reverse—a red cross on a white background.[3]

National Red Cross societies in various countries began to prepare for the inevitability of war by training personnel and stockpiling supplies such as surgical instruments, dressings for wounds, and horse-drawn ambulances. All too soon these committees were pressed into service for the frequent wars and armed conflicts that were typical throughout the remainder of the nineteenth century. Their mission in each case was to protect the wounded and "establish the principle of universality for the rights of all soldiers 'recognizing man as man, without any distinction whatever.'"[4]

As the business of warfare and armed conflict became ever more sophisticated, deadly, and sweeping, humanitarian law evolved from a series of multilateral treaties throughout the remainder of the nineteenth century and for the duration of the twentieth century, which was punctuated by two world wars. A significant response was an international movement to distill the body of humanitarian law into some signature conventions. What has become known as the Geneva Conventions is a series of international treaties that first focused on the treatment of soldiers who had been rendered incapable of fighting because of their wounds. Later attention was focused on prisoners of war. The first convention was initiated by what was originally called the International Committee for Relief to the Wounded but later came to be known as the International Committee for the Red Cross and (subsequently) the Red Crescent.[5] Its purpose was to protect wounded and infirm soldiers and medical personnel against attack, execution without judgment, torture, and assaults upon personal dignity. It also provided soldiers with rights to proper medical treatment and care. The second convention extended the protection of soldiers enumerated in the first convention to shipwrecked sailors and other naval forces, as well as affording special protection to hospital ships.[6]

Following World War II, the establishment of the United Nations, and the promulgation of the Universal Declaration of Human Rights, two additional conventions were added to the Geneva Conventions in 1949. One of the treaties further clarified the definition of prisoner of war (POW), reiterated the proper and humane treatment specified in the first convention for them, and prohibited the use of torture to obtain information from POWs.[7] Eventually, the need to address the treatment of civilians in conflict-ridden areas became apparent. A significant advancement in humanitarian law was incorporated in the fourth convention, reflecting a new international focus on the issue of vulnerable persons during war.[8] Here for the first time civilians were afforded the same protection from inhumane treatment and attack that had been bestowed upon sick and wounded soldiers in the first convention. The fourth convention specifically prohibits attacks on civilian hospitals and medical transports and specifies the rights of interned persons and those who commit acts of sabotage. It is at this particular point that a nexus between humanitarian law and human rights becomes most apparent, as this convention also addresses the issue of how occupying forces are to treat an occupied (and civilian) population.

Two additional protocols to the convention were adopted in 1977 to further elaborate the four earlier Geneva Conventions. The first protocol brought supplementary clarification to the issue of how protected persons are to be treated and to the terminology utilized in the conventions. New rules were developed regarding how the deceased are to be treated and cultural artifacts are to be respected. The protocol also incorporated a discussion regarding the handling of dangerous targets such as dams and nuclear installations.[9] The second protocol sought to clarify the issue of "humane treatment," and the rights of interned persons were more specifically enumerated, especially for those who were charged with crimes during wartime. New protections and rights for civilian populations were also identified.[10]

Even as international humanitarian law was developing, the notion of gender-based violence as a growing issue of concern was also attaining significant attention within the international human rights community through such documents as the UN Declaration on the Elimination of Violence Against Women (DEVAW) and the 1992 General Recommendation No. 19 in the Convention on the Elimination of All Forms of Discrimination Against Women (CEDAW). This recommendation insists that "gender based violence is a form of discrimination that seriously inhibits women's ability to enjoy rights and freedom on a basis of equality with men."[11] The UN Security Council even weighed in on this critical topic in 2000 with Resolution 1325 on Women, Peace and Security. This international attention to the rights of women serves to sharpen overarching definitions of patriarchy through focusing attention on the devastating impact of gender-based violence. The international community is moving toward recognizing that gender-based violence encompasses a multitude of patriarchally sanctioned conduct directed at people because of their gender, especially women and girls, that serves to impede or deprive them of their capacity to exercise their full complement of human rights, including first-, second-, and third-generation rights.[12]

Gabrielle Kirk McDonald

I interviewed Judge Gabrielle Kirk McDonald in her high-rise condo with a panoramic view of Houston, Texas, in 2004. Born Gabrielle Kirk on April 12, 1942, in Saint Paul, Minnesota, she is the daughter of an African American father and a biracial mother who appeared to be white but identified as Black.[13] She grew up in New York and New Jersey and attended Boston University (1959–61), later transferring to Hunter College in New York (1961–63). Although scheduled to graduate in June 1963, she found herself short of credits as a result of the transfer. Rather than complete her undergraduate degree with an additional semester of work, she chose, for a number of personal reasons, to apply to law school instead.

Earlier that year, Kirk had attended a conference at the New School in New York commemorating the one hundredth anniversary of the Emancipation Proclamation. At that conference, she became aware of the long and illustrious history of the Howard University Law School in training civil rights lawyers and in developing strategies to challenge de jure segregation in the courts. She learned that it was to Howard University, the school of Thurgood Marshall and Charles Hamilton, that civil rights attorneys came to practice the arguments that they would present in cases before the courts, including the US Supreme Court. Indeed, Howard was often referred to as the laboratory of the civil rights movement. Intent on becoming not just a lawyer but also a lawyer who specialized in civil rights, Kirk applied to the Howard University Law School. At that time, some law schools were willing to consider applications from students who had completed three years of undergraduate education if they had maintained very good grades. If the student was accepted and she or he successfully completed a law degree, the student would then be awarded both a law degree and an undergraduate degree. Howard was willing to admit an advanced undergraduate to its law school; however, it was unwilling to award an undergraduate degree to that student if she or he had not matriculated as an undergraduate at Howard University. Despite that caveat and in a rush to gain admission to law school, Gabrielle Kirk went to Howard in 1963 and graduated at the top of her class in 1966 with a bachelor of laws.[14] She describes herself as quite content to be in the unique position of holding one university degree—a law degree.

Just as Kirk was intent on attending law school at Howard University, she was equally determined to join the National Association for the Advancement of Colored People (NAACP) Legal Defense and Educational Fund (LDF) after graduation. She joined the staff of the LDF in 1966 and traveled throughout the South—Alabama, Georgia, Louisiana, Mississippi, and Texas—for the remainder of the 1960s, primarily handling employment discrimination cases under Title VII of the 1964 Civil Rights Act.

Kirk's career as a civil rights attorney began in the wake of the 1964 Civil Rights Act, which became effective in 1965. Developing the law around the statute became the focus of the LDF and of Gabrielle Kirk. As new law, there was no direct precedent as to how to interpret the statute, so the LDF "borrowed" from other case law. For example, according to Kirk, the LDF "incorporated some of the concepts developed in the voting rights cases regarding the issues of test requirements for employment discrimination cases." Following the Civil War, laws in the South were rewritten in a manner that required potential Black male voters (and, after the Nineteenth Amendment to the Constitution was adopted in the early twentieth century, Black female voters) to pass arbitrary and capricious tests designed to exclude them from voting or at least limit their participation in the electoral process. Meanwhile, white males who had been registered to vote prior to the war were not required to pass reading tests of their knowledge of the US Constitution; thus, they were effectively "grandfathered" into the electoral process. Eventually, grandfather clauses were successfully challenged in court, because, as Kirk McDonald observed, such requirements "disproportionally and undoubtedly intentionally impacted Blacks, who were previously denied the right to vote because of their race" and their prior condition of servitude. Likewise, in the field of employment, Kirk McDonald noted that if they were employed, African Americans usually found themselves restricted to certain jobs in companies. Prior to passage of the Civil Rights Act of 1964, in order to be considered for the higher-paying jobs reserved for whites, once again Blacks were required to pass tests, a prerequisite that whites did not have to satisfy. The LDF found "analogous reasoning" in the voting rights cases and "borrowed" the precedent to apply to discriminatory employment cases in what Kirk McDonald described as a "creative use of the law."

After marrying Texas attorney Mark McDonald in 1968, Kirk and her husband moved in 1969 to Houston, where they established the McDonald and McDonald law firm. She recalled that when they brought a case against the Houston Police Department for racially discriminatory hiring and promotional practices, she and her husband "were both harassed by members of the police department, which was then led by the notorious Herman Short." She also recollected, "Once I was followed by a police car into my driveway when I had my five-year-old son in the car . . . [and] was also subjected to so-called routine traffic stops." Her husband, Mark, and another Black attorney were also physically abused by the police.[15]

As a practicing attorney in Houston, McDonald sued most of the petrochemical companies and labor unions as she continued her work in civil rights. The employment discrimination cases required her to appear regularly in federal court, where she litigated scores of class-action employment cases against major employers and unions. This was at a time (the 1970s) when Black people rarely appeared in federal court as litigants. Her work attracted the attention of President Jimmy Carter, and in 1979 she was nominated for a federal judgeship in the United States District Court for the Southern District of Texas, becoming the first African American appointed in Texas and the third African American woman in the nation appointed to the federal bench. She served in that capacity until her retirement in 1988.

Perhaps one of her most memorable cases as a federal judge occurred in 1981, when Vietnamese American fishermen filed a lawsuit against the Ku Klux Klan under the Sherman Antitrust Act.[16] The Vietnamese fishermen alleged that the American Fishermen's Coalition and the Klan were violating the law by interfering with their ability to fish for shrimp in the Galveston area.[17] The Texas Klan, under the direction of its grand dragon, Louis Beam, had burned several Vietnamese boats between 1979 and 1981 and conducted a "boat parade" to threaten and intimidate the fishermen on March 15, 1981, the official beginning of the shrimping season. The Texas attorney general intervened, seeking to shut down a paramilitary camp operated by the Klan because it was providing weapons training to members of the American Fishermen's Coalition to be used to intimidate the Vietnamese fishermen. When the case was randomly assigned to McDonald's court, the Klan sought to have her removed, claiming that she as "a Negress" would be biased against the Klan. Although at that time she was the only African American judge in the southern district, she refused to recuse herself, noting that a defendant "is not entitled to a judge of his choice, he is only entitled to a fair and impartial judge."[18] She went on to say that "if race was an issue, then being white was an issue too. I may be a Negress, but I'm a Negress with a black robe and the gavel and the law." She later ruled in favor of the Vietnamese fishermen, ordering the paramilitary camp closed despite the fact that during the course of the trial she and her family were the recipients of death threats and "gifted" with one-way tickets to Africa.[19]

Her expertise in civil rights litigation and her position as a federal judge presiding over criminal cases—specialized knowledge that in turn informed her teaching at the Thurgood Marshall School of Law at Texas Southern University—converged in 1993 to secure her nomination to the International Criminal Tribunal for the former Yugoslavia. McDonald described herself as a member of the "good ol' boy network, [even though] she was not a good ol' boy," adding this to the list of her unique qualifications. A former colleague from the LDF, Conrad Harper, was at that time a legal advisor for the State Department and was therefore privy to information that the State Department was seeking people with prior judicial experience. At the same time, an influential group of women who were permanent representatives to the UN supported her candidacy. They were determined that there would be a war crimes tribunal for the former Yugoslavia, and they were also alarmed by reports of many egregious cases of sexual violence against women. Convinced that it was critical for women to hold some of the judicial positions, they lobbied the UN Security Council, insisting that female judges be appointed to the tribunal.[20]

With the above endorsements, Judge McDonald's name was submitted to the United Nations by the Clinton administration in 1993. Elected in May by the General Assembly, she was the recipient of the highest number of votes cast and became one of two female judges and the only African American among a total of eleven judges on the court at that time. Later, she would meet an African who had been with the UN during the period when she was nominated to the court. He recalled that when some of the African representatives became aware that she was, as he put it, "a sister," they rallied to support her candidacy. McDonald noted, "Even though there are some countries that are at odds with the United States, I was in a unique position, at least with African states, because I was an African American. And when they found out about my civil rights background, they were even more supportive."

Officially titled the International Tribunal for the Prosecution of Persons Responsible for Serious Violations of International Humanitarian Law Committed in the Territory of the Former Yugoslavia since 1991, the ICTY is a specialized agency established by the UN Security Council acting under the auspices of the UN Charter with particular reference to chapter 7, "Action with Respect to Threats to the Peace, Breaches of the Peace and Acts of Aggression."[21] The territorial jurisdiction of the ICTY includes the territory (land surface, airspace, and territorial waters) of the former Socialist Federal Republic of Yugoslavia (FRY), and the ICTY has the power "to prosecute persons responsible for serious violations of international humanitarian law committed in the territory of the former Yugoslavia since 1991.[22] It may prosecute persons who commit or order to be committed grave breaches of the Geneva Conventions, including such acts as willful killing, torture or inhuman treatment, causing suffering or serious injury to body or health, employing poisonous weapons, taking civilians as hostages, depriving prisoners of war or civilians of their rights to fair and regular trials or forcing them to serve in the forces of a hostile power, and the extensive destruction and appropriation of property.[23] The ICTY also has the power to prosecute persons who commit genocide as it is defined in paragraph 2, article 4, including killing or causing serious bodily or mental harm to members of a group, deliberately inflicting conditions of life calculated to bring about the physical destruction of a group in whole or part, imposing measures that are intended to prevent births within the group, and forcibly transferring the children of one group to another. Under article 5 the ICTY is also given the power to prosecute persons who commit "crimes against humanity," including murder; extermination; enslavement; deportation; imprisonment; torture; rape; persecution on the grounds of politics, race, and religion; and other inhumane acts.

According to the statute, the ICTY at that time consisted of three organs: the Chambers, comprised of two Trial Chambers and one Appeals Chamber; the prosecutor; and the Registry, which serviced both the Chambers and the prosecutor. The Chambers were composed of eleven independent judges from different nations. Under article 13 the judges were to be "persons of high moral character, impartiality and integrity who possess the qualifications required in their respective countries for appointment to the highest judicial offices." Additionally, the overall composition of the Chambers took into account the experiences of the judges in criminal and international law, including humanitarian and human rights law. The judges were elected for four-year terms and were eligible for reelection. According to article 14 of the statute, the judges elected a president from among their ranks. The president was a member of the Appeals Chamber and presided over its proceedings. In consultation with the other judges, the president also assigned them to the Appeals and to the Trial Chambers. Three judges were assigned to serve in each of the Trial Chambers, while the other five judges served in the Appeals Chamber.

Inducted as a judge in November 1993, Judge McDonald recalled that the ICTY had "none of the facilities necessary for a criminal justice system to function. We didn't have a courtroom, no rules, no detention facility, and no staff." Indeed, she and another judge accompanied the first president of the ICTY, Antonio Cassese, to look at available space in the Aegon insurance building in The Hague. They took half of the building, but there was no courtroom, so they had to meet in what was called the Winston Churchill Conference Room, an ironic designation that was not lost on McDonald, as she was aware of Churchill's antipathy to the idea of international tribunals. This eventually became their first courtroom. In addition to having to "build everything from scratch," the ICTY also faced budgetary constraints, as this was the first criminal court operated by the UN. McDonald observed that when she served as a federal judge, she "had the benefit of an established infrastructure and staff, with rules of procedure and evidence and clear precedent to look to."[24] Fortunately, prior to becoming an ICTY judge and during her tenure at the Thurgood Marshall School of Law, McDonald worked with attorneys from the US State Department and the Departments of Justice and Defense, who visited her at the school to draft a proposal on rules and procedures of evidence for the ICTY. This proposal-drafting process was also the beneficiary of suggestions from other states and from NGOs. From that endeavor she was prepared to present a full set of rules of procedure in evidence to the other judges at her first meeting in The Hague. That proposal, in turn, assisted the judges in their own process of drafting rules in their plenary meetings. Eventually, the judges adopted some seventy-five pages of rules for a total of 125 rules.[25] The ICTY was finally functional in the fall of 1995 with a staff of more than two hundred, a functional courtroom, a jail, and nine indictments that charged forty-three people of all ethnicities. One defendant, Duško Tadić, had been arrested and was already behind bars.[26]

In an article titled "Problems, Obstacles and Achievements of the ICTY," McDonald distinguished the ICTY from municipal criminal judicial systems and the international tribunals of Nuremberg and Tokyo. Unlike the former, "the Tribunal is not a part of a framework that ensures its arrest warrants and other orders will be executed." Furthermore, unlike the Nuremberg and Tokyo tribunals, the ICTY does not enjoy "the support of the allied powers that wielded full authority over Germany and Japan. Rather the Tribunal must rely on states and international organizations to carry out these functions."[27] Despite the binding obligation of states to cooperate with the ICTY as mandated by the Security Council under the auspices of the UN Charter, the ICTY itself did not possess the direct power to compel states to cooperate. Indeed, in the (all too frequent) event of noncompliance, the ICTY was forced to rely upon the Security Council to enforce its orders and requests.

Christopher Greenwood insisted in an article titled "The Development of International Humanitarian Law by the International Criminal Tribunal for the Former Yugoslavia" that the very manner in which the ICTY was established was problematic, resulting in several important consequences. Unlike that of the Nuremberg tribunal, the source of the ICTY's authority is from "the act of an organ of the UN which possesses no criminal jurisdiction at all." Furthermore, he argued that although the ICTY is the creation of the Security Council, it is "dependent upon the cooperation of states and its relationship with the states and ability to require their assistance are bound up with the extent of the powers of the Council under Chapter VII."[28]

Because the former Yugoslavia was still embroiled in war when the ICTY was convened, the judges anticipated a lack of cooperation and even assumed that compliance would be difficult to achieve. McDonald, along with her colleagues, worked to design measures that would "ameliorate the consequences of non-cooperation." One example of this endeavor, in addition to presidential reports of noncompliance to the Security Council, was the adoption of Rule 61, which "enabled a Trial Chamber to receive evidence of the commission of crimes when an arrest warrant was not executed."[29] A proposal had been advanced for trials in absentia because of the critical problem of non-cooperation. However, McDonald was opposed to the idea of a trial in the absence of the accused unless the accused absconded after having submitted to the jurisdiction of the ICTY. Instead, she proposed a procedure that would preserve the evidence in cases where the accused failed to appear.

> Pursuant to Rule 61 if a state failed to execute an arrest warrant, a Trial Chamber may conduct a public proceeding, in which it receives documentary and testimonial evidence from the Prosecutor. If it finds that there are reasonable grounds to support a finding that the accused has committed any or all of the crimes charged, the Chamber essentially "reconfirms" the indictment and an international arrest warrant is issued. Further, the Chamber may find that the state has, therefore, failed to cooperate with the Tribunal and, in such a case, the President can notify the Security Council.[30]

The chamber may then issue an international arrest warrant, which in turn is sent to all states and to the NATO Stabilisation Force (SFOR).[31]

At a time when states regularly refused to execute the ICTY's warrants and orders, McDonald felt that this procedure was invaluable for at least three reasons. First, during the proceedings, victims could be provided with some solace because they were afforded an opportunity to testify about the atrocities they had allegedly suffered, and this in turn was a way to inform the international community of the egregious violations that were occurring during conflict. Second, despite the fact that these proceedings were not trials, they did provide an occasion for the work of the ICTY to be publicized. Finally, the proceedings provided one way in which a presidential report to the Security Council on noncompliance could be triggered.[32]

While Rule 61 and other rules adopted by the ICTY judges seemed to encourage enforcement of their warrants and orders, in reality such rules of enforcement were largely ineffective because they were reliant upon the Security Council to provide a meaningful response to the judges' reported concerns. Often, the Security Council responded by (in order of significance) issuing a resolution, issuing a statement, or not responding at all. Indeed, McDonald noted that by the spring of 1998 the ICTY had issued some 205 arrest warrants, out of which only 6 had been executed by the states.[33]

McDonald presided over the Duško Tadić case, the first international war crimes trial since Nuremberg and Tokyo. Described as a freelance local thug, Tadić, then a forty-one-year-old Bosnian Serb, was a former café owner from Prijedor in northern Bosnia. He was charged with thirty-one counts of murder, sodomy, and torture at the Omarska concentration camp and other camps where Bosnian Croats and Serbs had been tortured and murdered. His trial began in May 1996. The charges lodged against him constituted crimes against humanity, which are defined as crimes that are committed as part of a widespread or systematic attack against civilians. Likewise, they were also characterized as violations of the law and customs of war, again because they were violent crimes against civilians. Finally, they were defined as grave breaches of the Geneva Conventions because they deprived civilian prisoners of war of their rights. Tadić was to have been charged with rape as well, which would have made his case the first rape trial before a war crimes tribunal. Those charges were dismissed, however, when the only witness was too frightened to testify.[34] Because the original focus of international humanitarian law was international armed conflict, there has been some reluctance to include internal armed conflict as an appropriate subject of humanitarian law. Thus, in the case of the former Yugoslavia, it was necessary for prosecutors to prove that Bosnia was an international armed conflict in which Serbia played an important role.[35]

After five months of deliberation, McDonald, along with her two colleagues in the Trial Chamber, rendered a verdict in May 1997. Of the thirty-one charges, Tadić was found guilty of eleven counts of persecution and crimes against humanity but not of murder. On eleven counts of violating the Geneva Conventions, it was found that the charges did not apply, because it was determined that the war in Bosnia did not rise to the criteria of an international armed conflict.[36] In a verdict delivered by Judge McDonald, Tadić was sentenced to a total of ninety-seven years in prison, but because the sentences were to run concurrently, the maximum sentence would be twenty years unless there was a successful appeal. In her statement, she described his acts as "brutally sadistic" and told him that he had to bear the responsibility for his criminal conduct. Even though Tadić played only a minor role in the wider campaign of persecution, McDonald insisted that he was no less culpable; further, she stated that a more tolerant treatment of the case threatened to ratify "a base view of morality and invite anarchy." As previously mentioned, she had been deeply involved in the process of establishing the rules of evidence and procedures to be used by the ICTY; thus, she viewed the Tadić trial as the test case. She likened it to "seeing an airplane you built fly."[37]

Traditionally, the subject of international law, including humanitarian law, has been the relationship between nation-states. But international human rights law also provides opportunities for individuals and groups to attain standing within the context of international law so that they can seek redress for abuses that they may have suffered. This first trial conducted by the ICTY was of critical importance because it breached the boundaries between humanitarian law and human rights through exploring the possibility of individual responsibility in the commission of war crimes. Thus, war crimes were no longer strictly confined to the realm of relationships between nation-states. McDonald acknowledged the broader implication of Tadić's sentence when she explained that she "wanted to make it clear that we were sentencing the individual, that we were holding him accountable for his crimes."[38]

Drafted by her peers later that same year, McDonald was elected to the presidency of the ICTY and served in that capacity from November 1997 through November 1999. Her presidency was quite productive, as the efforts of the judges to construct the ICTY system were finally beginning to bear fruit. During the first year of her presidency, the ICTY had a record number of twenty-seven persons in custody. This was in large part due not to any actions of the Security Council but rather to support from the SFOR in detaining the accused. The tribunal prosecutor engaged in the practice of issuing sealed indictments, which meant that the SFOR was in a position to arrest unsuspecting inductees. As a result, two suspects were arrested in Bosnia-Herzegovina by the SFOR, while another suspect was arrested by troops in the UN-administered area of Croatia. These arrests attracted considerable international attention and served to enhance the reputation of the ICTY.[39] There was also available a procedure that was euphemistically referred to as "voluntary surrender," a procedure encouraged by the United States.[40]

During McDonald's presidency, the ICTY expanded its infrastructure and caseload and increased the number of judges. The number of courtrooms also increased, from one to three, and the construction of two additional courtrooms was initiated. She presented a proposal to the Security Council to augment the number of judges, and as a result an additional Trial Chamber of three judges was added. At the same time, the number of accused in custody doubled.

During the second year of McDonald's presidency, the war in Kosovo exploded. At that time, she felt compelled to make six reports of noncompliance to the Security Council. The council finally adopted Resolution 1207, which was described at the time as the strongest response by the Security Council to a president's report. Despite a strongly worded resolution ordering the

FRY to transfer three indicted persons and facilitate ICTY access to Kosovo, the noncompliance continued—a blatant violation of international law. McDonald used all the avenues at her disposal to address the critical issue of state noncompliance, including the Contact Group, the Peace Implementation Council, and the North Atlantic Council. In her final report to the Security Council she strongly condemned the fact that some territories had become safe havens for individuals who had been indicted for serious crimes against humanity. She described the behavior as both legally and morally wrong and forcefully urged the Security Council to use its authority to rectify the situation. Unfortunately, her appeals and those of others fell on deaf ears, as the violence in Kosovo escalated with seeming impunity, and the world was once again confounded by the horrific atrocities that were being committed in the region. Despite the lack of definitive support and thwarted by the lack of specific enforcement powers, the ICTY continued to try to fulfill its mandate. Clearly, as McDonald concluded, "states, individually, and the international community, collectively, would determine whether the Tribunal realized its full potential."

Even as she engaged in the critical processes of institution building and the adjudication of cases, it soon became apparent to McDonald that despite the groundbreaking importance of the judges' work, there was an unacknowledged problem of detachment. The ICTY was located in The Hague rather than within the former Yugoslavia, just as the ICTR was located in Arusha, Tanzania, in both cases hundreds of miles away from the sites of war. Furthermore, both tribunals were applying unfamiliar laws that were often viewed as being imposed by biased judges from the West. More often than not, the very people who were the victims of the atrocities of these conflicts were usually uninformed or even erroneously informed about the work of the tribunals. Indeed, not only were the survivors of these war crimes frequently unaware of the proceedings, but even when the perpetrators were held accountable it seemed to have no immediate and visible impact upon the lives of those who had survived these atrocities either in the former Yugoslavia or in Rwanda. Concerned about this disconnect, McDonald suggested that there was a need for an outreach program whose purpose would be, in a sense, "to bring the tribunal to the former Yugoslavia, inform the people what it is that the tribunal does, how it goes about doing this, and what it hopes to accomplish."

While the obvious purpose of a trial is to ascertain guilt or innocence, McDonald insisted that these trials must also serve a larger purpose. In the former Yugoslavia, some two hundred thousand persons were killed, and perhaps two million persons were displaced, while in Rwanda it is estimated that eight hundred thousand to a million people were killed. In addition to the critical work of litigating humanitarian law, judges in the criminal courts are also engaged in the business of creating a historical record to guard against the problem of revisionism so that people will be unable to deny that these atrocities actually occurred. It is in that sense, according to McDonald, that documenting the scope of the atrocities accurately is a critical component of the wider role of social justice. She insisted that "people need to understand what happened, because until you know what happened, how can you go beyond the experience and try to forgive?"

While McDonald was president of the ICTY she also served as the presiding judge of the Appeals Chamber for both the Yugoslav and the Rwanda tribunals. She recalled visiting a genocide site and meeting with many of the local people when she was in Africa to consult with the ICTR. She was deeply concerned to learn that so many of the people she encountered were opposed to the ICTR because they did not see its relevance to their lives. "I tried to explain that one of the major contributions of the ICTR was that it had the resources to try these complicated cases and funds to develop an historical record in the process so that no one could deny what had happened in Rwanda."

As she contemplated this sensitive issue, McDonald applied her prior experiences as a civil rights attorney and a federal judge. When she was sworn in as a federal judge in 1979, she characterized the court as a "people's court" in her remarks because "we're here to solve problems that can prevent people from living together peacefully, and we address obstacles that prevent people from utilizing and having the opportunity to fully utilize their capabilities." Thus, she posited the notion that federal judges were truly on the front lines with the broad mission to give "meaning to the fabric of our society." She observed that although it is stated in the Declaration of Independence that we are all created equal with certain unalienable rights, it is "even at this late date a promise that is often honored more in its breach." The federal courts, then, are dealing with issues around the fact that our society has failed to come to grips with "a kind of dichotomy between the promises of the . . . Declaration of Independence and the reality of everyday racism and arbitrary obstacles. How can we all as a people interact with each other with respect and dignity and equality?" She pointed out that at the international level, both the Yugoslav and the Rwanda tribunals perform a similar function. That is, they are "exacting accountability after ethno-religious conflicts and helping survivors to put aside their difference and thereby lay the foundation for the beginning of reconciliation." How can people begin to live together, interact, and go forward with their lives?

The UN Security Council acted in the belief that prosecuting persons responsible for the commission of these serious violations of international humanitarian law could help bring about an end to such violations. Furthermore, it was believed that the establishment of the tribunals would also serve to promote and maintain international peace and security. McDonald argued, "Before the Tribunal can be truly effective and achieve its mandate, the people in the region must share a consensus that the Court is legitimate. They must know, understand and appreciate the work of the Tribunal," and "this was the goal of the Outreach Programme."[41]

McDonald described this time as the most fascinating, exciting, challenging, rewarding, exhausting, and wonderful period in her life. (And she admitted to eating lots of peanut butter sandwiches for dinner before getting up early the next morning to start all over again.) Although her passion lay in trying cases, she had willingly accepted the position of tribunal president, despite the fact that it required so much administrative work and travel; indeed, she felt that there was also a critical yet unstated ambassadorial character to the position. She recalled one four-week period in which she traveled to Cairo to speak at the American University, to China to speak at an International Criminal Court conference, to Tanzania to meet with the ICTR, and to Rome for a conference on the establishment of the International Criminal Court. Such travel was physically demanding, and that combined with the sense that her "experience was full" informed her decision to retire yet again. She has a keen appreciation of the opportunity to participate in the creation of an important international institution, including drafting the first rules of procedures and all the other provisions necessary for a court to function. She collaborated with an array of judicial colleagues from around the world with impressive résumés of legal experience in a shared vision of creating a new and important international institution that would transform both the conceptualization and application of international humanitarian law and international human rights.

Patricia Viseur Sellers

When Judge McDonald first arrived at The Hague, she was the youngest judge, at age fifty-one, and an African America woman at a time when there were very few women and no other African Americans who had been or were employed by the ICTY. Although deeply engrossed in the fascinating business of constructing the institution and trying cases, McDonald admitted to feeling isolated from, and missing the company of, other African American women as she worked and crafted a life in a European city. Attorney Patricia Viseur Sellers applied for a law clerk's position with McDonald, though at that time no provisions had been made to support a program for law clerks, so she referred Sellers to the Deputy Prosecutor's Office. Sellers joined the Office of the Prosecutor in July 1994, serving until 2007.

I traveled to The Hague to interview Patricia Sellers. On July 31, 2002, we met for dinner in one of her favorite restaurants and then returned to the quiet of my hotel room for the interview.[42] I learned that Sellers, too, brought a wealth of experience to her work in the tribunals. Born and raised in Camden, New Jersey, she received her bachelor of arts degree in political science at Rutgers College, Rutgers University, in 1976 and was awarded a doctor of law degree from the University of Pennsylvania Law School in 1979 with an emphasis on criminal and international law. Along the way she also obtained a certificate in Latin American studies from the National Autonomous University of Mexico in 1975. She was a public defender for a short time in Philadelphia, a position that helped strengthen her background in criminal law. She volunteered with the American Friends Service Committee, the service arm of the Society of Friends (the Quakers), and was also engaged in outreach work with the Philadelphia branch of the National Conference of Black Lawyers (NCBL). She had also served as the Directorate-General for External Relations at the European Commission.

Sellers was a program officer for the Ford Foundation in Latin America during the early 1980s. While she worked in the Rio de Janeiro, Brazil, office, she included women's projects in her funding portfolio. She supported programming in women's rights at a time when Brazil was just emerging from its dictatorship phase of government, and she included early funding of many of the initiatives created by Afro-Brazilian women. She learned that projects dealing with women's health were among the few issues that could be brought forward while the country was transitioning from dictatorship to democracy. Sellers credits this work with providing a basis for her understanding of profound events such as genocide that take place during periods of armed conflict, although she firmly declared that "no one has practice in genocide." In our interview, she acknowledged an ability "to work with the NGO community as they interact on the crisis issues but from a legal point of view." Those educational and professional experiences, including living outside the United States for several years and her fluency in French, Portuguese, and Spanish (along with English), served to prepare her for her work in international humanitarian law with the tribunals.

As Sellers reflected upon her social justice endeavors at the local level, she contemplated their relationship to international human rights, observing that one has to acknowledge that it is a complex and multifaceted area, even as "we pretend that we can talk about it in nice simple terms." She insists that those who are engaged in doing large-scale international human rights work do so "because it relates to a local social justice issue or various local social justice issues put together. Big issues often remind me of some of the local issues . . . that I have lived. Had we known it, we would have called it that. [For example,] had I known that I was talking about torture, I wouldn't have kept using the word 'police brutality.'" In acknowledging that this torture was often seemingly unknown at the local level, she observed that frequently the focus is different, the vocabulary is different, the method of addressing the issue is different, and even what may be considered a resolution to the issue may be different. She recalled attending a conference in India on torture and coming to the startling realization that despite the fact that she usually addressed it within the context of war, most of the torture that happens in the world occurs outside of the context of war. She also realized that police brutality should be understood as a form of torture.

The Deputy Prosecutor's Office opened in the ICTY at the beginning of 1994. Sellers explained that "the Office of the Prosecutor is mandated with investigating and then bringing to trial the cases we have investigated." She described her position in the Office of the Prosecutor as twofold: she was both the legal advisor for gender-related crimes to the ICTY and one of the trial attorneys. Her first title was acting senior trial attorney. She was later confirmed as the trial attorney, a position she held from 1998 to 2002. During her tenure at the ICTY, she was also the deputy head of the legal advisory section, which advises the Trial and Appeals Chambers team on international law (basically, the international law section). Her main function was "to develop and . . . assist in the execution of strategies to investigate and . . . prosecute sexual violence as war crimes or crimes against humanity or as part of a genocide within the Yugoslav tribunal and as a prosecutor to bring forward cases."

Sellers stated that she dealt on a daily basis with "violations of humanitarian law of armed conflict or of crimes of humanity against humanity and genocide":

> My work is to make certain that there is a viable and sustainable jurisprudence on the books to declare that raping women during war is not inevitable, it's a crime. Sexually abusing or threatening to abuse women as a manner of attacking a civil population is part of a basis for a crime against humanity. Women in Rwanda who were raped prior to being killed, those rapes were part of the genocide. Perpetrators didn't stop committing genocide when they raped the women, then go back to the genocide. The definition of genocide now includes sexual assault violations.

Sellers was fully committed to ensuring that women and girls impacted by all the events of war are neither disregarded nor treated as if they are nonvictims because they are somehow excluded from the interpretation of the law. She sought to eliminate from interpretations of humanitarian law the appalling rebuff that "'we wish we could do something for you, but rape is not a war crime, sorry.' We must make sure that the gap is not only narrowed but that the myth [the idea that rape is not a war crime] that it ever existed is something we should recoil in horror from."

In her position as the deputy head in the Office of the Prosecutor, Sellers was directly involved in some of the most important cases to come before the Yugoslavian and Rwandan tribunals. Most notably, she was co-counsel on the Jean-Paul Akayesu case and an advisor on the Alfred Musema case before the ICTR. In the groundbreaking Akayesu case, the defendant was charged with rape as a "constituent act of crimes against humanity, outrages upon personal dignity as a war crime, and sexual violence as a constituent act of genocide." In their paper "The Jurisprudence of Sexual Violence," K. Alexa Koenig, Ryan Lincoln, and Lauren Groth described the two most significant aspects of this case. In an unprecedented development in international law, the Trial Chamber articulated a relationship between sexual violence and genocide by acknowledging that sexual violence could be done with the intent of *killing members of a group*, could constitute *serious bodily or mental harm*, could be composed of *measures intended to prevent births within the group*, and could amount to *forcibly transferring children of the group to another group*.[43]

For the first time in international law, the Trial Chamber identified the specific elements of the crime of rape and distinguished it from sexual violence. The elements of rape were defined as "a physical invasion of a sexual nature committed on a person under circumstances which are coercive."[44] A definition of sexual violence that emerged from this case broadly defined it as "any act of a sexual nature which is committed on a person under circumstances which are coercive," an act that could involve harm to a person's dignity regardless of whether there was penetration or physical contact.[45] Based on these carefully constructed judicial enunciations, Akayesu was ultimately convicted of genocide based on evidence of sexual violence. Decided approximately two years later, the Musema case affirmed much of the jurisprudence found in the Akayesu case.

Sellers was also the trial attorney on the Anto Furundžija case, which came before the ICTY. Furundžija, the commander of a special military police unit of the Croatian Defense Council, was convicted of rape and torture as war crimes. Interestingly, the decisions of the tribunals are not necessarily binding upon one another. In this case, the ICTY decided to establish its own definition of the elements of rape in part to ascertain whether rape could also actually constitute torture. Ultimately, the tribunal developed the violation as "(i) the sexual penetration, however slight, of the vagina or anus of the victim by penis of the perpetrator; (ii) by coercion or force or threat of force against a victim or third person."[46] Based on this definition, Furundžija was convicted of outrages to personal dignity and of rape as torture, another significant development in international law. Similar to the case of Akayesu, this case also "eschews the non-consent of the victim as a prerequisite to the commission of rape." In fact, the case reinforced the notion that "any form of captivity vitiated consent."[47]

In addition to the above, Sellers was the trial lawyer on the Dragan Nikolić case, the first person to be indicted by the ITCY and the first to be the subject of an international arrest warrant. She was an advisor to the Dragoljub Kunarac case, the first case in which the accused was convicted of the crime of rape as a crime against humanity and the first time that an international tribunal prosecuted sexual slavery. The Kunarac case was also notable for departing from the definition of rape established in the Furundžija case by mandating "a two-pronged lack-of-consent requirement." This requirement included, first, an assessment of whether the victim gave voluntary consent based on free will and, second, the perpetrator's knowledge that penetration occurred without consent. This decision differed from the prior Furundžija decision because the Kunarac decision was considered to be broader, thus requiring that the "'non-consensual or non-voluntary' element of the crime needed to be calibrated to reflect the appropriate scope of the norm against rape under international law." Its significance arises out of the inclusion for the first time of "an explicit and affirmative inquiry into the consent of the victim rather than an inquiry into the presence of force or coercion, which would imply non-consent." The Trial Chamber found that the "basic principle" that underlies the crime of rape is a violation of sexual autonomy, which is subsumed within the consent prong of the definition of rape.[48] This definition was upheld in the Appeals Chamber, although the justices recognized that when victims were held in detention centers, that amounted to "circumstances that were so coercive as to negate any possibility of consent."[49]

Sellers was an advisor on the complicated Čelebići prison camp case, a joint trial of four defendants who occupied different positions of authority at the camp. She was also an advisor on the previously mentioned Tadić case, the first to be tried in an international tribunal since the German and Tokyo tribunals following World War II. Other cases in which she was involved included those of Radislav Krstić, Momčilo Krajišnik, Slobodan Milošević, Ramush Haradinaj, and Naser Orić. These and other cases combined to carefully construct the necessary precedents for a gender-sensitive humanitarian law that was also responsive to the contributions of international human rights.

In her work at the ICTY, Sellers, along with McDonald and the other judges, lawyers, and investigators, were "challenged to deliver gender-competent interpretations of humanitarian norms that govern war crimes, international crimes, and doctrines of individual responsibility, such as command responsibility or procedural safeguards of due process, especially in light of the plethora of evidence submitted by witnesses recounting gender-based violence."[50] Sellers's efforts on these and other cases that came before the tribunals during her tenure are profound contributions to international humanitarian law because they provide critical definitions of sexual violence. Prior to the deliberations of these international tribunals, sexual violence was understood historically to be a violation of a man's property rights in a woman, and under such conceptualizations, women were afforded only vague protection against sexual assaults. These tribunal cases are indicative of a profound shift in international norms that clarified and defined sexual violence as an egregious crime in a manner that moved "towards respecting the human dignity and bodily integrity of the victims themselves."[51] Sellers argues forcefully that rape is a core violation of humanitarian law, and prosecution of rape serves as a way to measure protection offered under international law from gender-based violence. Further, prosecution affords women and girls with much-needed protection of their rights to equal access to a judicial forum.[52]

The International Criminal Tribunals for Rwanda and Yugoslavia have been described as the "primary engines driving the development of an international jurisprudence prohibiting rape and sexual violence."[53] Subsequently, the International Criminal Court, established in 1998, relied upon the jurisprudence around rape and sexual violence produced by the ICTY and ICTR (and later the Special Court for Sierra Leone). The founding treaty of the International Criminal Court, referred to as the Rome Statute (2002), has moved to distill the definitions of rape and sexual violence in a manner that clarifies critical notions of accountability while also providing greater procedural protections to those victims who have agreed to participate in the court's proceedings.

Through her scholarly endeavors, Sellers has made crucial and important contributions to the jurisprudence of international humanitarian law and human rights and to the development of a synergistic articulation of these fields. She has authored numerous articles for legal journals and for the UN, including "Wartime Female Slavery: Enslavement?," "Sexual Violence and Peremptory Norms: The Legal Value of Rape," and "The Prosecution of Sexual Violence in Conflict: The Importance of Human Rights as Means of Interpretation." Building upon her practical experience as a trial lawyer with the international tribunals, she continues to provide brilliant analyses that serve to explore the critical complexity of issues of rape and sexual violence within the context of armed conflict and to offer innovative, well-grounded approaches for the protection of the rights and dignity of women and girls.

The Women's International War Crimes
Tribunal on Japan's Military Sexual Slavery

Attorney Patricia Viseur Sellers and Judge Gabrielle Kirk McDonald also participated in another historic and innovative event in the amalgam of international humanitarian law and human rights: the Women's International War Crimes Tribunal on Japan's Military Sexual Slavery. Convened in Tokyo from December 8 to 12, 2000, its mission was "to establish the criminal liability of high-ranking Japanese military and political officials," including the late former emperor Hirohito, and "the separate responsibility of the state of Japan for rape and sexual slavery as crimes against humanity arising out of Japanese military activity in the Asia Pacific region in the 1930s and 1940s."[54]

This tribunal was a belated response to a system of slavery devised by the Japanese military as a tactic to build troop morale through supplying them with "recreational" sex from enslaved females from other Asian countries and at least one woman from a European country. They were called "comfort women," a ludicrous misnomer that belies the horrifying brutality of such ordeals in a systematic organization.

In an article titled "Wartime Female Slavery: Enslavement?," Sellers describes aspects of the Japanese administration of this system, which included the routine medical examination of the enslaved females and soldiers to protect against sexually transmitted diseases because they could have an adverse impact on the soldiers' fighting ability. Furthermore, the military saw the system of comfort women as a way to decrease the possibility of espionage and potential leaks about military operations and tactics. Oddly, an additional rationale put forth by military officials at the time was that enslaved females would prevent the invading Japanese soldiers from raping women and girls in occupied territories. Ironically, it was felt that such behavior would create ill will among occupied populations. Although the system ceased at the end of World War II, a Japanese version of an Emancipation Proclamation for the enslaved women was never issued. Rather, when the Japanese army retreated, it simply left the women and girls behind. Thus, they were never officially released from bondage, nor were they transported back to their countries of origin. Those who managed to survive either remained where they were left or had to figure out their own ways of returning to their homes. Profoundly affected physically and emotionally by their horrendous experiences, the women were left to cope in silence and shame with their shattered lives. When the Japanese finally admitted the existence of such a system, they insisted that the women and girls were really prostitutes who had volunteered their services as their patriotic contribution to the war effort.[55]

After World War II, the International Military Tribunal for the Far East (IMTFE), was created; however, it "was bereft of any evidence of the enslavement of over 1,000,000 Burmese, Indonesian, Chinese, Japanese, Korean, Taiwanese and Filipino 'comfort women.'"[56] Sellers argues that the IMTFE Charter should have resulted in multiple convictions for war crimes and crimes against humanity in regard to the comfort women. The IMTFE could and should have pursued convictions for crimes such as rape, imprisonment, murder, torture, inhumane treatment, and slavery. It did, however, indict some individuals for other sexual crimes, including rape and sexual assault of female prisoners of war, as well as the rapes of female and male inhabitants of occupied territories.

For many years, Korean professor Yun Chung-ok had been engaged in investigating the brutal treatment that women had undergone in "comfort stations" at the hands of the Japanese military before and throughout World War II. By 1988 the women's movement in the Republic of Korea had become aware of her work and sought additional details. Slowly, elderly women began to speak publicly about their experiences as comfort women and about the lives of isolation, shame (due to sexist patriarchal beliefs that this was somehow their fault), poverty, and mental and physical illness that they as survivors endured after the war. Finally, in 1991 the first lawsuit for damages and compensation was filed in Japan, and the issue was raised before the UN Commission on Human Rights in 1992 and subsequently brought before other UN bodies, including at the 1993 Vienna World Conference on Human Rights. Public hearings were also held in Tokyo. The International Commission of Jurists provided legal analysis based on its investigation of the issue through examining the documentary evidence and collecting the testimony of survivors.[57]

The shameful response of the Japanese government included denial that there was any official governmental involvement in the establishment and operation of the comfort system. However, as more and more women came forward to offer testimony about their experiences, the government finally made a carefully limited acknowledgment and expressed some guarded remorse, even as it continued its denial of any legal responsibility. The government sought protection under the peace treaties concluded in the 1950s, arguing that those treaties had terminated any claims and, further, that individuals had no standing under international law. Although the Japanese government continues to deny its legal responsibility, it has acknowledged a moral responsibility. In addition to some formal and informal apologies, it established a semiofficial organization, the Asian Women's Fund, on the fiftieth anniversary of the end of World War II. The fund was to be a vehicle for compensation to the victims and survivors of the system. However, rather than providing governmental funds, the Japanese government relies on private donations. Rumi Sakamoto has observed, "The Asian Women's Fund was largely regarded as a 'charity payment' designed to obscure the state's official responsibility."[58]

Frustrated by the lack of appropriate responses to their plight and concerned that the remaining frail and elderly survivors were running out of time, other organizations created other avenues for redress. A people's tribunal called the Women's International War Crimes Tribunal was spearheaded by the Violence Against Women in War Network, Japan (VAWW-NET, Japan), which was founded in 1988. The establishment of the Women's International War Crimes Tribunal was proposed by VAWW-NET at the 1998 Asian Women's Solidarity Conference in Seoul. Its purpose was to provide a judgment on the system of sexual slavery conducted by the Japanese military prior to and during World War II under the auspices of international law and based on gender justice. Following the International Conference on Violence against Women in War and Armed Conflict Situations, held in Tokyo in 1997, planning for the tribunal commenced with two preparatory conferences, one in Tokyo in December 1998 and the second in Seoul in February 1999. The International Organizing Committee was formed to conduct research and investigation, draw up the tribunal charter, and prepare for the tribunal's meeting in Tokyo.[59]

A panel of judges, including Gabrielle Kirk McDonald (by then the former president of the ITCY, now acting as the chief judge of the Women's Tribunal), Carmen María Argibay (a criminal law judge in Argentina and president of the International Association of Women Jurists), Dr. Willy Mutunga (a human rights lawyer from Kenya), and Christine M. Chinkin (professor of international law at the London School of Economics and Political Science) presided over the Women's Tribunal. Eight regional teams of prosecutors presented cases on behalf of the former comfort women who were able to testify either in person or via video. The two lead prosecutors were Patricia Sellers (the chief prosecutor) and Ustinia Dolgopol (senior lecturer, Flinders Law School, South Australia). Together they led the prosecutorial team, which developed and presented a common indictment. Interestingly, Sellers indicated that the ITCY had given her formal permission to attend the Women's Tribunal, and by doing so, they, in essence, provided public international support for it.[60] Gay McDougall, who appears elsewhere in this book, was a UN special rapporteur at the time, and she was invited to participate as an expert witness.

Chinkin, who described the overall prosecution strategy as "simple but subtle," explained: "The prosecutors argued that trials at the end of the Second World War with respect to the Japanese conduct of war, including the proceedings of the International Military Tribunal for the Far East, were incomplete in that they had inadequately considered rape and sexual enslavement and had failed to bring charges arising out of the detention of women for sexual services. Accordingly, this tribunal could be seen as an addendum to those earlier proceedings and the named indicted persons were those who had been tried earlier."[61] Over the course of three days, the IMTFE heard evidence presented by many of the seventy-five survivors of the comfort stations who were present. Prosecutors also presented affidavits and submitted videos as evidence to the court. Additionally, two former Japanese soldiers testified to their involvement in and use of the comfort station facilities.

The Japanese government was unresponsive to an invitation to participate in the proceedings, although police protection was provided for the participants. This was not a UN-sanctioned activity. Rather, this could best be described as a people's tribunal—but one that strictly observed procedural constraints on the officers of the court. Despite the lack of legal authority, judges and prosecutors were separated throughout the proceedings, and the registry recorded all evidence. Chinkin characterized it as "a striking example of the developing role of civil society as an international actor."[62]

Chinkin argues that law does not belong to governments; instead, it is actually an instrument of civil society that has the right to step in when governments fail to meet the obligation of ensuring justice for their people. She goes on to observe that even though a people's tribunal is not able to guarantee due process in the same manner as a state or international court of law, nor is such a tribunal able to impose sentences or order reparations, it is able to make recommendations "backed by the weight of its legal findings and its moral force." Chinkin explains that "such a forum constitutes a form of public acknowledgement to the survivors that serious crimes were committed against them," and such acknowledgment in turn is "recognized as being essential to redressing feelings of shame and guilt and providing healing and closure." Chinkin concludes that a people's tribunal "combine[s] in a single process elements of both war crimes trials and truth commissions."[63]

The Women's International War Crimes Tribunal made significant contributions to the development of both international humanitarian law and women's human rights. As Sakamoto observed, this tribunal recognized the right of individuals to act under international law; furthermore, prior peace treaties and bilateral treaties between Japan and other states could not diminish an individual's right to compensation for governmental abuse. In addition, it found that the failure of the postwar Japanese government to prosecute the responsible parties and make reparations along with the wartime violence itself constituted a legal basis for compensation claims.[64] Perhaps most important, the Women's Tribunal provided a public international platform for the stories of the victims and survivors. They were finally able, through publicly sharing their memories, to transfer their crushing burdens of unwarranted shame to the Japanese government, the party responsible for the harm inflicted on them.

Conclusion

The brilliant contributions of Gabrielle Kirk McDonald and Patricia Viseur Sellers to the rights of women under international human rights and humanitarian law are truly exceptional yet, unfortunately, unheralded. Just as we have engaged in the project of retrieving the important contributions of Black women to the US civil rights movement, it is imperative for us to retrieve the unknown or little-known stories of Black women's contributions to the development of international law.

3

Localizing International
Human Rights

Our feminist identity is not qualified with "Ifs," "Buts," or "Howevers." We are
Feminists. Full stop.

> Charter of Feminist Principles for African Feminists, 2006

[We are] struggling to actualize visions of women's rights, social justice, and
democratic development.

> Ayesha Imam, interview with the author, 2004

Ayesha Imam and Loretta Ross are firmly avowed feminists committed to the transformative power of global human rights, which began at the local level in their own communities. While one is Nigerian and the other American, they nevertheless share a passionate commitment to the development of holistic, inclusive, and effective human rights that will improve and enhance the lives of women, children, and men.

Feminism, both African and Black, and the commitment to human rights education are deeply integrated into their respective ventures. Ayesha Imam was among the more than one hundred self-identified African feminist activists who congregated in Accra, Ghana, from across the continent and the diaspora to participate in the African Feminist Forum in November 2006. Together these activists drafted and adopted the Charter of Feminist Principles for African Feminists, which "sets out the collective values that we hold as key to our work and to our lives as African feminists." Additionally, it defined their "individual and collective responsibilities to the movement and to one another within the movement."[1]

The feminist analysis that suffuses the charter insists upon thoroughly interrogating patriarchy. Essential to African feminism, then, is a holistic understanding of the ideology of patriarchy. In turn, the charter provides a framework for understanding the totality of oppressive and exploitative relations that African women must contend with. The charter defines patriarchy as "a system of male authority which legitimizes the oppression of women through political, social, economic, legal, cultural, religious and military institutions." It recognizes that as patriarchy varies across histories and cultures, manifestations of class, race, ethnic, religious, and global-imperial relationships and structures, as well as the interrelationships of those factors, are also negotiated through patriarchy. The charter insists that African women's capacity as feminists to effectively challenge patriarchy relies upon their abilities to "challeng[e] other systems of oppression and exploitation, which frequently mutually support each other."[2]

African feminists are also dedicated to their membership in "the global feminist movement against patriarchal oppression in all its manifestations." Just as important, they deny the notion that feminism was imported into Africa from the West and insist upon "reclaim[ing] and assert[ing] the long and rich tradition of African women's resistance to patriarchy in Africa."[3]

The charter provides a list of "individual ethics," and African feminists agree to commit themselves to that list. They believe in feminist principles based on gender equality, including but not limited to the following:

- The indivisibility, inalienability and universality of women's human rights.
- The effective participation in building and strengthening progressive African feminist organizing and networking to bring about [transformative] change. . . .
- The practice of non-violence and the achievement of non-violent societies.
- The right of all women to live free of patriarchal oppression, discrimination and violence. . . .
- Freedom of choice and autonomy regarding bodily integrity issues, including reproductive rights, abortion, sexual identity and sexual orientation.
- A critical engagement with discourses of religion, culture, tradition and domesticity with a focus on the centrality of women's rights.
- The recognition and presentation of African women as the subjects not the objects of our work, and as agents in their lives and societies.[4]

Just as Imam identifies as an African feminist, Loretta Ross defines herself as a Black feminist. She subscribes to the acclaimed 1978 Black Feminist Statement from the Combahee River Collective. It succinctly declares a shared belief that "black women are inherently valuable, that our liberation is a necessity

Localizing International Human Rights

not as an adjunct to somebody else's but because of our need as human persons for autonomy." The collective's definition of feminism emerges not only from historical and contemporary abuse and mistreatment, particularly of US Black women, but also from the disheartening fact that other progressive movements have failed to prioritize and address their specific forms of oppression. For that reason, members of the collective understood that "the only people who care enough about us to work consistently for our liberation is us." Thus, "[our] politics evolve from a healthy love for ourselves, our sisters and our community, which allows us to continue our struggle and work." Black feminists embraced the concept of identity politics as a profound and potentially radical politics because it centralized their oppressions, as opposed to working to end the oppression of others: "It is obvious from looking at all the political movements that have preceded us that anyone is more worthy of liberation than ourselves."[5]

Despite almost three decades of separation, both the Combahee River Collective and the African Feminist Forum identified patriarchy as pervasive, interrelated, and difficult to separate from such forms of identity as race and class. Their advocacy of a radical liberation for all oppressed peoples is premised not only upon the destruction of patriarchy but also upon the demise of the political-economic systems of capitalism and imperialism. Members of the Combahee River Collective embrace socialism based on their beliefs that work must be organized for the collective benefit of the people and that material resources must be distributed among those who have created those resources. They insist that class relationships can only be understood if they account for the specific class position of Black women—what is more recently referred to as the intersectionality of gender, race, and class.[6]

bell hooks has long been central to the project of defining US Black feminism, and her work has directly informed Loretta Ross's politics and activism. hooks distilled our understanding of feminism into the following pithy definition: "Feminism is a struggle to end sexist oppression. Therefore, it is necessarily a struggle to eradicate the ideology of domination that permeates Western culture on various levels as well as a commitment to reorganizing society so that the self-development of people can take precedence over imperialism, economic expansion and material desires."[7] Both Ross and Imam, committed international human rights advocates, are unusual in that they have also insisted upon integrating human rights education into their feminist activism. Article 26 of the Universal Declaration of Human Rights, adopted in 1948, pronounces education a human right, and that right is further elaborated in paragraph 2 of the article: "Education shall be directed to the full development of the human personality and to the strengthening of respect for human rights and fundamental freedoms. It shall promote understanding, tolerance and friendship among all nations, racial or religious groups, and shall further the activities of the United Nations for the maintenance of peace."[8]

Although the Universal Declaration of Human Rights provides a right to education, it was not until the 1980s and 1990s that the international community moved to strengthen human rights through integrating human rights education into the right to an education. The 1993 Vienna World Conference on Human Rights reaffirmed and sought to accelerate the implementation of the right to education. In response to that imperative, the UN General Assembly declared 1995–2004 the Decade of Human Rights Education. Human rights education (HRE), described as a "long term strategy with its sights set on the needs of coming generations," is an essential contribution to the long-term project of preventing human rights abuses and achieving a just society that respects and strives to implement human rights standards.[9]

The Office of the High Commissioner for Human Rights has declared: "Human rights can only be achieved through an informed and continued demand by people for their protection. Human rights education promotes values, beliefs and attitudes that encourage all individuals to uphold their own rights and those of others. It develops an understanding of everyone's common responsibility to make human rights a reality in each community."[10] During the decade, HRE was to be introduced into all levels of formal education, but, equally important, it was to be adopted in "nonformal" or popular education as well. A general methodology to promote HRE favors "interactive, participatory and culturally relevant learning methods" as various NGOs focus on their specialized constituencies.[11] Ultimately, HRE is committed to the construction of a "universal culture of human rights." As Eleanor Roosevelt so presciently stated in 1948:

> It will be a long time before history will make its judgment on the value of the Universal Declaration of Human Rights, and the judgment will depend, I think on what the people of different nations do to make this document familiar to everyone. If they know it well enough, they will strive to attain some of the rights and freedoms set forth in it, and that effort on their part is what will make it of value in clarifying what was meant in the [UN] Charter in the references to human rights and fundamental freedoms.[12]

Imam and Ross are not only familiarizing their constituencies with the power of human rights through HRE but are also deeply engaged in the project that Sally Engle Merry refers to as "remaking human rights in the vernacular."[13]

In her book *Human Rights and Gender Violence*, Merry explores how international human rights law is translated through activists serving as intermediaries from the global to the local context. As Imam and Ross conceptualize and perform the role of intermediaries, their roles are actually multidirectional; that is, as they engage in introducing international human rights to their local constituencies, they also insist that the grass roots can and do provide input that is invaluable to the ever-expansive development of the corpus of international human rights. Their stories of human rights advocacy and activism follow.

Ayesha Imam

Ayesha Imam, the daughter of a Nigerian father and a Chinese mother, was born in 1957. She is married to a Senegalese man, and they are the parents of a son. Her siblings and extended family members are the quintessential twenty-first-century globalized family. They too are married to spouses from other countries, so Imam has relatives living and working on every continent except Antarctica. As a result, travel is a family custom, as they regularly visit each other in the countries where they reside around the world. My initial and primary interview of Ayesha took place one Sunday afternoon in 2004 in the comfortable living room of her home. At the time, she and her family were living in New York City while she worked as a consultant with the United Nations. Over the years, we have informally met and spoken on several other occasions.

Imam has an impressive résumé that traces a complex journey along the contested paths of social justice and social transformation. Her formal training includes a bachelor of science degree in sociology from the North London Polytechnic (which has since merged into the London Metropolitan University in England) in 1980; a master's degree in sociology and mass media from Ahmadu Bello University in Zaria, Nigeria, in 1987; and a doctor of philosophy degree in social anthropology from the School of African and Asian Studies at the University of Sussex, England, in 1994. She would argue that certainly of equal importance is the informal training that she has also acquired through her human rights activism over the course of her career.

Imam, who rarely uses the pronoun "I," appears to be most comfortable using the pronoun "we" in a manner that emphasizes the collaborative nature of her (their) endeavors. However, despite this collaborative ethos, there are some who are threatened by her passionate dedication to human rights. In fact, she was the recipient of her first death threat in March 1985, soon after she issued her first public statement on the potential of women's liberation in Islam.[14]

Imam and her colleagues engage in something they have termed "double claiming critique strategy." Speaking with a soft British accent, during our interview she described "discourses about rights, about gender relations, about the notion of who can do, speak for, what are ours whether they come from 'local contexts' in the sense of ideologies or religious ideologies which may themselves become international of course. Or whether they come from the formal international level, like international human rights discourses and treaties." She insisted, "They are ours in the sense that we have the right to participate in defining them. So we claim them; we have the right to participate in defining them and insist that there's a space for us to do that. And we have therefore also a right to critique them at all levels."[15]

More specifically, in Nigeria the women initially began by examining the "construction of rights and particularly [the construction] of women's human rights in gender discourses." Imam observed that although Nigeria is host to many cultural contexts, Nigerians also share similar colonial and postcolonial histories and experiences. Imam and her colleagues were convinced that they had the right to draw upon not only those histories but also the formal secular constitutional laws of Nigeria. Furthermore, they recognized that they had access to international human rights discourses, particularly those found in such documents as the Convention on the Elimination of All Forms of Discrimination Against Women (CEDAW), the Vienna Declaration on Women, and the Beijing Plan of Action.

Imam asserted the "criticality of (re)claiming," because as she and her associates have pursued the business of championing women's issues, they have often been accused of being Westernized and therefore traitors to their communities, their own cultures, and their heritages. Thus, it became important for them to do two things. First, they have insisted that, indeed, "cultures are complex, changing, and imbued with power relations." Second, they are attentive to the fact that those people who have had the power to define the current cultural traditions, rights, and religion "have usually been men and have always been upper class."

The women insist that African social formations were always imbued with what were formerly referred to as "class relations" but more recently are termed "socioeconomic statuses." Furthermore, Imam observes, "there are always, and always have been, lots of different strands of elements at the same time which are understood by, promoted by, pushed by groups that have perhaps less power at that current time." The basis of their project was and still is, in part, to "historicize dominant culture and reclaim, if you like, progressive elements in past cultures." Such an endeavor allows them to craft a powerful counter to charges that they are somehow betraying their culture by supporting women's rights.

They demand to know "which one" and go on to point out, "We like this one, you like that bit." Thus, she laughs, "as members of the community we have as much right as anybody else to be participating in defining it!"

As important as the recognition of their membership in local communities is, they insist on their right to engage at broader levels as well, including at the national and international levels. Interestingly, Imam finds that challenges are more pronounced at the local level than at the national level in Nigeria, but then the challenges become much more pronounced at the international level. Moreover, it is at that level that "those people who are particularly opposed to women's human rights issues again label [the] whole corpus of international discourse . . . on human rights as being Western, external, and imposed on us." She acknowledges that "white, Euro American, middle class, educated, males who had a roof over their heads" were the first to advocate the formal elaboration of what is now known as international human rights. She reminds us that "discourses of rights pre-dated these in many parts of the world, such as the Sundiata Keita Mande Charter of the thirteenth century against slavery (amongst others)."[16] However, if the practice of historicizing the international human rights discourse is applied (much like the women's efforts within Nigeria), what becomes obvious is that rights are a product of struggles to overcome oppression—and oppression has not been limited to a European American context. Indeed, Imam insists that oppression might best be understood as not just the ultimate resident of globalized neighborhoods and communities; instead, it has the capacity to shape-shift to reflect the specific cultures in which it is embedded. Thus, while "oppression[s] in many senses are also culture and context specific, [so too] the notions of rights are also context specific."

Imam has argued that struggles around oppression resonate across cultures around the world because they are really about being able to live a good life. "And therefore, the idea of international and universal rights is not just a principle that human rights apply to all human beings but should also be a process that brings together the viewpoints, the experiences, the contexts of more and more people in a way that builds resonances across the world, that can be claimed across the world." Thus, the "international human rights discourse is not itself a finished discourse, it is not perfect, even if in some issues, it is the best that we have at the moment. It may well be and quite often is, but then on other issues, different local contexts are in fact way ahead." Imam insists that universalization "is not simply top down, it also has to work its way back up." Just as Nigerian women are claiming their rights to reclaim the progressive aspects of Nigerian culture, Imam insists on claiming rights to universalizing human rights.

From this perspective, Imam, along with other feminists in the developing world (more recently referred to as the Global South), has reviewed the history of international human rights. From that process, they "discovered" that proselytizing for CEDAW did not just emerge from the West. Rather, "twenty-two . . . Eastern European and 'developing countries,' of which twelve had Muslim communities, and eight of them were Muslim-majority countries," lobbied for CEDAW. She explained that after the Universal Declaration of Human Rights, during the 1950s and 1960s, when the shackles of political colonialism were being discarded, those countries began to make demands for a universal declaration of rights for women, which would ultimately become CEDAW. Furthermore, she insisted that the reasons CEDAW has a section specifically devoted to rural women was precisely because "people who were not white, middle class, Western were finally participating. The reason the Beijing Platform of Action has a section on the girl child comes directly out of the African women's movement." Indeed, African feminist women have claimed international human rights by pointing out that it is not only Western but also theirs: "We participated in making it, we have a right to claim it, and you can't simply say it was imposed on us. We want it, and it's ours, while at the same time saying it's not perfect, and we still need to improve it, and yes, there are many ways in which the continuing political and economic hegemony of Euro-America means that their issues are taken up before ours." Laughing ruefully, she affirmed that "as you can imagine, we get it from both sides."

Ayesha Imam has been intimately involved in the processes of creating a number of critical and instructive organizations, including Women in Nigeria (WIN), Women Living under Muslim Laws (WLUML), and BAOBAB for Women's Human Rights.

Women in Nigeria

Women in Nigeria (WIN) came into existence in the early 1980s as Nigeria was just emerging from military rule into the Second Republic; thus, it was a period of great hope and excitement among the people. In Kano State and Kaduna State there was even a radical populist movement called the People's Redemption Party. At the time, Imam was a lecturer in the Sociology Department at Ahmadu Bello University (ABU) in Kaduna State. She recalled a very heated conversation with a colleague, Sule Bello, at that time also a lecturer, over whether women's oppression existed or whether all oppression was class oppression. Before coming to blows they decided, in true academic fashion, that the question deserved to be addressed in a seminar. At first it was to be an interdepartmental seminar within the Faculty of Arts and Social Sciences at ABU, and then as more people at the university heard about it, it grew into a university-wide seminar. At the time, Imam was active in the Academic Staff Union of Universities (ASUU), and at the national meeting of ASUU people heard about the seminar and were also interested in participating, so it then became a national university seminar. Subsequently, people outside the university heard about the seminar, and they also wanted to attend. What had begun as a small interdepartmental seminar at one university morphed into a national seminar purely through word of mouth. Imam was in charge of organizing it and was given 500 naira (at the time, that was the equivalent of $500) from her department. Other departments provided in-kind support, such as designing and making posters and offering to print papers. Local people opened their homes and provided meals for those who traveled to participate in the seminar. The first Women in Nigeria Seminar was held in 1982.

The seminar included two and a half days of formal sessions of discussion, debate, and arguments, and at the end of each day's formal sessions the discussions continued for hours afterward in the staff club. Toward the end of the second day, the group was coalescing around the position that women were oppressed as members of the oppressed class but that they were also oppressed, in the vernacular of the day, "as women." The group therefore concluded that both sets of oppressions were intertwined and had to be addressed together rather than separately or sequentially. Once they had come to this understanding, they turned to the question of what to do about it. A group of people, including Imam, were "sort of nominated by popular acclaim," as she put it, as opposed to exactly being elected, to spend the next year working on developing a structure. The process was to include the formalities necessary for establishing an organization that could work on the issue with particular regard to the areas of research and dissemination of information, policy and engagement in policy formation, and direct action and campaigning.

Imam observed that the emphasis on research was fairly obvious, as so many of the members were at universities. They were especially interested in using research to address myths and stereotypes about the positions of women and men. Information generated from their various research projects was disseminated, because there was a strong belief that research was only beneficial if it was made accessible. For example, according to Imam, there was a belief that polygyny (the practice of one man being married to more than one woman at the same time) was necessary because there were so many more women than men. It was generally believed that without polygyny many women would not have an opportunity to marry. As seminar participants looked into the practice of polygyny, they not only sought answers to the question of whether polygyny was the only avenue available to women for marriage but also examined the age cohorts of women. In other words, were only younger women more likely to be married into polygynous situations? Were older, perhaps widowed or divorced women less likely to (re)marry even in a polygynous marriage, and if so, why not? The group discovered that in fact there was a higher number of older widowed women who were not remarrying. But they also discovered that younger and younger girls were being married five to ten years before their male cohorts of the same age brackets: "This data demonstrated that polygyny cannot be justified as helping an 'overabundance' of women to marry but results in younger men unable to marry and early marriage with all its deleterious consequences for girls and very young women."

As previously mentioned, Nigeria was emerging from military rule, and it was assumed that the new government was in need of input, which the seminar participants were quite willing to provide. There was also a feeling that if such input were not enough to bring about social change, then direct action would take care of everything else. Imam observed that much of the direct action by WIN was actually local action in the different states. She recalled that ABU had a policy that so-called fringe benefits for married women were different from those for either married men or single people. For example, married women were not allowed to bring their children to the health center for medical treatment. That was one issue addressed locally by WIN in Zaria; however, different branches of WIN focused on issues that were of specific concern to married women.

Interestingly, men were always involved in WIN. In fact, men's participation was debated at the 1982 and 1983 meetings, when the organization was formally established. It was thought that women's liberation was not simply something that only women were responsible for—men also had to accept the responsibility of working toward that goal. Therefore, as WIN advocated for women's rights, it was believed that such advocacy should not necessarily be restricted to women only. WIN felt it was important that "real men with proper understanding" should work for the rights of women. Unfortunately, Imam felt that in the long run this was not successful, perhaps because of the group's naivete in at least two areas: "The strength of the male left belief that they have all the answers. The arrogance, if you like. And for not building that [reality] into the structure." She did describe the men who worked in WIN the first few years as by and large "extremely gender sensitive," meaning that they did not impose their patriarchal or class views. Rather, while they might express disagreement, they would also acknowledge that it might be a situation where they did not have all the answers.

Imam noted that it was frequently suggested that men in some states were even in the majority, especially in those Islamic states where women were living in seclusion. However, Imam, who kept the membership records for the first four years and was traveling extensively throughout Nigeria at that time, stated categorically that "men were never more than one-third of the total membership, although in some states male membership might be up to fifty percent." She noted, for example, that in Sokoto and Bauchi States, men had even taken the initiative to establish WIN chapters, but in other states, including Zaria and Kaduna, men were distinctly in the minority.

Imam observed that male membership later became a problem, especially as Nigeria was experiencing the "increasing authoritarianism of military rule and crackdown on discussions of democracy and possibilities of democracy, and criticism of the structural adjustment program, and so on." In fact, she mentioned that at the 2003 WIN meeting, for the first time many women finally began to admit that male membership had become a problem. She charged, "A number of men in Left groups decided to use WIN, in the classical Leninist doctrine, as their front organization." The men formed little caucuses that met, unbeknownst to the broader membership, one or two days prior to a WIN meeting to strategize around ending military rule. Unfortunately, members of the government heard about these secret meetings and then tried to shut down the entire WIN meeting. Imam noted that this fostered a great deal of uncertainty, especially among the women in WIN, about why this was happening.

Imam recalled that up until the late 1980s WIN relied on membership fees and internal fundraising. They also were the recipients of in-kind donations. So, for example, they never used hotels, because people would be accommodated in the homes of their sympathizers when they had their meetings. They rarely had to pay for such things as posters, because printers would usually work for the cost of the paper or perhaps the ink but would provide the labor for free. Often the use of community halls, churches, or mosques was freely donated for meetings. However, when the Nigerian Structural Adjustment Program (SAP) was introduced in 1986, many laborers lost their jobs or their wages were cut, subsidies were withdrawn, and more people experienced difficulty purchasing the necessities of life.[17] This situation led to the second aspect of what Imam described as WIN's naivete, which was that for the first time WIN began to receive major external funding mostly from private US foundations, especially the MacArthur Foundation: "And then there came huge fights within about how the funding should be used, about who controlled it, about whether it was selling out to use funding at all."

Even as WIN was beset with these critical issues, it was also once again confronted with the original concerns about working on issues of women as a gender group intertwined with the issues of women as members of a class or of other oppressed groups. When Imam returned from pursuing her doctorate in the UK in 1990, she found WIN embroiled in a huge debate over "whether or not it was frivolous to look at violence against women as opposed to the effects of structural adjustment on women." The people at that annual meeting divided almost completely along gender lines on the question of whether violence against women should be the theme of their next year's work.[18] More men than women were in attendance at that meeting, so Imam felt compelled to raise some important issues. She pointed out that "because men can travel easier, because they usually are not the ones staying around looking after the kids, if there are kids, because they are less shy about speaking out in public, then they had to recognize that they should not always take the floor and make the decisions." Although she was defeated at that meeting, the discussion continued a few years later, and at that time many women withdrew from WIN. It did continue to exist, however, with branches in a number of states. For example, WIN sponsored programs for rural women in Bauchi and Edo States. Imam speculated that because it became possible to be more openly political in Nigeria, more men withdrew their energies from working with WIN. Nonetheless, Imam continues "to believe that men must be involved in the struggle for gender equality (recognizing both their privileges and their losses in patriarchy)—and particularly that men need to focus on addressing and mobilizing other men on this."[19]

Women Living under Muslim Laws

Ayesha Imam has also been deeply involved with the work of Women Living under Muslim Law (WLUML). Although this initiative was established in 1986 at a meeting in Aramon, France, the organizational initiative actually began in 1984, when a group of women from Muslim countries and communities happened to meet in Holland at another meeting. At that meeting, they began to recognize a number of commonalities, so they formed what was then called the Action Committee on Women and Muslim Laws, which later became the International Solidarity Network.

Although invited, Imam was not in attendance at either meeting because at that time she was heavily involved in WIN in addition to working full time. She admits to also feeling uneasy at the idea of being associated with what she felt was a specifically religious group, unlike WIN, which was a secular multireligious body. She learned that in fact WLUML is not a religious group; rather, "it's a group that works on issues of women living under Muslim laws." She notes that "many of the women do come from Muslim communities—some of whom are devout believers, while others might be slightly less orthodox believers. Still others may not be believers at all but claim Muslim as a cultural identity." Thus, it also "includes people of any and no religion who happen to live in places, in communities, or in states where Muslim discourse is a full part of the laws or part of the social practice. . . . So it's not in fact a religious group."

Imam, who is also a member of the Association of African Women for Research and Development (AAWORD), met Algerian feminist Marieme Helie Lucas briefly in 1982 at an AAWORD meeting. Following that meeting, Helie Lucas sent information about the work that AAWORD was doing to "increase understanding of the ways in which religion is abused for political identity, for creating legitimacy, and particularly to abuse and violate women's rights." Finally, Imam agreed in 1984 to coordinate what was at that time an action research project called Women in Laws Program for Africa and the Middle East. Little by little, she became more involved until she was coordinating the Women in Laws Program not only for Africa and the Middle East but for the entire WLUML.

According to Imam, WLUML operates under a number of different assumptions, including the necessity for historicizing Islamic laws and discourse along with an insistence on WLUML's diversity across the world. Members began by bringing together representatives from fifteen different Muslim countries and communities for discussion. They discovered that although they might be using the same terminology, those terms were often used differently, they did not necessarily mean the same things, and they did not elicit the same effect in different contexts. From those discussions two programs were born: "One was the planned interpretations program, which was, strictly speaking, . . . a theological program. That is, [members] would examine verses of the Koran and the Hadith and how they have been interpreted and what other interpretations they might, could, and have had in the past," a process that harks back to Imam's notion of reclaiming, as practiced in the double claiming critique strategy.

The second program was the Women in Laws Program, and this is where Imam became engaged. The program was

> an empirical survey of laws in Muslim countries and communities that affect women as family members, as citizens, as individuals. So for Africa certainly it meant that we looked at laws influenced by Muslim discourses, Muslim laws, but also secular laws, particularly secular laws where they have Muslim prefaces, but also at customary laws, at British and French colonial law and how these might combine to affect women. So as families that [included] marriage, divorce, child custody, inheritance and community land, and so on. As citizens that meant education, access to loans, banking. And as individuals that includes bodily integrity, sexual orientation, personal autonomy that you have. And over a historical time frame so we can see where these laws were coming from and how they've changed.

This research also employed a comparative perspective so that the women could begin to see how the laws differed from country to country. And, according to Imam, this was "action research." That is, the women were determined to ensure that this research was "guided by the needs of women activists working for women's rights in the communities." To that end, Imam declared, "the idea was not, and never was, to produce papers that would go into some thesis or be published and then sit in libraries. It always was information that we could turn into manuals and brochures and pamphlets."

According to Imam, all the research teams were deliberately composed of people who, like Imam, were trained social scientists but who also saw themselves as activists rather than only as academic social scientists. Teams also purposely included people who were not academics (e.g., ordinary citizens such as teachers and porters) but who were active in the field of women's rights. They strongly believed that if the research was going to be both flexible and useful, then the teams had to include the people who would be using the results of their research, because they were the ones qualified "to judge there and then, do I need to know this? Is that a way that's helpful for me?"

In regard to the coordination of the research teams for Africa and the Middle East, she observed, "Unlike in Asia, the development of women's ideas in particular in Africa is relatively new." She went on to suggest that the "Asians were working with preestablished ideas which were part of the WLUML network, or they found NGOs and brought them into the network." In many places in Africa, on the other hand, "it meant setting up groups, three or four, five of whom then went on to become their own NGOs, such as BAOBAB for Women's Human Rights in Nigeria." Just as she had traveled throughout Nigeria when working with WIN, Imam began traveling to many countries within Africa seeking out at least one person from each community "who was a feminist, activist, willing to be involved and give the time, and then going around and finding more people so they could put together a team and doing a lot of training with groups." Her work was very comprehensive and included research and methodologies training, grant proposal writing, project management, and envisioning missions and objectives. It became painfully clear as she engaged in these endeavors that, structurally, Africa was not in a position to be able to raise the necessary funds for these endeavors. Rather, women would have to rely on external funding at a time in the 1980s and 1990s when external funders were extremely reluctant to provide such support.

Often, she would be invited to attend a conference or a meeting, where she would begin to meet people. Frequently, she would stay on for a week or two after the meeting to meet other people. This was what she called "piggybacking," that is, staying to work in places to which the travel fares had already been paid, working with people on their own time and with their own money. Although this was a slow and arduous process, with donors only later beginning to provide some support, Imam also found it to be an incredibly empowering process. She characterized the project as empowering in part because it allowed them to say to people, "We are not looking at what Islam says, we're looking at what Muslims have done. What Muslims have done is as susceptible to critique as anything else in this world!"

This project's innovativeness relied upon its ability to be comparative. So, for example, when Indian women were challenging their lack of access to divorce they were able to argue that Muslim women in Nigeria have easier access to divorce. The most classic example is the issue of female genital cutting. People who were opposed to such practices among Muslims in West Africa were able to argue that genital cutting was not practiced in the birthplace of Islam, Saudi Arabia, nor in Iran, which Imam argues for many people was the "symbol for anti-imperialist, anti-Western resistance and struggle and victory." The capacity to make such a strong argument based on the women's research was in itself empowering. Imam laughed when she recalled that, based on their research, they were even able to challenge the practice of secluding women in the privacy of home out of public view, arguing that it had only begun in northern Nigeria in the 1950s!

Much of her work for WLUML was of course done in Nigeria, which exemplified the complexity of this project. Nigeria, the largest country in Africa, is estimated to have a population of about 200 million people in 2020, according to the World Population Review. It is about twice the size of California, or the size of California, Nevada, and Arizona combined. While it is a multiethnic state of more than 250 ethnic or nationality groups, the largest and most influential of those groups include the Hausa-Fulani of the north (Imam's father was a member of that group), the Yoruba of the southwest, the Igbo in the southeast, and the Ijaw in the Niger Delta region. The Nigerian Muslim population is primarily located in the north, including Muslim majority states in the northern part of the country, Muslim minority states in the north-central and northeastern parts of the country, and Muslim minority states in the southwest. The Christian population largely resides in the middle and southern areas of the country.

Because it is such an immense country with a wide range of cultural contexts, not surprisingly, Nigeria fielded a huge research team with hundreds of members to ensure that its diversity was well represented on the research teams during the series of training workshops for WLUML. There were three research teams. The largest was the fieldwork team, which focused on what people were actually doing and what people believed the law to be. The legal team researched what the courts had been saying. Prior to this undertaking, Imam stated, "Muslim laws were not legislated," so the team members had to rely on court records. The historical team examined archival records and other documents to ascertain what had been happening on the street, as well as in Muslim law. Once each team had completed their work, they collated the information in a report in a manner that would support direct action. The group recognized a necessity to build an institutional framework that would utilize the information that had been collected, and that, in turn, led to the founding of BAOBAB for Women's Human Rights.

Imam noted that for a number of reasons, there were many young men on the Nigerian research teams. Of course, some were on the team because they thought this work would help women, but, perhaps even more important, many of the men spoke Arabic. This was critical, because so many of the older records are written in Arabic script or were written in Hausa using Arabic script.

Imam often reiterated in meetings that "we are not looking at Islam, we are looking at what Muslims do." She recalled that, especially at the early meetings, young men would regularly begin their comments with "But Islam says . . . !" and everyone, with the exception of Imam and a few others, was immediately silenced. However, she recalled a significant incident two years later at the third workshop after people had begun to do the research and returned to discuss what they had learned as a group. A question arose regarding the dress requirements to maintain women's decency in Islam vis-à-vis Muslim laws and practices. As Imam began to refer to what the Koran had to say about the issue, a young man stood up to say that Islam says that women must cover their heads and dress in a certain manner. Imam responded by saying that "there are more Muslim women in India than in the whole of Nigeria, and they don't think it." His response was "No, no, no, Islam says. And how can you say this, and you're against Islam!" Imam recalls that literally to a woman, and some Ethiopian young men as well, the members of the group shouted out, "First of all, she [Imam] didn't say that! And secondly, how do you know what Islam says? We are all Muslims here!" Imam proudly recalls that transformative moment as a result of two years of empowering research work of and for the people.

At about that time, Imam moved to Senegal, where she initiated and directed the Council for the Development of Social Science Research in Africa (CODESRIA), the first gender institute in Africa, along with two other renowned African feminists, Amina Mama and Fatou Sow. The move to Senegal meant that she was no longer only involved in Nigeria but was also engaged in this work with the teams that were developed in Senegal, Mali, Sudan, and Cameroon.

After more than ten years of activist engagement in more than twenty countries supported by substantial amounts of secondary research, in 2003 WLUML was finally able to publish volume 1 of *Knowing Our Rights: Women, Family, Law and Customs in the Muslim World* (which has since been updated in 2006).[20] The volume is composed of brief, analytical sections written in accessible language, along with tables that compare what is actually happening with Muslim laws across the world. It became very clear that laws, depending on where they were enacted, could provide women with autonomy, could defend and promote their rights, or could be extremely restrictive on the same issues even though all of them were called Muslim laws. The book includes sections on tactics and strategies for law, as well as on the potential for and limits to legal reforms.

Imam's assessment of WLUML (and also of WIN) is quite thoughtful. On the one hand, she noted that it "encouraged the recognition of diversity within the commonality . . . of having our lives defined by somebody's understandings and constructions of Muslim laws. But on the other hand (and as part of that WIN was very insistent, I think rightly so), that only people working on the ground could define, ultimately, what the correct strategy or tactic was. Because they were doing the work, they were living with the consequences, and they were in the contexts." Although WIN was similar, it was not quite as structured as WLUML, according to Imam. As previously mentioned, WIN was structured with state branches, and although each year a national theme was chosen, each state branch was free to choose the issue it would focus on. Imam felt that WLUML had a much more formal structure, although at the same time it provided for the recognition of diverse contexts and situations, as well as the ways in which different individuals and groups within WLUML were linked despite their different priorities, structures, and possibilities. She concluded that even more so than with WIN, which was, after all, a national organization, WLUML "was very, very clear" that being a network meant working together on the things that brought people together but allowing for autonomy on everything else. "So, if you like, solidarity without, not precisely without judgment, but certainly without being judgmental."

WLUML, then, was structured in such a way that it could accommodate working with people who were utterly opposed to the idea of working within religious discourses, as well as those who were only able to see themselves as working within religious discourses. Ultimately, the first principle of WLUML was a capacity to agree to disagree, even as members continued to share information with one another. They were able to either support or not support each other's solidarity campaigns and could do so without rancor. Imam acknowledged that there were of course disagreements, but people recognized that one person cannot define for others what is correct and what they have to do, even when people disagree. A second clear principle, according to Imam, was that WLUML "would have to be in solidarity around promoting women's rights against the use or abuse of religion and politics of identity." These principles meant that there will be some groups of specifically Muslim women who choose not to work with WLUML precisely because they think the organization is not religious enough, while others will refuse to work with the network because they feel it is too religious.

Imam also insisted that WLUML "always saw itself as part of the international human rights, women's human rights movement"; therefore, Muslim women are not ghettoized under a false assumption that they would have nothing in common with other women in the world. In fact, they had much in common with other groups that were dealing with the identity politics of the religious Right, including, for example, Women Against Fundamentalisms and Women in Black in the former Yugoslavia. Other groups were also grappling with religious fundamentalism among Hindus, Sikhs, Jews, Catholics, and Protestants, as well as within ethnic nationalisms. As its global connections evolved, WLUML also expanded its mandate through researching other critical issues, including militarization, terrorism, and sexualities.

Imam noted that the manner in which WLUML is organized is also quite innovative. For example, the network does not have members per se because, according to Imam, membership implies unitary structure and dues. Instead, people are linked to one another through the network, and those linkages are envisioned as a spiral. On the inner part of the spiral is what they would call the core group, which is composed of about six people—roughly equivalent to a board. Then there is the coordination group. Neither the core group nor the coordination group is elected; instead, they are "self-selecting by consensus." The next group within the spiral is the program implementation committee (which has gone through a series of name changes). That committee has a membership of about twenty-five networkers "who are," according to Imam, "willing to put in the extra time and effort required to run programs, do solidarity work, collect information, respond to queries, and generally take responsibility for helping to define and implement policies and programs of WLUML." This is the group that does the actual work. The next group, the active networkers, is made up of people who are very often running the country projects, writing articles, and responding to requests for information, help, or solidarity. They sometimes issue requests for alerts that are international appeals. They use their own contacts to pass on any information that would be useful to others. Outside of this spiral there are people who get the emails or the publications and may or may not respond and may or may not pass the information on. Imam noted that the spiral is designed to recognize that people are always immersed in their own personal life cycles and that there are times when they may or may not be able to participate in the work. They can move in and out of the spiral as necessary but "always with the sense that we don't want you to go, but if you have to, we understand," laughed Imam. This organizational structure respects the fact that most of the members are human rights and women's rights activists working within their own NGOs in their own countries, so the work they do must be directly useful to that work as well.

WLUML does have a small office in London that is called the International Coordination Office (ICO). It was located in London because at the time it was believed to be necessary to have an office in a place that was not likely to be either directly attacked by the religious Right or constrained by the local statutes. Imam mentioned that the group had considered Pakistan; however, it was felt that the military regime there would not be conducive to their work. Over time it became clear that this was an important consideration, because in Nigeria, for example, the rise of the terrorist group Boko Haram has resulted in violent attacks in villages and towns, especially in northern Nigeria and more recently in the kidnapping of young girls from their schools. There are, however, regional coordination officers in Pakistan (Asia) and Nigeria (Africa and the Middle East). Imam noted that there is increasing concern that perhaps some attention should also be directed toward Muslims in the African diaspora.

BAOBAB for Women's Rights

In 2002 Ayesha Imam and BAOBAB for Women's Rights were the recipients of the prestigious John Humphrey Freedom Award, conferred by the Canada-based International Centre for Human Rights and Democratic Development. BAOBAB was formed in 1996, and "the BAOBAB vision is to defend, promote and develop women's human rights in customary, secular and religious laws." The group is engaged in research to determine "what rights and/or constraints exist in laws, implementation and in social practice." BAOBAB has also disseminated the knowledge generated by their research even as they have felt it was critical to examine "whether law and their implementation are adequately protecting rights, and devising strategies to further develop laws, implementation and social practices where they do not."[21]

BAOBAB researched and reported on women's rights and law in Nigeria for the Human Rights Violations Investigation Commission, established in June 1999.[22] They have worked with other NGOs on Nigeria's record in fulfilling its obligations under the CEDAW and also produced a series of leaflets promoting legal literacy leaflets. They have designed strategies that draw attention to the issue of women's rights. For example, with the Civil Resource and Documentation Centre, they co-organized Nigeria's first National Tribunal on Violence Against Women.[23] They have also organized art competitions for youth around the theme of building a culture that respects and promotes the rights of women. Their work encompasses both national and international components. As previously mentioned, BAOBAB is the regional coordinator for WLUML for Africa and the Middle East. As such, they provide workshop training in a variety of areas, including for paralegals, leadership skills for women, and gender awareness in project management and research. BAOBAB also provides support to individual women and girls who are seeking redress in cases that have included domestic violence, forced marriage, rape and sexual abuse, and custody, guardianship, and maintenance rights (or what we refer to as child support) for their children.[24]

In her acceptance speech to the International Centre for Human Rights and Democratic Development, Imam acknowledged that BAOBAB was best known for "defending women's rights in Muslim laws and practices." She described BAOBAB'S Women and Laws action research team. Numbering around seventy people, the team consists of women's rights activists, legal scholars of Islam (called *ulema*), lawyers, social scientists, researchers, historians, and Arabic linguists. The team "spent over three years researching Muslim jurisprudence, the history of Muslim laws in Nigeria, Sharia court judgments (especially at the higher levels) and daily practices in diverse Muslim communities across Nigeria, as they affect women as family members, citizens and individuals."[25] As they conducted their research, it became apparent that many women did not know about their rights and so were unable to access them. As a consequence, in 1996 BAOBAB began to address the problem by providing legal literacy leaflets and activities, training workshops, and paralegal support.

In 1999, led by Zamfara State, twelve states in Nigeria started passing a series of new Sharia acts. Prior to that point, Muslim laws around family and personal status in Nigeria were largely uncodified. Unfortunately, most of the laws that were then being codified focused on "elaborating and executing punishment for offenses like theft, *zina* [adultery or fornication, depending on marital status] and drinking alcohol," despite the fact that such legislation could have also included other areas such as the collection and distribution of *zakat* (the charity tithe that is one of the five pillars of Islam) and the implementation of regulations prohibiting usury. Imam insisted that the laws had serious shortcomings in drafting, content, and implementation. What is even more troubling, these laws have been characterized as a universal God-given code; thus, to point out any defects or deficiencies in them is subject to attack on the basis of being un-Islamic and anti-Sharia and thus tantamount to apostasy.[26]

In her acceptance speech Imam reminded her listeners that "there are several 'schools' of Muslim legal thought (*fiqh*)" but that even the oldest of these schools only came into existence decades after the death of the Prophet and the revelation of the Koran. (The four main schools of thought are Hanafi, Maliki, Shafi, and Hanbali.) Thus "the laws they outline [commonly collectively referred to as Sharia or Islamic law] are clearly not direct divine revelations from Allah, but mediated through human judicial reasoning [*ijtihad* in Arabic]."[27] For this and other reasons, Muslim laws are diverse and should be subject to change through progressive development. Imam cited several examples attesting to this diversity, including the fact that under orthodox Shia, Sharia daughters who have no brothers are permitted to be residual heirs, while the Maliki school does not allow this. Also, while the Hanafi Sharia does enable a woman to choose a husband without her father's permission, Shafi Sharia does not. Some schools also permit family planning and/or abortion, while others do not. Even the question of polygyny has elicited a wide variation in Muslim law. While the Koran does permit polygyny, it does not require it, and the Koran specifies the conditions that must be fulfilled in order for it to occur.[28]

Clearly, according to Imam, the implementation of the new Sharia acts in Nigeria is discriminatory against women. She cited one extremely troubling incident, the postulation that by itself pregnancy outside marriage is evidence of *zina* (adultery or fornication). She noted that this constitutes a minority position that is held by neither the Hanafi, Hanbali, or Shafi school nor by a variant of the Maliki school. Under this law women are held to a standard of evidence different from that required for men: pregnant women are required to provide evidence of their innocence, while men are not. If an allegation of *zina* is made, the prosecution must provide independent evidence, such as four eyewitnesses. Without such evidence, men have been allowed to walk away from the charges, unlike pregnant women. Even though *zina* is understood to be a (heterosexual) act that necessarily includes one woman and one man, Imam pointed out that more women than men have been charged and convicted. Imam further argued that "women who ought not to even have been charged, have been convicted of *zina* and sentenced to death, by ignoring the well-established Maliki doctrine of the 'sleeping embryo' . . . whereby a child born to a woman within a set period after the end of her marriage (in some areas up to seven years), is assumed to be the child of that marriage." Imam also reminded us that under these new Sharia laws "women have been accused and convicted of *zina* as prostitutes, for instance, with neither confession nor the testimony of four witnesses to a willing act of sexual intercourse, nor even pregnancy, for evidence."[29]

Imam insisted that another consequence has been "to deprive women and girls of any protection under Sharia from sexual assault or rape." In fact, a woman who would make such a charge has to produce four male witnesses of impeccable character to testify on her behalf. This law ignores the fact that rapists rarely seek to commit crimes of sexual assault before an audience. Thus the victim of rape, according to Imam, is in double jeopardy, likely to find herself convicted of *zina* for having admitted to nonmarital sex and false testimony because she is unable to produce the requisite witnesses.[30]

Despite threats of violence and accusations of being anti-Islam, BAOBAB members have fearlessly responded, offering victims support and redress against this kind of discrimination. They have assembled a legal strategy team composed of independent Muslim attorneys and scholars, as well as rights activists to provide advice and information. They have also activated their international resources to acquire information on similar cases in other geographical locations and to raise funding to cover the costs of legal fees, including court costs and appeals, counseling, and the provision of safe houses for defendants. They also work in solidarity with the Nigerian human rights movement.

BAOBAB has offered a series of workshops that bring members of Muslim communities together for several days. Members of the *ulema*, ordinary Muslims, conservatives and progressives, activists, and people from different parts of the country and different walks of life have met to examine the Koranic *surahs* (chapters) and *hadith* (traditional sayings of the Prophet). They discuss dominant and less well-known interpretations and study how Muslim laws are constructed in other countries and communities around the world regarding some thirty different issues of particular importance to women. Imam stated, "These workshops thus examine the potential and actuality in Muslim laws and practices for establishing and promoting women's rights, as well as critiquing negative constructions and practices even when the latter are claimed to be Islamic." This process empowers the participants with knowledge to challenge Sharia laws that actually violate human rights and the confidence to envision and work toward the establishment of more progressive Muslim laws.[31]

Loretta Ross

My initial interview with Loretta Ross was in her home in Atlanta, Georgia, on July 8, 2002. The walls were painted in lovely shades of lavender and purple, and there were interesting artifacts throughout the house acquired from her world travels. Her home was comfortably open and flowing. The garage had been converted into office space, which was clearly separate from, yet easily accessible to, her living quarters. Our five-hour interview was wide-ranging, fascinating, and occasionally punctuated by laughter. The phones rang throughout the afternoon, and there were occasional quiet interruptions by her staff with questions or information. Ross's pleasant gaptooth round face is surrounded by long flowing dreadlocks. She has beautiful mahogany-colored skin and is what southern African Americans call "stout." Her physical weight serves to anchor and enhance her commanding intellect and presence.

Like Ayesha Imam, Ross is not only a feminist but one who proudly proclaims herself to be a "flaming feminist." She founded the National Center for Human Rights Education in Atlanta in 1996 because, she stated emphatically, "although the concept of human rights is centuries old and the Universal Declaration is [at that time] almost fifty years old, no organized entity existed in the United States with the purpose of teaching the American public about their human rights in general and to apply these human rights standards to issues of injustice in the United States."[32] Although she acknowledged that such organizations as Amnesty International and Human Rights Watch are deeply engaged in the struggle to implement human rights, she observed that with the exception of their work around prisons and the death penalty, their focus on human rights violation was in areas other than the United States. Americans, she declared, are unaware of the wide range of human rights available to them. She insisted that people will not stand up to fight for something that they are not aware they have. "So," she concluded, "before we can have effective human rights advocacy in the United States we have to have effective human rights education."

Her circuitous route to human rights education and advocacy began officially in the 1970s with social justice activism in the antirape movement when she was appointed the third executive director of the first rape crisis center in the nation—the Washington, DC, Rape Crisis Center. How she came to feminism and her work in a rape crisis center could be a textbook case for the 1970s feminist mantra "the personal is political." At the age of eleven, she was the victim of sexual assault during what normally should have been a safe activity for a young girl, a Girl Scouts outing. She was kidnapped from the rest of the group, dragged into the woods, and raped. At the age of fourteen, she became the victim of yet another rape by an older cousin who was supposedly babysitting her.[33] Impregnated during that assault, she endured a difficult pregnancy, becoming a mother at the age of fifteen. Despite what would normally be incapacitating circumstances, she managed to graduate from high school at the age of sixteen and was offered a full scholarship by Radcliffe College and Howard University. Radcliffe withdrew its offer of a scholarship once it learned that she was an unwed mother and that she had chosen to keep her child rather than put him up for adoption. Howard University, however, did offer her a scholarship, so in 1970, at the age of seventeen, she enrolled, majoring in chemistry and physics at a time when the campus was a hotbed of student activism.[34] During her three years at Howard, the deadly shootings at Kent State University and Jackson State College occurred, and she and her fellow students protested against those incidents and the Vietnam War while also advocating for Black studies classes on this historically Black university campus.[35] During her freshman year, she was introduced to two books that had a profound effect upon her developing consciousness: *The Autobiography of Malcolm X* and the groundbreaking anthology *The Black Woman*, edited by Toni Cade.[36] She quickly decided that she identified with what in those days was called Black Pan-Africanist feminism, a term she felt was broad enough to acknowledge some sort of global consciousness.[37] A woman named Nkenge Toure, a member of the Black Panther Party, invited her to begin volunteering at the DC Rape Crisis Center. Although Ross was at first skeptical about working with white women, Toure asked Ross to trust her and thus ushered her across the proverbial bridge into her life's work.[38]

While she was matriculating at Howard, Ross again became pregnant, but this time she chose to have an abortion. Realizing that she needed to use a more effective and less exacting form of birth control (she lamented the fact that birth control pills require one to remember to take them every day), she decided to use the Dalkon Shield, a form of IUD. Unfortunately, the shield had a dangerous design flaw that could cause acute pelvic inflammatory disease. In addition, it ruptured her fallopian tubes, resulting in permanent sterilization. Thus, after one pregnancy carried to term, one abortion, and an unintended sterilization, her reproductive career was over at the age of twenty-three.[39] When she learned from her OB/GYN that the company that produced the shield had research indicating that the shield was defective but chose to market it anyway, she brought a successful lawsuit against the manufacturer, A. H. Robins, becoming one of the first Black women to prevail against a multinational corporation. Other women joined a class-action suit against the company, and it was eventually forced into bankruptcy.[40]

Ross observed that by the time she was in her twenties, she had experienced many of the reproductive crises consistent with being Black, poor, and female in America. She has chosen to tell her own story because she believes "it is the deliberate combination of the personal and objective that creates the authority, authenticity and uniqueness of the African American female experience."[41]

In 1979 Ross became the director of the Washington, DC, Rape Crisis Center, the only center run primarily by and for women of color. During her tenure it would become what she called "a hotbed of Black feminist activity," even as it also provided her with on-the-job training.[42] She recalled that formal training for this kind of work did not exist at that time because the work was pioneering.

Throughout her career, Ross has sustained a relationship with the scholarship of Black feminists. Indeed, she remarked that she "love[d] the way the academics and theorists have begun to, in hindsight, describe what we were doing." In 1981 she discovered the seminal work *Ain't I a Woman?* by bell hooks and recalled how excited the DC Black feminists were about the book.[43] They had been "doing the work for nearly a decade without any theory to guide them, without anybody to affirm that, yeah, we are different from the white feminists out here. But we didn't know how different. We didn't know what it meant. . . . We knew we struggled against racism in the white feminist movement, but we struggled against sexism, so we weren't comfortable in the civil rights or the Black nationalist movement, so we were like women poised between two movements without the theory to guide us." Once they discovered *Ain't I a Woman?* they quickly raised money to bring bell hooks to Washington, DC, "to tell us what was going on. She was the first theorist to describe our work, and . . . it was like a revelation," Ross laughed.

The second expert they invited to talk with them was Paula Giddings, whose iconic book on Black women's history, *When and Where I Enter . . . : The Impact of Black Women on Race and Sex in America*, was published in 1984.[44] Ross recalled that it was only when the scholarship started to become available that the women began to realize "what significant actors we were . . . because we just didn't know." Ross noted one of the important things that she learned from engaging with feminist scholarship and that she practices in her own writing projects: how crucial it is to provide the names of the women who were active, because so often they are invisible in both the history and the media.

In 1985 Ross attended the UN World Conference on Women in Nairobi, Kenya, where she roomed with political operative Donna Brazile, who provided Ross with information about applying for a position at the National Organization for Women (NOW). Eventually, after some discussion, she was hired in 1985 by Ellie Smeal, then president of NOW, to be the minority rights staff person. However, Ross quickly disabused Smeal of that notion, and her title became instead the director of women of color programs. She helped Smeal to become engaged in a paradigm shift. While Smeal was under the impression that Ross's job was to bring women of color into NOW, Ross thought her job was "to figure out why women of color hated NOW. So," she laughingly stated, "I became more like an ombudsman than a recruiter, which I thought was a really important distinction."[45] As a NOW director, she organized women of color delegations for the prochoice marches sponsored by NOW in 1986 and

1989. She left NOW in 1989 to work for the National Black Women's Health Project, where she would become deeply involved in both reproductive rights and antiviolence organizing.

Ross describes herself as "the kind of person who wanted to organize larger and larger groups of people to participate in something." She began in 1980 by organizing the first national conference on Third World women and violence, which would later grow into the organization for women of color called INCITE! Women of Color Against Violence. In 1987 she organized the first national conference on women of color and reproductive rights because she "always felt so isolated doing the work as a feminist." Furthermore, and perhaps even more important, she "always felt that my particular gift was to organize women like me together so we could meet and greet and know each other." These first two conferences provided critical opportunities for networking, even though, she admits, the weakness of the conferences was a lack of documentation.

Ross's activist career took a decidedly different twist when she was approached by the Center for Democratic Renewal (CDR) in 1989. The CDR was at that time the only African American organization that was monitoring hate groups, including the Ku Klux Klan, Aryan Nations, and neo-Nazi organizations. She went to work for the CDR as a research director in 1990, engaging in what she described as "reactive work": visiting the states that had experienced violence from such hate groups and helping communities organize responses to that violence. She spent a lot of time in Washington, Oregon, Idaho, and Montana. The work was challenging for several reasons, including the fact that at that time most people who were doing the research on hate groups were white men, yet she, a woman of color, was in charge of a research department.

In Ross's opinion, the CDR had serious ethical lapses, even though it purported to be a civil rights organization dedicated to protecting everyone's rights. She characterized the work as essentially a spy network. She cited one particularly egregious incident regarding David Irving, a British Holocaust denier. Irving came to the United States to do a speaking tour, and some of Ross's colleagues who engaged in what she termed "I-spy games" happened to find his home phone number. One of them, pretending to be an employee of the airline on which Irving was traveling, called Irving's wife and informed her that either his flight had not arrived safely in the States or that Irving had not arrived in the States—that he was missing. When Ross's colleague came into her office

> cackling about what confusion he had caused in this man's household . . .
> I realized that there was a difference in how we approached doing [this]

work. . . . I thought that was the most disgusting thing I'd ever heard of. I don't care if I am opposed to the man. And I am passionately opposed to antisemitism and the Holocaust denial movement. . . . But it has gone beyond the pale . . . to call a man's family and create that kind of havoc just because you're in political opposition to the man. And it became clear that there are white boys who saw this as a big I-spy thing, who saw this as civilian cops versus the bad guys thing. Who really did not have a larger sociopolitical analysis of the fight [against] white supremacy. And, moreover, the way and the dignity in which it needs to be conducted.

The Oklahoma City bombing on April 19, 1995, was another important issue that the CDR addressed. Ross, who had heard about it before she even arrived in the office that day, immediately called her staff, because she felt that the bombing was the work of some of the people they were monitoring. April 19 was a very significant date to white supremacists because it was the anniversary of the Waco siege (1993) and it was one day before Hitler's birthday, a date that the Aryan Nations organization always tried to commemorate. In addition, a white supremacist named Richard Snell had also been executed on April 19. The recorded messages on the hotlines of the groups that were routinely monitored by the CDR were warning their listeners to watch out for April 19. So, unlike the US government and the media, which for a while had been attempting to blame some mysterious Arab terrorists for the bombing, the CDR's analysis pointed to home-grown suspects. The CDR held a big press conference in its office and released the tapes it had collected from the hotlines indicating that something big was scheduled to occur on April 19. As a result, the CDR, and especially Loretta Ross, immediately became highly visible.

A frightening experience would strike much closer to home for Ross, confirming her vehement response to the David Irving prank. Because she was engaged in monitoring the Klan's activities, she was at risk of "being made" (recognized) by them. Indeed, her photograph had already appeared in a Klan newspaper, and she became nationally visible because of the Oklahoma City bombing press conference. In Ross's considered opinion, there is a gender difference in monitoring work. She noted that the men who were monitoring were all married; a married man can disguise his identity by putting a house, utilities, and credit cards in his wife's name. But a single woman does not have a husband behind whom she can conceal her identity, which means that a single woman is much more vulnerable to being recognized, harassed, and even threatened for doing this work. Ross's assessment eerily confirmed Adrien Wing's analysis of why she had not been harassed in her home after the newspaper article about her appeared. She was protected because she used her married name in her private life.

About a month after the Oklahoma City bombing, Ross called her mother to wish her a Happy Mother's Day. Her mother, a senior citizen mostly confined to a wheelchair, innocently mentioned that she had been meaning to call Ross about a phone call she (Ross's mother) had recently received from someone who had identified himself as a member of the Texas Militia and invited her to attend one of their meetings. This was the same chapter of the Klan that had harassed the Vietnamese fishermen and whose case was tried before Judge McDonald. He said that they wanted to show her that they were not a racist organization and asked if she could relay that message to her daughter. Ross was, of course, deeply disturbed by the incident, because although she expected to be harassed, she had no idea that any group would have so carefully researched her that it would be able to identify and contact her mother in another state. She had been "doxed." At this point, Ross became personally concerned about continuing to do monitoring work not only because of the risk to her own safety but also because of the risk to her family.

Toward the end of her career with the Center for Democratic Renewal, Ross's job was to deprogram white supremacists who sought to leave the hate movement. By far her most notorious case was the Floyd Cochran case. Cochran, who had been a Nazi since he was fifteen years old, was in his early thirties when he became disillusioned. Floyd had a son who had been born with a cleft palate, and his Nazi friends had described his son as a genetic defective that needed to be put to death. It was at that point, when the hate came home, so to speak, that he began to question the beliefs of the Christian identity movement, which he had accepted without question since he was a teenager. Until that time, he had never disputed what he had been taught, including that Blacks were "subhuman" or "pre-Adamic" (i.e., beasts created before Adam) and that Jews were the spawn of Satan and Eve. Once he began to question those beliefs, he was ejected from the Idaho compound and spent the next few months homeless, sleeping on park benches and in trailer parks, trying to figure out what he should do. He eventually called the CDR because of their reputation for helping people who were seeking to leave hate groups. Soon he was assigned to Ross to help him through a rehabilitation process. Once he was deprogrammed, the first thing he wanted to do was very publicly apologize for having recruited young whites into the skinhead movement. So Cochran and Ross began a whirlwind tour of TV talk shows, including *The Jerry Springer Show*, on which he very publicly apologized.

Ross told this story because it signifies a personal epiphany. She discovered that as she came to know people who had previously been involved in hate movements, she could no longer hate them. She recalled that she used to compare Klansmen to roaches because they "only come out when you turned the lights out. . . . If you turned the lights on and shined the spotlight on them . . . they go running." She admitted that she had not realized "what an objectifying and dehumanizing explanation that was. And I used to offer it very glibly because it was cute. I totally obliterated their humanity." These people also had "their aches and pains and values and families that they care about. And though they are horribly wrong in why they think Johnny can't read and want to blame all black people . . . for that, they are poor white people who have been left out of the economic pyramid. And the only thing they have to rely on is white supremacy for their identity formation and to establish their sense of superiority because they know they are working as itinerant farmhands or manual labor." Floyd Cochran eventually formed an organization called Education and Vigilance, whose main purpose was to dissuade white youngsters from joining the hate movement.

Another haunting case was the Freeman family in Allentown, Pennsylvania. Brenda Freeman contacted CDR because she was afraid of her two older sons, who had joined the Church of the Creator, a white supremacist church, and had started to make serious threats against the family. Brenda had sought help from law enforcement and had tried family counseling for the children, who had been raised as Jehovah's Witnesses, were extremely religious, and had earlier been straight A students. Ross strongly advised Brenda during a phone call to practice some tough love—put the boys out of the home and change the locks on the door—because they were making threats against the family. The mother hesitated to heed Ross's warning, worrying that if she followed that advice, the boys would get into even more trouble. Tragically, the weekend following her conversation with Ross, the two boys returned home and murdered the entire family, including their twelve-year-old brother. They tried to escape to Ohio but were eventually captured and sent to prison.

While doing this work, Ross also came to question the messages that the CDR was delivering to the communities that were experiencing neo-Nazi and Klan violence. She noted that the CDR's basic message was "Just say no to hate." As the organization tried to support communities in their resistance to hate, it used phrases such as "Build a Firewall Against Intolerance" at the unity rallies, prayer vigils, and Rock Against Racism concerts it organized. The CDR was especially committed to dissuading young people from joining hate groups, even as it also reached out to progressive young people to dissuade them from attacking hate groups. In her opinion, "It was just a big liberal mess." About that time, the brainchild of the Southern Poverty Law Center, "teaching tolerance," was also introduced. "I actually thought that message was racist. Because tolerance is not a framework that I think should apply to human relationships. . . . [Tolerate] is something you do to a pair of shoes that hurt your feet until you can change them." Ross went on to argue that "tolerance . . . is inadequate for a lot of people because it maintains power and control in the hands of the white community that is asked to 'tolerate' all of those people of color. . . . You tolerate something until you no longer have to tolerate it anymore."

Even as she continued working with the Center for Democratic Renewal, Ross's attraction to international human rights was growing. She was a founding member of the International Council of African Women and of the Network of East-West Women. She helped organize a delegation of one hundred African American women to attend the UN International Conference on Population and Development in Cairo, Egypt, in 1994. She attended the UN World Conferences on Women in Copenhagen, Nairobi, and Beijing and the Conference on Race in South Africa.

At the Fourth World Conference on Women in Beijing, Ross participated in a workshop facilitated by Shula Koenig with an organization called the People's Decade for Human Rights Education. Ross and Koenig had met in Iowa in 1994 at a conference titled "The Future of Human Rights," sponsored by the Stanley Center for Peace and Security. Koenig, a former colonel in the Israeli army, the daughter of a rabbi, and an Israeli American, had been asked to leave Israel because of her work on behalf of the Palestinians and in support of a potential two-state solution. Gay McDougall, a highly respected human rights activist (discussed in more detail in chapter 6), had also been invited to the conference. Together, they functioned as "the wicked opposition," Ross chuckled, because they challenged the white men on their limited interpretation of the future of the human rights movement. They argued that the men's version of the human rights framework failed to address economic, social, and cultural rights—so-called second-generation human rights. Further, the women argued, "it failed [because] . . . it was totally aloof in many ways from the social justice movement of which we were a part." Koenig adamantly argued that the men were not even using the human rights framework to address what her country (Israel) was doing, while Ross and McDougall took the conference participants to task over racism and their failure to see the struggle against racism as a human rights issue versus a civil rights issue.

When Ross attended the Beijing conference, she met women from twenty-one other countries whom Koenig had persuaded to start human rights education programs in their home countries. Koenig had also been instrumental in the struggles to persuade the United Nations to declare 1995–2004 the World Decade for Human Rights Education. Koenig insisted that Ross attend the meeting so that she could meet other women from such places as Argentina and Bali and participate in the discussions about centers for human rights education.

Ross had realized that the tolerance framework she encountered in her work with the CDR was disturbing because it had become clear to her that "when you do hate group work you become very, very aware of what you are fighting against. You are fighting against hatred, homophobia, bigotry, etc., etc. But you lack a framework to tell the world what you are fighting for. And so when she [Koenig] introduced me to the human rights framework and showed me its richness and complexity and its applicability, which is even more important, that's when the 'for' question started working for me." Thus began a paradigm shift for Ross: "I began to describe myself as seeking to build a human rights movement that seeks a seamless garment of undivided justice so that my human rights as an African American, my human rights as a woman, my human rights as a peace activist, my human rights as a southerner, all of these are connected together. All of my identities are organized under one human rights roof."

The human rights framework intrigued Ross because it offered one lens through which to see multiple and interlocking oppressions. But it did more than call attention to what was wrong; in addition, it offered a vision of what could be right. She was also deeply concerned that no one seemed to be actively engaged in providing education about human rights abuses in the United States. While she does not deny that there has been human rights education in this country, she observed that historically the focus has been on letter-writing campaigns for tortured prisoners overseas, but "not necessarily to talk about stepping over the homeless man on your way to the mailbox to mail that letter." Ross took the "big leap of faith" and decided that she would establish the Center for Human Rights Education (CHRE) in the United States in 1996.

Ross invited the veteran civil rights activist Rev. C. T. Vivian to join the CHRE board, and from him she was shocked to learn that Martin Luther King Jr. had actually intended to build a human rights movement rather than a civil rights movement.[46] Indeed, the mythology surrounding King has served to emphasize only his role as a civil rights leader, even as it has failed to unearth and extol his vision of a holistic human rights movement. While King's ascendancy began with the Montgomery bus boycott, which challenged the segregation of public accommodations and expanded to include voting rights, Thomas F. Jackson argues that "King was adept at stretching the terms of civic nationalism toward ideals of social democracy. Equal rights to integrated education and political participation depended on the fulfillment of human rights to economic security and dignified well-paid work." Jackson goes on to insist that "King stretched the meaning of integration beyond desegregation and color-blind fairness to demand structural changes in the geography of home ownership, the relations and compensation of work and shared political power."[47]

Although Ross had long been a women's rights activist, she had not come to that position through the civil rights movement, as many other Black women had. Rather, she came late to the civil rights movement when she joined the Center for Democratic Renewal in 1990 and after nearly twenty years in the women's movement. Her assessment of the two movements is an interesting one. She argues that the women's rights movement has progressed toward understanding that women's rights are human rights and illuminating the connections between local violations and a global framework. On the other hand, Ross asserted, "I think the civil rights movement is one of the most backwards in terms of understanding that connection. They are resistant to new information and to change. I think they have become somewhat rigid and formulaic." She pointed out (as did Gay McDougall) that it was not until the UN World Conference Against Racism in 2001 in South Africa that a significant number of civil rights organizations realized that they needed to be connected to the global human rights framework. And even when they attended the conference, they came with the attitude that somehow they should assume leadership of the international movement for human rights despite the fact that they had no experience and extremely limited knowledge regarding how to build international solidarity with other antiracist struggles around the globe.

Ross did have a history of international engagement, since she had attended all four of the UN's women's conferences, the International Conference on Population and Development in Cairo in 1994, and the Conference on Housing in Istanbul in 1996 (Habitat II), in addition to the aforementioned racism conference in South Africa. She had also attended several of the preparatory conferences that met prior to each conference to negotiate the contents of the conference documents.

Once Ross made the decision to build the Center for Human Rights Education, based on a holistic approach to human rights, it became necessary to determine how to focus the organization strategically. Recognizing that this was "a kitchen table–based women's organization," Ross and the other organizers had to decide how to proceed. To that end, they held a retreat in 1996 for social justice activists representing women's rights, antipoverty, campaign finance reform, and environmental justice movements and asked them for their advice on what the CHRE should focus on. The group insisted that the first group that needed to be informed about their human rights was actually activists who were already engaged in struggle, because this information would provide them with a new tool with which to engage their activism. The CHRE began first by providing human rights education to people in the antipoverty movement who were struggling against the so-called welfare reform of the time. The CHRE also attempted to bring a human rights education program to the public schools because they felt strongly that children and young people needed to be taught that they possessed human rights and what those rights were. Additionally, they educated women's right's activists about human rights.

Ross emphasized that the CHRE was the only human rights education institution that was located in and focused on the Deep South. Members traveled to Alabama, Mississippi, and Tennessee, among other states.

By 2002, six years after it was established, the CHRE was involved in directly training between five and six thousand people annually. Also by that date they had distributed close to 275,000 copies of the Universal Declaration of Human Rights. The CHRE had three basic programs. The largest and most popular program was called Bringing Human Rights Home—Human Rights 101, if you will. These introductory-level training courses were offered to community groups, schools, churches, and whoever requested them. Within this program there was also a "train the trainer" program to prepare people who had received human rights one-on-one training to become human rights educators in their own communities.

The second major program was called the Human Rights and Social Justice Institute, which featured advanced think tank retreats focused on specific human rights issues. For example, in May 2002 Ross taught a workshop directed primarily to men of color about the framework for women's human rights and how it applied to their work. These men had worked in antibattering programs, AIDS programs, and community health programs. Most had heard about human rights but had never actually thought about applying them to their own work. The context for this particular think tank emerged from the first wave of the movement, which challenged violence against women between about 1972 and 1990. This era included a number of programs aimed at working with men who committed violence against women.

Ross recalled that the DC Rape Crisis Center had developed a program against rape that actually went into the prisons to provide feminist education to rapists so that when they reentered society they would have a different set of ideas about gender, power, and domination. Women who worked at the crisis center had come to the realization that most rapists would continue to rape once they were confined to prison, but in that setting, their targets were men. Because rapists only changed the gender of their victims, not their behavior, when they returned to society they would continue raping not only women but also men if their domination and control issues were not addressed while they were in prison. There was, therefore, a dire need for programs to address these issues. Feminists debated as to whether women or men should run such programs, but they finally came to the conclusion that men listen best to other men. Men of color began to work in these programs, and over time some began to identify as male feminists. Members of these kinds of groups were invited to participate in the Human Rights and Social Justice Institute think tank.

The Human Rights and Social Justice Institute held a three-day retreat titled "Fighting the Right with Human Rights," which brought together a wide array of groups, including those that monitored right-wing groups such as the Ku Klux Klan and neo-Nazis; the religious Right, including the Christian Coalition; the politically conservative Right, including think tanks such as the Heritage Foundation; and what the institute referred to as the institutionalized Right, including police officers who are guilty of brutality and the bankers and realtors who engage in redlining neighborhoods. The institute brought together people who were monitoring such groups with people who were most affected by such groups, including immigrants' rights groups, prisoners' rights groups, and those who were dealing with school reforms such as the teaching of creationism, advocated by right-wingers who had taken over local school boards. These two populations were, in turn, exposed to the human rights framework and then learned how they might use the framework to enhance their work.

The third program was called the Collaborative Action Projects. While the first two programs were educational and strategic in purpose, this program sought to activate the institute's theories. That is, the program developed partnerships with organizations in order to put the framework into practice. The primary partnerships were with the Southern Human Rights Organizing Network (SHRON), which holds a regionwide conference on human rights in the Deep South every two years. SHRON addresses seemingly intractable problems, including treatment of workers, police brutality, welfare reform, and environmental racism. Another very important collaborative relationship was with the SisterSong Women of Color Reproductive Justice Collective (see chapter 4). They also work with other women of color health groups in Puerto Rico and Hawai'i to increase their use of the human rights framework in the area of reproductive health advocacy.

The impact of the institute even reached into mainstream institutions. Ross recollected that the institute received an invitation from a national committee whose goal was to preserve Medicare and Social Security. The committee wanted institute members to build a training program for their staff on how to use the human rights framework to advance their case for protecting Medicare and Social Security. The participants wrote a statement of principles for human rights and aging and even felt empowered to discuss the human rights of staff.

The CHRE had a staff of five people, four full time and one part time, and an annual budget of about $400,000 by 2002. Ross recalled that during the first year of the CHRE's existence she made half the salary that she had earned the previous year; furthermore, the organization survived on the speaking fees and honorariums that she was able to generate until they were in a position to attract funding from foundations. Ross observed that most funders of human rights initiatives are less generous toward human rights projects based in the United States. While they are eager to fund proposals that address human rights in Eastern Europe or Africa or Asia, they are reluctant to fund projects closer to home. And if foundations choose to fund a domestic project, they have a tendency to compartmentalize, focusing on the civil rights movement rather than funding an organization that offers a holistic approach to human rights in the United States. In 2002 the Ford Foundation provided 74 percent of the CHRE's funding, but for the reasons mentioned above, this was a matter of concern to Ross.

Ross argued that women of color have a significant impact upon human rights because they are engaged in the creation of a more integrated, holistic understanding of human rights. For example, they insist that donors rethink their practices of establishing funding strategies that foster competition between organizations and that they stop limiting time frames. For instance, at one point Ross had attracted funding from a major women's foundation to support the CHRE's economic justice work in 1997. The project provided human rights education to antipoverty activists about the ways in which welfare reform was actually violating human rights. When the CHRE sought additional funding in 1998, they were told that the project they proposed to do was much too similar to the project from the previous year—as if the work of welfare reform could be completed within the strict parameters of a one-year time frame.

Social justice and Black feminism are deeply embedded in how Loretta Ross understands and performs human rights. She embraces the concept of social justice because it offers a strong radical critique of capitalism and of white supremacy, and it is anti-imperialist: "If it is not offering a critique of our economic system, then social justice gets reduced to identity-based groups seeking their equal opportunity to oppress by getting their turn to be in charge of the system." She charged that the liberal feminist movement has not sought to change the nature of capitalism; instead, it has been more interested in participating in the system and running it. By the same token, she charged that many Black people, rather than critiquing white supremacy, have wanted to join the black neoconservative movement and run it.

Social justice, she insisted, "seeks to eliminate all forms of oppression, not simply that one that affects you the most." Thus, she concluded, "My definition of social justice has pretty much morphed into the definition of human rights." She tends to view herself as a member of the human rights movement, which is educating the social justice movement, thus helping it become a human rights movement.

As a Black woman, Ross feels that she has a unique perspective because she offers a critique of white supremacy within the human rights movement, as well as the white supremacy in those they fight. She is critical of what she terms the old guard traditional human rights movement, which she characterizes as dominated by white men and lawyers, because "they tend to deprioritize the human rights that matter the most to people who are marginalized—economic rights." She argued, much as Imam did, that the old guard doesn't see the centrality of second-generation human rights because they are not the ones most likely to be at risk of not having housing or food or quality education for their children. Rather, as they prioritize first-generation civil and political rights, they tend to replicate issues of power, domination, and gender supremacy within the human rights movement. Ross asserted, "The positionality of Black women calls attention to internal contradictions in the movement as well as the external opponents to the movement."

Ross spoke of merging what she described as "the disciplines of human rights education and self-help" into a technique that is often used in the CHRE's training sessions. The technique relies on what she terms the "victimized violator paradigm." When asked, people are easily able to recall incidents when their human rights have been violated, but they find it very difficult to name a time when they themselves have violated someone else's human rights. She noted, however, that this is a difficult exercise for different people for different reasons. People of color and women have little difficulty in recalling the violations of human rights that they have experienced, but owning the responsibility of having violated someone else's rights is another story. She insisted, however, that it is impossible for them not to have been human rights violators, because "we live in a racist, sexist, homophobic society and," she laughed, "you cannot have escaped the virus!"

Oddly enough, Ross found when she was training white men, particularly police officers, that they were very quick to acknowledge that they have violated the rights of others. They seem to think that by definition of being white and male, they had to have violated someone else's human rights—especially a Black woman's rights. On the other hand, they are totally oblivious to people who have violated them. Ross, who finds this to be a very sad commentary, notes regretfully that police officers fail to realize that the manner in which they were socialized to be white men (to show no emotions, not to cry, to compete with rather than partner with people, to express fear and frustration as violence, etc.) was itself a human rights violation. They have internalized what they have been taught in what she calls the "white male syndrome," but they are unable to recognize this as a violation. She has encouraged leading white men in the human rights movement to talk about the victimized violator paradigm:

> I'm convinced that until we stop white men from accepting the banality of human rights violations which start with them, then the rest of us will never be safe! . . . [Things will not change] until they understand that it is not all right for people to go without food. It is not all right for people to get beaten as a form of parenting. It is not all right for people to have cold and distant relationships with their parents and their siblings. Until they accept [that] this . . . is where the stage is set for all of the disconnection from the rest of humanity, nothing is going to change!

But, she said, trying to get them to have this fundamental conversation is almost impossible. Despite feminist recognition decades ago that the personal is political, white men continue to insist on separating the personal from the political—in essence, they argue that how they treat their wives and/or their children is different from the political work that they do. As she put it, "They want to compartmentalize and separate. But when you ask them about their lives in a human rights way they run screaming. If they had skirts, they'd throw them over their heads," she laughed. Becoming serious, she went on to state that if white men do not take responsibility for challenging these routine violations of human rights, then all of their and our human rights efforts will continue to meet "a very resistant wall of incomprehension."

Black women, then, are bringing a particular positionality to this struggle. She references Kimberlé Crenshaw's work on the "intersectional matrix," which does not allow one to leave race, class, gender, or sexuality off the table. Thus, Ross believes that women of color, particularly Black women, are shifting the entire human rights debate. Their impact is much less UN-centric; that is, their human rights educational process does not begin with the UN documents but rather with the lived experiences of the people. Black women ask, What are your housing, educational, and health care needs? How have these needs been addressed in this thing called human rights? Ross argued that the UN-centric legalistic approach disempowers rather than empowers people because it is difficult to maneuver through the bewildering array of documents and committees and structures. Interestingly, Ross acknowledged that while the UN's emphasis on human rights education is critical, it has also led to recognition that there are too few organizations actually engaged in doing human rights advocacy. The CHRE began receiving dozens of calls from people who, having read their copies of the Universal Declaration of Human Rights (which the CHRE was distributing), found out that they had, for example, a right to a living wage and wanted to know whom they could go see to get that taken care of! Sadly, the CHRE was forced to admit that no such organization exists at this time that can help a person to do that. Thus, the critical level of advocacy is missing in the United States that would transform the promise of human rights into the actuality of human rights.

Just as Imam was committed to integrating and implementing the African feminist philosophy, Ross has also struggled to incorporate a human rights Black feminist intersectional matrix into the organizational structure of the CHRE. She described their organizational chart as "a web-like structure of power and leadership . . . a hybrid somewhere between bureaucratic and the collectivist model of feminist organization." She imagines herself as a doctor of Black feminist philosophy, the spider in the center of the web. "But if you notice about the structure of a web, that a lot of points are interconnected with each other without necessarily being connected to the center. They are anchored to the center but allow for a lot of lateral or horizontal connection." What she attempts to do is to find and empower people at the management level with autonomy to make decisions and to develop great relations with each other, not just with her. Indeed, she feels that as they strengthen their relationships with each other, their relationships with her will diminish. The rationale here is that people function better as a team if they are not required to filter everything through her. Returning to the web analogy, if one part of the web is touched, then the entire web shakes. Decision-making happens for people in this way; that is, they tend to make decisions collectively, but each person has a different point of entry into the web, and they take different responsibility for implementing those decisions.

Ross mentioned that she discovered the web structure in a book titled *The Female Advantage: Women's Ways of Leadership*.[48] She has found this model to be useful in protecting women's values around empowerment while at the same time offering a management style that, as she put it, actually accomplishes something. Thus, the web is most appropriate to that dual need for both empowerment and accomplishment. Ross noted that she also makes it a point to hire superstars, because "the brighter they shine, the brighter I look." In a web structure, she observed, "you really don't want women who lack self-confidence or feel totally disempowered, because they are too dependent on others to help them shine. But if that internal fire comes from within, then they fit well within a web structure, because at every point of that web they have a sense of empowerment, entitlement that they can do what they need to do within where they are."

Ross also observed that people who were extremely subordinated in their previous employment history do not usually work well in the CHRE's system. She believes it is "because they do not know how to work without threats and coercion." Such a motivation for job performance is incompatible with the goals and methods of the CHRE: "People who are self-motivated, self-directed, who want to pioneer stuff, who want to shine, who can take responsibility for their failures, as well as their success, they love this. They love this model because they don't feel that they are in competition with each other in order to get the higher salary or get the best salary or get the most praise or the rewards or the great trip."

The CHRE has also established a human rights–based set of personnel policies that, she laughingly stated, "changes how you run a nonprofit." She noted that many nonprofits actually replicate the corporate model; however, when you begin to apply human rights standards to how employees are treated, it makes for some differences. She offered the fact that the salary structure for the employees of the CHRE is divorced from their positions. Much like the Marxist concept, what one is paid is not dependent upon one's position but on one's human need. So, for example, the secretary who is the single parent of two children receives the same salary as the senior program director. By this same logic, the Native American communications director receives money from her tribe's casino disbursements; thus, she has fewer material needs than the secretary does, so she is paid less, even though their total incomes work out to be the same. Such conversations are brought into the workplace, thereby alleviating secrets about anyone's salary. Salaries are an open subject for staff meetings, and decisions are collectively made about who is paid what. And in those "difficult dialogues," workers are invited to share personal concerns. For example, if someone's spouse just lost his or her job, then that employee's needs have changed and should be included in the decision-making process about salary.

Ross acknowledged that this attempt to manage the organization on the basis of human rights presents some challenges. By far the biggest challenge is the issue of health insurance. The cost of health insurance was (and still is) extremely high, so the CHRE was only able to offer coverage for an employee. They were unable to offer dependent coverage. Even so, Ross mentioned that the employee coverage was about to bankrupt the organization because it was so expensive.[49] She was dissatisfied with this solution because she believes that a human rights organization should offer full family coverage, but at that point it was the best that they could do.

Ross mentioned that "we also democratize who gets to do foreign travel."

So that the secretary went with us to South Africa . . . [in 2001 for the UN Conference on Racism]. Of course, it is neither possible nor appropriate for everyone to do everything. For example, everyone should not be doing a press interview. It is, however, a collective when the business of the organization and the needs of their people are put on the table for discussion and decision-making. Thus, out of respect for and in conformity with the Black feminist concept of intersectionality, CHRE strives to be interconnected, universal, and indivisible and to be, internally as well as externally, accountable and consistent as it lives into the promise of the human rights framework.

In December 2004, eight years after she founded the CHRE, Ross retired as executive director. In January 2005 she became the national cofounder and national coordinator for the SisterSong Women of Color Reproductive Justice Collective. Their endeavors will be discussed in the next chapter.

Conclusion

Although they have only "met" through this chapter, Ayesha Imam and Loretta Ross are kindred spirits in their absolute allegiance to claiming and implementing international human rights for and with their local constituents. They are accomplished multidirectional players operating in a movement from the commanding heights of the international all the way to the gritty level of the local. They are engaged in the creative processes of domesticating and applying the lofty principles of international law to the realities of their respective corners of the world. These processes rely upon extensive educational dialogue (some would say "multilogues") that emerge from their understanding of social justice within the comprehensiveness of the human rights agenda. They not only share their specialized knowledge of international human rights but also translate it even as they negotiate appropriate interpretations of those rights in a manner that resonates with and expands to meet the needs of people. Their innovative feminist methods of bringing human rights to bear on the challenges of abuses, discrimination, and oppression are having an immediate impact on the lives of women, their children, and men. Their work, then, is representative of the best efforts of individuals within groups around the world that are engaged in the critical task of both claiming and (re)defining their human rights.

4

Grassroots Praxis

Show
reflections of girls
not fully formed
Show
thieves of innocence their blood . . . drenched deeds
no hiding place
no escape from choices of desperate cries
. . . .
Their punishment is our redemption . . . our liberation
impunity is the last comfort station
shake it
rattle it
tear it down

Jaribu Hill, "Haunting Mirrors," 2000

"Fraught" is the word that best captures the relationship of the US government to international human rights. Despite US leadership in the founding of the United Nations and the critical role the United States played in the drafting of the Universal Declaration of Human Rights, US endorsement of human rights during most of the last half of the twentieth century was constrained by the Cold War and inhibited by a jealous defense of our national sovereignty. Additionally, our historic emphasis on civil and political rights along with our cavalier dismissal of economic, social, and cultural rights has resulted in what Martha F. Davis has described as an "awkward waltz . . . [a] three-part dance of ambivalence, rejection and embrace."[1]

Nevertheless, the global human rights movement is quietly being ushered into the United States through the work of human rights practitioners such as Linda Burnham, Dazon Dixon Diallo, and Jaribu Hill. Each has moved beyond ambivalence and rejection to embrace human rights through their vital grassroots work. They seized upon the opportunities offered by the international human rights framework to invigorate and inform struggles for the rights of marginalized and disenfranchised members of the US population. As they have struggled to develop crucial sociopolitical possibilities, they have also battled to attain some space to extend the scope of the social implications of human rights in a reluctant, often hostile, political landscape. As seasoned activists, they bring to these critical endeavors sophisticated toolboxes of multi-layered advocacy in the organizations they have founded and/or direct. They occupy the role that Karen Sacks terms "center woman" and describes as "key actors in network formation and consciousness shaping."[2]

In her analysis of social movements, Belinda Robnett provides a racially gendered conceptual framework that serves to structure our understanding of the significance of the work of the grassroots practitioners of late twentieth- and early twenty-first-century human rights discussed in this chapter and the social movements that have been facilitated by their due diligence. Despite the fact that most were too young to be activists in 1960s civil rights movements, these center women are arguably descendants of the women bridge builders whom Robnett describes in her book *How Long? How Long? African-American Women in the Struggle for Civil Rights*. She explains that "women bridge leaders" were much more than community organizers; instead, they were the critical "micro mobilizers" of civil rights activities of the 1960s. According to Robnett, micro mobilization has been identified by theorists as the critical processes of social movements through which consensus is formed and action is mobilized.[3] Bridge leaders transgress the boundaries between the public life of a movement organization and the private spheres of potential constituents and adherents.

Robnett developed a list of ten characteristics exhibited by women bridge leaders. The women who are the subject of this chapter demonstrate at least four of the entries on her list. First, they employ a one-on-one interactive style of leadership for mobilization and recruitment. Second, they exhibit leadership mobility in nonhierarchical structures and institutions. Third, they are closely bound to the wishes and desires of their constituency because, unlike formal leaders, they do not require the state to legitimize their activities. And fourth, they tend to advocate more radical or nontraditional tactics and strategies, again because legitimacy from the state is not a prerequisite for them.[4]

Robnett asserts that bridge leaders operate in "free space," a niche that should be understood as "an unclaimed space that is nevertheless central to the development of the movement, since linkages are developed within it." Bridge leaders, according to Robnett, "operate through one-on-one community based interactions," and their power is derived largely from their autonomous pioneering activities rather than from their titled or hierarchical position within an organization.[5]

The stories of the center women in this chapter demonstrate the critical ways in which effective and innovative activism can be constructed.

Linda Burnham

When I interviewed Linda Burnham, the first "center woman" in this chapter, in June 2002, she was the director of the Women of Color Resource Center in Berkeley, California, which she had cofounded with long-time colleague and friend Miriam Ching Louie in 1989. The office, with colorful posters on the walls and stacks of pamphlets and other publications on shelves and desks, was small yet busy: women of a rainbow array of races moved around and phones rang. Linda Burnham has a serious demeanor and an air of controlled passion about her causes. Loretta Ross (see chapter 3) also interviewed Burnham in 2005. Together, these two interviews provide a more complete portrait of Burnham's career.

A longtime activist, Burnham has been involved with organizations such as the Venceremos Brigades, the Alliance Against Women's Oppression, the Angela Davis Defense Committee, and the Line of March.[6] She was also active in both of Jesse Jackson's presidential campaigns (1984 and 1988) and the Rainbow Coalition.[7] More than any of the other respondents in this chapter, Linda Burnham and the Women of Color Resource Center can be described as direct descendants of the civil rights movement, specifically, the Student Nonviolent Coordinating Committee (SNCC) and its Black Women's Liberation Committee (BWLC).

A brief review of SNCC history is useful at this point. Established in 1960, SNCC emerged as a response to the student sit-in movement that erupted in North Carolina when four students from North Carolina A&T State University decided to protest the segregation of a drugstore lunch counter in Greensboro. Often referred to as the "beloved community," SNCC was characterized in its early years by ideological openness and a loose administrative structure. By 1964 the organization was moving from an emphasis on the creation of an integrated beloved community toward Black nationalism along with a more centralized administrative arrangement. Within the debates around the structure of the organization, nascent feminist concerns were also beginning to be tentatively expressed by Mary King and Casey Hayden, white members of SNCC who anonymously drafted a "Position Paper" in 1964 and "A Kind of Memo" in 1965, both of which were presented at SNCC conferences. The second paper especially represented the first overt critique of the sexism that the women argued was endemic to the organization. According to Kristen Anderson-Bricker, Black women, for a number of reasons, either ignored or responded negatively to both memos.[8] Meanwhile, Black consciousness, racial separatism, and an international perspective were attaining currency as the organization moved beyond its earlier herculean efforts to desegregate public accommodations and attain voting rights. SNCC deepened its commitment to the antiracism struggle, which members were forced to acknowledge was even more obdurate than had previously been recognized.

As a result of internal ideological debates, somewhere around 1966 SNCC began declining just as many Black women in SNCC began deliberations around a different and more complex agenda. In December 1968 Frances Beale, Gwen Patton, and others founded the Black Women's Liberation Committee (BWLC) in New York City. Beale and colleagues began calling attention to the fact that the Black nationalist movement was not addressing the specific concerns of Black women. In 1969 her iconic essay "Double Jeopardy: To Be Black and Female" appeared first in the critically acclaimed anthology *The Black Woman*, edited by Toni Cade, and was later reprinted in the also important anthology *Sisterhood Is Powerful* in 1970. In it, Beale critiqued the white women's movement for focusing only on the oppression caused by male chauvinism and the civil rights / Black nationalist movement for not realizing that any revolutionary struggle must be not only anticapitalist and antiracist but also feminist. In the parlance of the day, the revolution must "be about the business" of creating a new world dedicated to destroying all forms of oppression. Thus, "living for the revolution means taking on the more difficult commitment of changing our day-to-day life patterns."[9]

Clearly, Black women were in need of a forum to address their unique problems, including their relationships with Black men and children and their role in the Black struggle and women's inequality. Moving from their personal experiences of gender discrimination in the SNCC toward a well-conceptualized critique of what was then termed the "male chauvinism" characteristic of Black nationalism, the BWLC embarked upon an ambitious group study and community education program. Members met throughout 1969 and then decided to expand the group by admitting to membership Black women who were not already members of SNCC. Early in 1970 the BWLC transitioned into the Black Women's Alliance (BWA). Although still a component of SNCC, the BWA evolved into both a think tank and an action-oriented organization dedicated to improving the lives of Black people in general. More specifically, it focused on the condition of the Black woman and sought to promote "educational, cultural, economic, social and political unity, and sisterhood among

Black women." Additionally, it sought "to collect, interpret, disseminate and preserve information about the Black community" and to use this knowledge in educational programs. Ultimately, the BWA's mission was to eliminate "any and all forms of oppression based upon race, economic status or sex."[10]

As their understanding and critique of capitalism and imperialism were refined through study, BWA members became cognizant of the fact that Third World women both at home and abroad (i.e., Native Americans, Chicanas, Asians, and Africans) were experiencing similar forms of exploitation and oppression. Thus, the next move was to extend an invitation to Third World women to join the organization, and that in turn led to the assumption of yet another name: Third World Women's Alliance (TWWA). By November 1970 the New York City–based TWWA had grown to around two hundred women, and there was a growing interest in establishing chapters in other states. At that point, a small group of activist women in the TWWA went on retreat to formulate a workable administrative structure and to establish an ideological platform that would address the needs of its growing and diverse membership. They emerged from the retreat with a well-defined independent organizational structure based on democratic centralism and a detailed ideological platform designed to facilitate the growth of an alliance into a national Third World women's organization. In short, the organization would be completely distinct from SNCC and governed by a national centralized administrative structure. At the same time, members embraced a decentralized local structure responsible for implementing the national program. "In other words," as Anderson-Bricker observed, "individual members and chapters were directly responsible to the National Coordinating Committee for carrying out its directives, program and ideological platform, but how each chapter chose to do this depended upon local conditions and decisions. The organization supported collective leadership, collective decisions and input from all members, but abhorred individualism and disregard for the will of the majority. Unity and the revolution would be achieved only if the part submitted to the whole and chapters acted as one in principle, program and tactics."[11]

The TWWA's definition of its feminism differed from that of white feminism and even some other forms of Black feminism because of its focus on a simultaneous struggle to eradicate economic exploitation, racism, and sexism (which would later be captured within the concept of "intersectionality"). The TWWA insisted on embracing socialism as opposed to capitalism and advocated armed revolution to attain the goal of a socialist society that would eliminate all forms of oppression.[12]

Linda Burnham became involved in the Bay Area chapter of the TWWA, established in the early 1970s. She attributes her affiliation with the TWWA as providing an opportunity for her to begin thinking "in a slightly more systematic way about the kinds of issues that women face, and solidify a more developed gender perspective." Burnham noted that the organization was composed of African American, Asian, and Latina women. Interestingly, the membership did not include any Native American women, and it included only one Arab American woman; nonetheless, Burnham described it as "a really rich mix. . . . We learned a lot from each other, a lot about each other, a lot about each other's communities." The Bay Area TWWA addressed issues such as the high rate of infant mortality and peace, as members were vehemently opposed to the Vietnam War, and they developed educational celebrations around International Women's Day and South African Women's Day.[13]

They eventually did grapple with the issue of sexuality. Burnham recalled that when she first joined the organization, it was primarily composed of straight women who were not prepared to deal with issues of sexuality, although many were probably open to accepting lesbians into the organization. Nonetheless, they were challenged about their homophobia and their unwillingness to place that issue on their agenda. They were again challenged several years later about their heterosexist and homophobic orientation, but by that point they were willing to struggle internally to address the issue using the tools of education and discussion.[14]

At some point in the early 1980s the TWWA moved through yet another metamorphosis and became the Alliance Against Women's Oppression. The alliance "brought white women came [sic] into the organization and was much clearer on, and more publicly articulated, an anti-homophobic politic." Burnham reflected on how her work changed in the 1980s. She described herself as part of an aging generation that had not previously been career oriented: "We basically tried to figure out how am I going to get myself a little gig that will keep a roof over my head and bread and butter on the table so that I can do what I'm really about doing, which is trying to figure out how to make a revolution or win women's rights or, you know, fight for black liberation or whatever it was. So, we were not inclined to follow a career path." Furthermore, the organizations that she had been involved with had managed to survive on volunteer energy and willpower rather than depend upon foundation funding. However, by the end of the 1980s, she observed that the "model of organizing at least for those of us who were hitting our forties, was no longer really a viable model."[15]

The 1980s brought with it the demise of both the Third World Women's Alliance and the Alliance Against Women's Oppression. Meanwhile, Burnham worked as a legal secretary in various offices around the area as she confronted the questions of "how and in what form might I be able to . . . sustain a political orientation and vision, that, again, traces itself back to the Third World Women's Alliance and then the Black Women's Caucus." In 1989 she brought together something that she called a "project development team" to discuss "in what form we might be able to transition these politics and stabilize them in an organizational setting." It was from those conversations that the decision was made to establish the Women of Color Resource Center.[16]

Cofounders Burnham and Miriam Ching Louie of the center were intent upon creating an organization that had a holistic perspective about "how racism works in our country, how economic justice and class bias and class discriminate against women, misogyny and . . . all kinds of challenges that women face, how do those things all work together. So, it was basically about figuring out how to sustain those politics in an activist way." Given the times, they felt it was important to develop the center as a nonprofit organization in hopes that it would be more durable. During the first two or three years of the organization, Burnham held down a part-time job and shared a small office space with the National Network for Immigration and Refugee Rights. She and the project development team attained nonprofit status, found someone to work for them on a pro bono basis, and began work on their first project.[17]

Their initial projects included developing a national directory of women of color organizations and their projects, and learning how to raise money as a nonprofit organization, skills they developed through on-the-job training. It was difficult to raise money in those early days. Burnham laughingly recalled "having what you think is a fabulous idea and not being joined in the opinion of its fabulousness by people who are in the position to give you some money." Despite those kinds of roadblocks and with the assistance of their excellent board, which had developed out of the project development team, the organization did develop programmatically over time.[18] At the time of our interview in 2002, their funding came from a combination of membership dues, individual donors, foundations, the sale of their publications, the proceeds from fund-raising events, and sometimes fees from the workshops they ran. Although funding was problematic for many years, they managed to support a staff of six or seven, some of whom worked part time. Burnham noted that they were barely able to pay themselves, and at that point they were unable to provide health insurance for the staff. (See chapter 3 for a description of Loretta Ross's struggles with this issue.)[19]

When asked about the formal training she brought to her work, Burnham laughed and stated that she had been an English major in college. She attended Bennett College in North Carolina, one of only two Black women's colleges in the country, for one year, but she found it a bit too socially conservative for a girl who grew up in Brooklyn. While in North Carolina, she did participate in the voter registration project before she transferred and graduated with a bachelor of arts degree in English literature from Reed College in Portland, Oregon. In 1969, soon after completing school, she moved to the Bay Area. Later she returned to school at Cal State University, East Bay, in Hayward to pursue a master's degree. She mentioned that she felt compelled to return to school because she was determined to develop and refine her understanding of African American women and the issue of homelessness. She felt that a return to a more formal educational environment would provide a systematic opportunity to study the subject. She wrote her master's thesis on African American women and homelessness and attained a master of arts degree in sociology.[20] Her informal education, on the other hand—learning how to build and develop an organization—was the result of many, many hours of volunteer labor in a variety of different organizations.

Burnham characterizes her work as social justice work, and she described it in the following manner: "At the broadest it means looking at issues of inequality and inequity in terms of economic, gender, and racial issues . . . and how those interrelate. And trying to figure out how those function structurally in our society, how they are manifested politically, and how they are sustained, how those inequities are sustained politically. And then try to figure out programmatically how we can go at either educating people about structural injustice and/or try and do something to change it." It was her opinion that nearly everyone who worked with the resource center "is convinced at one level or another that there are deep structures of our society and that it will take a pretty substantial radical transformation of some sort or another to transform them." She laughed and admitted that "what that transformation looks like or how it might come about, all of that, no telling."

Burnham went on to provide examples of some of the resource center's current projects. In 2002 they were organizing around foreign policy issues and the War on Terrorism soon after September 11 and contemplating why women should oppose the War on Terrorism: "What do women have to lose, . . . [and] what do women of color have to lose in particular? . . . And really trying to figure out how to raise the voices of women of color, including and particularly the voices of Arab and Muslim women." (These issues continue to resonate to this day!) They were focusing much of their International Women's Day work around how Arab and Muslim women were being impacted at that time.

As a part of its racial justice emphasis, the resource center was also collaborating with other small nonprofit grassroots racial justice organizations in an attempt to understand how best to respond to the current political climate, in which racial justice issues had been removed from the agenda. They were concerned that communities that were already suffering were being impacted in even worse ways. Thus, they collaborated in focusing on foreign policy issues and, from the Women of Color Resource Center's particular perspective, emphasizing gender issues to ensure that these issues were included on the social justice agenda. Additionally, they were deeply concerned about the move to reform welfare. In 1996 there was a national effort to eliminate the long-standing Aid to Families with Dependent Children program and replace it with the Temporary Assistance for Needy Families (TANF) program.[21] The resource center was quite concerned about the manner in which the issue of welfare actually bundled together inequities based on class, race, and gender. The resource center members argued that race and misogyny comprised the critical subtext beneath the processes that result in such policies, "so we kind of feel like it's our job to, in that case, to kind of state the unstated."

Burnham also has a history of engaging with women's international human rights. She was a member of a delegation from the Alliance Against Women's Oppression that attended the 1985 UN Women's World Conference in Nairobi, Kenya. They learned much from attending their first world conference on women's rights. They went to Nairobi prepared to discuss the issues of reproductive rights and the wars in Central America, but it was also their first opportunity to engage with women from around the world.

Burnham ruefully admitted, "We kind of come at [human rights] sideways." The process of their engagement in human rights began when they attended the international women's conference and only afterward realized the importance of those rights. They learned how organized the conferences were around the concepts of human rights and the instruments to achieve human rights. "And it's only then that we started to try and understand better what the human rights framework is and what's positive and useful about that framework. And also, where it might be limiting." They also began to interact with the Bay Area chapter of Amnesty International, which included a focus on human rights education. Burnham was quick to note that "it's not as though we function or even necessarily consider ourselves in a structural way . . . [as] part of the human rights community." In fact, she questioned whether the resource center as an organization was really involved in human rights or if, as they focused on specific issues, those issues fell under the purview of human rights: "So it is interesting to me, anyway, to get, to try to get, a sense of how people come into or what kind of a relationship they try to develop with this whole idea of what human rights is. Because it varies."

Burnham expressed concern about how a small organization with limited resources and no lawyers on staff might be able to participate in the international arena of the UN. She questioned how human rights education could be accomplished in grassroots settings: "At the UN a lot of that space is consumed by experts . . . legal experts or people who sort of work the UN setting for decades on end." She described the center's attempt to work out how to insert itself into the UN setting and how to function within that setting without being a lawyer as a "pretty steep learning curve." Other crucial issues the center confronted during its attempt to participate in the international setting included the relationships that needed to be developed and sustained outside the UN "so that when you get to the UN setting you have more capacity to move." Burnham also pointed out concerns around document language: "There's only a certain set of people that have either the patience or the skills or the orientation to . . . sit and work a document. And then the patience and the skills to take that work and figure out a lobbying strategy around it." Indeed, her experience with the UN Conference on Racism led her to conclude, "It's really to the detriment of those caucuses [especially in the women's caucus] that the space has been basically monopolized by experts. And the ability to . . . integrate a more grassroots perspectives is underdeveloped, I would say." However, she acknowledged, "I'm interested in anything that advances and improves the condition of women. So," she laughed, "if human rights does it, I'm for human rights. If something else does it, I'm for that too."

> To me the human rights instruments and the sort of programs that come out of these major conferences provide us with powerful tools to do important work both domestically and internationally. And especially powerful tools because at one level or another they represent an international consensus . . . and I think they are underutilized in the US. And it would be an advance for us in the women's movement and in many other movements if we were able to incorporate a human rights perspective more effectively in our organizing work. . . . Human rights instruments represent . . . a profoundly progressive orientation to relations between citizens and states, responsibilities of governments to their citizens. . . . And you know if they were, if the human rights instruments were actually implemented, we'd be in a whole different situation.

As the Women of Color Resource Center prepared for the Beijing Conference on Women, it made the decision not only to bring a delegation of one hundred people to the conference but also to develop a range of positions on issues so that they might be better prepared for what they would encounter at the conference. Thus, attendees arrived at the conference prepared to discuss immigrant women and their rights in the United States and other places around the world, as well as welfare rights and homelessness, especially by drawing connections between the status of low-income women and the pressure on housing. The center included some homeless women within the delegation so that they could provide authentic voices of experience about this problem. Burnham noted that this issue was of particular interest to women from around the world because many were astonished to learn that the United States had a problem with homelessness. Burnham stated, "For us, at the Women of Color Resource Center, it was an opportunity both to do that kind of work, and in doing a lot of the preparatory work for it, I think it forced us to engage with issues having to do with the impact of globalization on women around the world and also to start to understand how global economic policies, or the parallels to the kinds of global economic policies that were impacting women in other places, how they were impacting women here in the US." Furthermore, according to Burnham, the gathering provided a crucial opportunity for them to really begin to understand that "for many women in other parts of the world, their thinking and understanding and work around women's issues was framed by how they understood the impact of transnational capital on their communities. . . . There tended to be a more integrated approach to the variety of different issues on a woman rights agenda than was the case for those of us from the US who tended to have a more fragmented . . . approach to our agenda."[22]

As she reflected upon the Beijing conference, Burnham mentioned that while the powerful statement "women's rights are human rights" emerged from that conference, she felt that an equally powerful but underreported statement that also emerged from the conference was that "women's rights are compromised by the processes of corporate globalization." She insisted that this was the message from the grassroots women who were in Beijing. Clearly, they felt that their communities were being destroyed by the policies of the World Bank and the IMF, and the slogan "women's rights are human rights" did not capture their profound concerns about economic, social, and cultural rights.

Burnham acknowledged that the opportunity to attend an international conference was a privilege that carried with it a responsibility to "translate and transfer" the information and experiences they attained back to their constituency in the United States. To that end, they compiled a popular education workbook titled *Women's Education in the Global Economy*, which examined the impact of World Bank and IMF policies of structural adjustment on women. It also focused on work in the informal sector of the economy, trafficking in women, violence against women, and the impact of environmental toxins. As they explored those issues, they also addressed what Burnham described as "parallel questions," such as women's double- or triple-day work requirements (paid work outside the home plus work within the home for the family) and the impact of US privatization policies: "So, the point of all that is, I feel like it was both a continuation and a deepening of an orientation, a long-standing orientation, towards the international arena and towards placing the work that we do in an international context."[23]

By the time the women began to prepare for the "Beijing + 5—Women 2000: Gender Equality, Development and Peace for the Twenty-first Century," a special session of the UN General Assembly at UN Headquarters in New York in June 2000, they had become engaged in framing the issue of US welfare reform within a human rights context. The UN Platform of Action called for governments to develop programs that would improve the conditions of women living in poverty. As mentioned previously, the TANF legislation had been passed by Congress and signed into law between the Fourth World Conference in Beijing in 1995 and the UN special session in New York in 2000. The Women of Color Resource Center explored a variety of ways in which the welfare legislation directly contradicted the Beijing Platform for Action and then tried to disseminate that information in as many ways as they could to the American public.

The resource center also hired a scholar with a legal background to assume responsibility for a welfare rights education and advocacy program. While acknowledging that the legislation was extremely complex, nevertheless, the resource center was especially concerned with those aspects of the legislation that would have a particularly egregious impact on women of color. Burnham cited the example of the family cap issue, which denies additional welfare benefits if a woman has another child while she is already a welfare client. Burnham noted that this aspect of the legislation emerged from an erroneous belief that women have children in order to collect more welfare benefits. She mentioned another problematic issue found within the legislation: the drug felony ban, which barred a woman from receiving welfare if she had been convicted of a drug felony. The resource center collaborated with other groups that were concerned about the legislation and especially how it would be implemented at the state and local levels. "I think what many have recognized, I think belatedly, is that women of color have a very muted voice in public policy. Very muted. At all levels."

Because of her participation in several UN world conferences, Burnham was able to provide some insightful commentary on the relationships between domestic and international arenas within the context of human rights and the reciprocal impact of Black feminism and international human rights. Those reflections began with a brief critique of the mainstream women's movement "and understanding that there was a way in which that movement was not going to be capable of reflecting and articulating certain sets of issues and interests." She asserted that the emphasis on intersectionality, which was particularly evident in the UN conference on racism, provided a framework that attempted to account for "the complexity of women's lives and the varied and distinct ways in which they experience discrimination or exploitation or oppression . . . the experience of being a marginalized voice here in the US . . . and understanding that a perspective that comes on a unilateral front can't—and won't—account for that reality." This realization in turn led to an impulse to determine how the human rights framework could be made more complete. There were what Burnham called "tiny baby steps along the way." She recalled that progress from the period of the Beijing conference to the race conference was made in confronting the difficulty of developing language that was inclusive of minority or marginalized women. Despite the fact that the Beijing Platform for Action was a profound document, she argued that the conference participants had not yet achieved language that reflected and integrated the issues of racial/ethnic minority women. She did note that a measure of progress from Beijing to Durban, South Africa (location of the UN World Conference against Racism, Racial Discrimination, Xenophobia and Related Intolerance in 2001), was how much more centralized the emphasis on racial/ethnic minority women had become. Indeed, she attributed much of this emphasis on a more integrated feminist analysis as filtering in from Black feminist theorizing. No doubt the thoughtful engaged activism of the Women of Color Resource Center and other similar organizations also contributed to the progress toward a more nuanced international understanding of the family of "isms" that the concept of intersectionality strives to capture.

Dazon Dixon Diallo

Dazon Dixon, born in Fort Valley, Georgia, the child of parents with advanced graduate degrees who were themselves educators, learned to read by the time she was three years old. In addition to their emphasis on education, her parents were also Episcopalians who were active members of the first integrated church in Fort Valley. They were deeply committed to the church's mission of human rights, justice, and peace and instilled that fierce commitment in Dazon. Because she was born in 1965, Dazon was too young to be active in the civil rights movement of the 1960s, although she would later become active in the antiapartheid movement in college. Neither of her parents had chosen to participate in the overt activities of organizations such as SNCC, perhaps because both came from extremely poor rural backgrounds and were first-generation college students.[24] After graduating in 1982 from the newly integrated Fort Valley school system, Dazon matriculated at Spelman College in Atlanta.

I interviewed Dazon on July 9, 2002, in the home of Loretta Ross. She brings a humorous demeanor to the seriousness of her work, so we occasionally shared some hilarious moments as she informed me about her work. Loretta Ross is a colleague and friend of Dazon Dixon Diallo, and they have worked closely together over many years. Ross interviewed Dixon Diallo in 2009 for the Voices of Feminism Oral History Project, housed in the Sophia Smith Collection at Smith College. Ross's extensive interview not only confirms much of what I learned from my own interview with Dixon Diallo but also provides additional information that enriches and deepens my appreciation for her critical endeavors.

Dixon Diallo's grassroots praxis weaves together several important strands, including (but not limited to) feminism and women's rights, health advocacy, reproductive justice, and international human rights, in a manner that both culminates in and is sustained through her work with SisterLove. The odyssey of her life's work began during the summer between her freshman and sophomore years, when she was employed on the Spelman campus. That summer of 1983 the first national conference on Black women's health was held on campus. Intrigued by the conference and excited by the prospect of meeting so many important women in attendance whose work she was reading in her classes, she missed an entire week of work in order to participate. Armed with a mandate provided by the highly successful conference, the renowned health educator and advocate Byllye Avery would move to establish the National Black Women's Health Project (NBWHP) in 1983 (it would later be renamed the Black Women's Health Imperative). This was and is a critical intervention that continues to be "committed to defining, promoting and maintaining the physical and emotional well-being of women and their families."[25]

Inspired by the conference and its participants, Dazon began volunteering at the Feminist Women's Health Center in Atlanta in 1984, her sophomore year in college. "So I was the youngest and, well, glow in the dark, I was one of the few that were dark on staff at the Atlanta Feminist Health Center," she said with a laugh. She described the center as inclusive of both activism and advocacy that "provided contraceptive care, family planning assistance, [and] well-woman gynecological services. Eventually we even added services of artificial insemination for women, particularly lesbians, who wanted to become pregnant." She described this work as her "entrée into the practical, into the practical application of feminist theory . . . in [the] everyday lived experiences of women."[26]

Dazon was not only the youngest worker on the staff but also the only woman of color, but this, she felt, helped her connect with the women of color who were seeking help from the center. The issue of AIDS as a health issue not just for gay men but also for women began to attract public attention. As women began to discover that they might have been infected with HIV, they sought help from AIDS Atlanta, a local gay male health organization. Fielding calls from women, especially Black women seeking help, and unsure of how to respond appropriately, the men asked for assistance from the Feminist Women's Health Center. As these concerns evolved into an important issue, the center felt compelled to engage it.[27] The two organizations collaborated on a women's education program called the Women's AIDS Prevention Project (WAPP). Dixon recalled that the health center not only had begun a donor insemination program for lesbians and other women but also was creating programs in the areas of reproductive and sexual health education that seemed to parallel the WAPP project.

Dazon started volunteering at AIDS Atlanta with the WAPP, but oversight of the program vacillated between AIDS Atlanta and the health center before finally settling into its home in the center. By the time the Democratic National Convention was held in Atlanta in 1988, Dixon Diallo had graduated from Spelman and was a full-time employee of the center. The health center (along with other centers that provided abortion services) attracted the attention of Randall Terry and his group, Operation Rescue.[28] They not only brought hundreds of volunteers with them but also trained hundreds of Atlanta residents who remained in Atlanta after the convention to continue demonstrations for a year. The center was effectively under siege, and its resources were severely depleted, as funds were necessarily diverted to physically shield clients and the clinic and to support the clinic's legal defense. Dixon Diallo also recalled that this was the Reagan–Bush era, so during this time funding was limited. This meant "there would be no AIDS prevention money coming to an abortion provider"; therefore, the difficult yet pragmatic decision was made to end the project. In an interesting aside, Dazon mentioned that the donor insemination program was allowed to continue because although it too required self-funding, the rationale was that, unlike the AIDS program, it was an income generator.

Dixon Diallo, the youngest woman on the staff, had become the WAPP director and been left to run the project on her own because it was felt that neither she nor it needed much attention. She created an advisory board, and it soon became very clear to the board's members that AIDS was not just a Black woman's issue, a woman of color's issue. At the same time, it was not the primary concern of the health center. When the center dropped the program, anger fueled the board members' determination to make sure that the women in their own communities were served. This was the impetus that resulted in the establishment of their own organization, SisterLove Women's AIDS Project, in 1989, which would become SisterLove Incorporated by 1992.

Dixon Diallo describes SisterLove as "a women's organization focused on the eradication of HIV/AIDS and other reproductive health and human rights challenges on women in the United States and around the world." The organization pursues its mission through "education, advocacy, support, and self-help." Ultimately, its programs and initiatives are designed to transform the lives of women and the communities around them so that they are able to live healthier and better lives.

In her interview, Loretta Ross asked Dixon Diallo to retrospectively examine the challenges that SisterLove had addressed over the previous twenty years of its existence. Dixon Diallo pointed out, with justifiable pride, that Sister-Love was instrumental in raising the level of awareness around AIDS and HIV in the late 1980s and early 1990s: "We started the first women's support group for women living with HIV and AIDS . . . that continues today at the clinic where most of the women who are diagnosed with AIDS go for their HIV treatment and care. We started the very first HIV/AIDS housing program for women and their children . . . in the entire Southeast."[29] SisterLove's long-term transitional housing program for HIV-positive women and their children is focused on what Dixon Diallo refers to as a "woman's place in her own life, as well as in her community." So a series of workshops and fieldtrips, for example, have been organized to involve the residents. While some workshops are very basic, including parenting skills and journaling classes, there are also civics lessons and opportunities to attend city council meetings and to learn about neighborhood planning units. SisterLove also works to make sure that the women learn how to represent themselves in community decision-making and policy development.

Dixon Diallo recalled that early on in their endeavors, many of the "women were dying very rapidly once diagnosed with AIDS, but were dying from opportunistic infections that were not necessarily associated with AIDS." The Center for Disease Control (CDC), located in Atlanta, had not readily associated such opportunistic infections with AIDS because they did not fall within the range of the CDC's definition of an AIDS diagnosis. Dixon Diallo insisted that this was clearly a gendered issue, citing the example of cervical cancer, which was more prevalent in women who had been diagnosed with AIDS, and noting that women were dying from this disease. Furthermore, SisterLove learned that "one particular form of pneumonia was also deadlier in women than it was in the men who were living with AIDS at that time."[30] She described their struggle:

> So, we fought—SisterLove at a very local level, as part of ACT UP Atlanta—we fought very hard alongside other national activists to get the

CDC to change its definition, to make sure that women's issues, women's critical conditions as a result of having HIV were also included in that definition. That was a major mark, to make sure that from that point on, the HIV surveillance, the treatment modalities, how fast women were being diagnosed, how quickly they could get on certain treatments—all of that has been impacted by the change in definition.[31]

According to Dixon Diallo, one of SisterLove's hallmark workshops is a safe-sex workshop called the Healthy Love Party. While the organization focuses on such practical issues as sexually transmitted diseases, risky sexual behaviors, and HIV and AIDS and provides information on the use of condoms, latex barriers, and safer-sex negotiation, the women also discuss identity and sexual conversation. Dixon Diallo clarified that "when I say sexual identity, not just orientation but just being able to find space that's safe and, . . . I don't want to say empowering, but there's power there that you find and use." The parties are important because they creatively support the very serious intention "to level the playing field on consciousness about talking about sex. We are going to have fun. We're talking about people having sex like you are talking about soap operas," she said with a laugh. "And it works!" Dixon Diallo insisted that "a lot of our ills particularly are related to disease, violence, all of that . . . because we have not yet created a way to mainstream and normalize our concepts and practices of sex and sexuality." She went on to state, "I want to be able to sit around a nice table and talk as normally about my sex and sexuality as I do about my hair, my nails, my teeth, my eyes, my ears, my feet, my feet hurt, my coochie hurt. You know, it ought to be all in the same conversation." Furthermore, she insisted that this would lead to a different consciousness about so many things, including contraceptive technology.

> It would lead to a different consciousness about who needs to be more protected when it comes to sexual risk behavior. It would lead to a different consciousness about what insurance companies can't cover contraceptives but they cover Viagra. I mean, it would lead to a whole different level of conversation about what is justice and what isn't. Who's got access and rights to health care and who doesn't? What's a healthy lifestyle and what isn't? And it would be so far beyond this who is bad and who is good that it wouldn't make any difference.

Shame and stigma around the disease often lead to higher infection rates, as people may be fearful of telling their partner or their family and friends about their status. Black communities and especially Black churches have traditionally suffered from homophobia and heterosexism. Dixon Diallo noted that often it could be up to five years after diagnosis before women were willing to go public with their diagnosis for fear of the reaction they would receive from their families, churches, and communities. Another critical partner to shame and stigma is the issue of violence against women. Women are also reluctant to publicize their status because frequently, even prior to a diagnosis of AIDS, many women have experienced domestic violence, and that violence may very well escalate if their partners become aware of their health status.

Dixon Diallo noted that the program has risen to another level through incorporating a number of critical strategies, including the Black women's self-help model that SisterLove adapted from the original NBWHP. The definition of self-help may be a difficult concept to grasp because it is so often viewed as a kind of "amorphous project," but it was originally designed to meet the needs of Black women both individually and collectively. The "mothers" of the NBWHP, Byllye Avery and Lillie Allen, believed that Black women were living in a "conspiracy of silence." They needed not just health education but also a way to confront the internalized oppression and negative sense of self inflicted by racism and sexism. Thus, they sought to develop programs that combined empowerment with information and that would foster change in individuals, who could ultimately impact change in the communities where they lived. While a holistic approach is characteristic of self-help, equally as important is the concept that self-help groups will vary because they necessarily respect the differences in individuals and communities and reflect what they determine is important and must be addressed.[32]

Ten years after graduating from Spelman, Dixon Diallo returned to graduate school to pursue a master's degree in public health at the University of Alabama, Birmingham. Her long-term involvement in the women's health movement through SisterLove brought her to the realization that she was engaged in more than "just" community organizing; she was also working within the realm of public health. She understands that much of what the women were doing at SisterLove was critically important for others in the world beyond SisterLove, so she felt compelled to return to school in order to

> put some theory in my practice, which is usually the opposite of what people do. Normally folks are looking for the practice to go along with the theory; that's how science works. But in my case, which is really the grassroots, the lived—the power and the credibility of the lived experience within the grassroots is that theory really comes from what's already happening out there; you simply put some translational knowledge to it and some . . . long term questions that you can look at and come back to and say, "You know, here's how you can intervene in a given situation." Right? Because we look at theories, this is how it works. And on the ground, this is how it should play out. When, actually, things are already being played out and

driving the questions. And that's what I thought. We're already playing it out. Now let's go find out how we're driving these questions.[33]

Dixon Diallo commuted 150 miles to Birmingham every weekend for two years to complete the degree. Her work, not unexpectedly, was focused on an HIV-positive women's prevention intervention, which she continued for three additional years after graduation.[34] For her, graduate studies illuminated the interrelationship of community and theoretical work even as they clarified her conviction that "in the realm of doing public health work, it truly is where the issues of justice and community bridge when we're talking about health and wellness."[35]

An interesting and disturbing issue became apparent to her while she was in graduate school. She noticed that reproductive and sexual health was not integrated into women's health, and because classes in women's health were not offered, she found that she had to choose maternal and child health as her concentration. Thus, the only area where she could explore reproductive health was through pregnancy and motherhood, which, she insisted, was insufficient to the critical necessity of examining women's overall health throughout their lives. Dixon Diallo argued that the lack of comprehensive public health programs arises from the way that we are also failing to create the learning spaces that would support appropriately addressing women's sexuality and women's sexual health and rights in a manner that does not contribute to the sexual objectification of women.

This perspective relates to Dixon Diallo's work with HIV and AIDs, particularly when it comes up against the seeming conundrum regarding whether to teach abstinence or to provide comprehensive sex education. Laughing, she marveled that one "can actually have a conversation about abstinence and sex without ever talking about sex!" She insisted that we must be able to discuss "a continuum of experience that includes communication with people, that includes feelings, that includes beliefs and ideas that go along with that physicality. And unless we can put all those things in one place, it's very, very difficult to teach how to have those conversations."[36]

This is the rationale and praxis behind the Healthy Love Parties designed by SisterLove. This community-based organization was created to provide women, particularly women of color, with a space where women could come and feel safe as they participated in conversations where they could learn about AIDs, HIV, prevention, sex, sexuality, safer-sex negotiation, and empowerment—issues that we have been socialized not to discuss, as they say, in polite company.[37]

SisterLove branched out internationally, carrying the self-help initiative to South Africa in 1999. There were, and still are, distressing parallels between sub-Sahara Africa and Africa America in that both communities were struggling with the AIDS epidemic or pandemic. While at the end of the twentieth century, sub-Saharan Africa was inflicted with 62 percent of all AIDS cases in the world, well over 60 percent of all HIV infections in the United States were found in African American communities. Southern Africa especially suffers from the AIDS epidemic, with 25 percent of its population infected.[38] With support from the CDC, SisterLove embarked upon what was then a five-year project to do capacity building in a very rural area of South Africa. They began working with NGOs that were addressing mother-to-child transmission and youth prevention. The SisterLove branch was established in Mpumalanga, about an hour and a half away from Johannesburg and, as Dixon Diallo ruefully noted, about thirty years behind as well.

Because the SisterLove practice is to craft its approach to the specificity of location, its work in South Africa is not a mirror of its work in Atlanta, even as it remains "sensitive to the needs of Black women and families."[39] The survival of Africans is very often tied to farming, so access to land was crucial to SisterLove's endeavors in South Africa. The women have established the Thembuhlelo Cooperative (loosely translated as "Trust Your Program"), which operates a seven-hundred-acre dairy farm. Dixon Diallo observed: "That happened because we bridged the notion of women's Empowerment and rights with HIV and AIDs service delivery. And [with] the land-reform policies that are going on to help restore the land that originally belonged to local people from the hands of the white farmers and the white government regime under apartheid—to reclaim the land and put it back in the hands of the people it should belong to."[40] By 2009 SisterLove no longer received US funding for this project; thus it was unable to continue staffing the program. Dixon Diallo feels responsible for the program, however, so she often travels to South Africa, staying for three or four months at a time.[41]

In addition to adopting the self-help initiative, SisterLove is firmly ensconced in the reproductive justice movement, which operates within the context of a human rights framework. Loretta Ross stated that the SisterSong Women of Color Reproductive Justice Collective introduced the term at its first national conference in 2003.[42] It emerged from a well-crafted critique of an unfortunate emphasis on the "prochoice" movement, whose primary concern was the right to abortion. This is, Ross argues, "a paradigm shift beyond demanding gender equality or attaching abortion rights to a broader reproductive health agenda." Thus, the reproductive justice movement is not simply a substitute for what are sometimes referred to as either reproductive or sexual rights.[43]

Ross defines reproductive justice as a "positive approach that links sexuality, health, and human rights to social justice movements by placing abortion and reproductive health issues in the larger context of the well-being and health of women, families, and communities." Ross applies intersectionality theory to reproductive justice in a manner that clarifies our understanding of women's reproductive destiny as so much broader than only a matter of individual choice and access. Rather, it attends to the actuality of women's multilayered, intersectional experiences of gender, sexuality, race/ethnicity, religion, abilities, class, and so on. Therefore, the intimacy of each individual's experience in concert with the broader experiences of communities impacts the effects of this complex of simultaneous identities and oppressions differently even across their similarities.

Zakiya Luna and Kristin Luker in their article "Reproductive Justice" argue that reproductive justice "highlights the dynamic yet often tenuous relationship between the law, social movements and academic scholarship." Furthermore, they argue, "legal scholars straddling the boundaries of the academy and social movements have contributed key concepts that the emerging reproductive justice movement has drawn on in its challenge to improve upon reproductive rights. In a relatively short time, [reproductive justice] has moved from the streets into academic and public discourse." They note that reproductive justice "contains multiple modes: analytic framework, movement, praxis and vision." Luna and Luker also insist that there are critical issues with the prochoice movement, especially the core premise of the right to privacy: "Privacy assumes access to resources and a level of autonomy that many people do not have. A privacy approach cannot accommodate that many people rely on government support for their daily activities, whether they be education (e.g., student loans), family formation (e.g., tax credits) or employment. The concurrent reproductive disciplining and reproductive privileging of different groups produce a linked set of experiences that point to devolution of the state in providing for the welfare of its members, the resolution of which requires more than protections of abortion rights."[44]

SisterSong continues to insist that every woman has the human right to

Decide if and when she will have a baby and the conditions under which she will give birth.
Decide if she will not have a baby and her options for preventing or ending a pregnancy.
Parent the children she already has with the necessary social supports in safe environments and healthy communities, and without fear of violence from individuals or the government.[45]

SisterSong has also adopted the definition of reproductive justice formulated by the Asian Communities for Reproductive Justice (ACRJ): "the complete physical, mental, spiritual, political, social, and economic well-being of women and girls, based on the full achievement and protection of women's human rights."[46] This definition expanded on the SisterSong analysis through evaluating the three main frameworks that challenge the problem of reproductive oppression. Ross defines reproductive oppression as "the control and exploitation of women, girls, and individuals through our bodies, sexuality, labor, and reproduction." She argues that "the regulation of women and individuals thus becomes a powerful strategic pathway to controlling entire communities. It involves systems of oppression that are based on race, ability, class, gender, sexuality, age and immigration status."[47]

In a 2005 discussion paper, the ACJR advanced three frameworks, "the matrix of reproductive activism," that "provide a complementary and comprehensive response to reproductive oppression as well as a pro-active vision articulating what we are fighting for and how [to] build a new movement to advance women's human rights."[48] The first framework is reproductive health, which critiques the lack of health care, service, information, research, and health data and seeks to improve and expand services, research, and access. It also focuses on prevention and seeks to promote culturally competent care for communities of color. The second framework is reproductive rights, which is the legal and advocacy-based model. It seeks to protect an individual woman's legal right to reproductive health care services. ACRJ intends to ensure that all individuals have universal legal protections, because these protections are their constitutional rights. Finally, reproductive justice "is the movement-building framework that identifies how reproductive oppression is the result of the intersections of multiple oppressions and is inherently connected to the struggle for social justice and human rights." It recognizes and then addresses the actuality that "a woman's societal institutions, environment, economics and culture affect her reproductive life."[49]

Dixon Diallo reflected upon the importance of integrating the use of the human rights framework "so that our conversation is, for lack of better words, we can deal with a lot of these issues at the macro as well as at the micro [levels]." Dixon Diallo insisted that this is not only a different way of orienting folks to healthy decision-making but that it provides a way of thinking of this

> as more of an entitlement or a right to be healthy and well versus a struggle or something that some people have and some people don't, and you just live with that, then, you know, it takes on a different flavor. Or that you actually have some level of protection in your ability to negotiate your sexual activity versus it's your personal responsibility to do this. You know, it takes on a different tone. And it motivates people to make change in different ways. Folks start talking about HIV and safer sex and all of that in a different way.

The activism charted by SisterLove was transformative not only for the cause that it championed, that of women of color and HIV/AIDs, but also for the holistic and continuously evolving manner in which the organization addresses multifaceted challenges, including its grounding in reproductive justice integrated into women's international human rights. It has served to empower women through providing them with the necessary knowledge of their human rights and the skills to advocate for their lives, the lives of their families, and the lives of other members of their communities.

Jaribu Hill

The third "center woman" of this chapter, Jaribu Hill, is also deeply engaged in the struggle to secure space in which to extend the scope of international human rights. Her work is in Mississippi, a venue that is perhaps most in need while at the same time least likely to welcome the establishment of a beachhead for international human rights. She founded the Mississippi Workers' Center for Human Rights in 1996 in Greenville.[50]

I interviewed Jaribu Hill on June 24, 2002, in Greenville. I was struck by the flat, dusty landscape in this part of the state and saddened by the poverty so apparent in the many small and dilapidated houses that were closely situated on dusty and poorly paved streets in the Black neighborhoods. Our interview took place over several hours throughout the day in several locations—in her office, over lunch in a lovely feminine southern restaurant, over dinner in a popular working-class restaurant, and in her home. The office was housed in an older high-ceilinged house that had been converted into office space. Her home, comfortably appointed, was surrounded by a large lawn in a middle-class neighborhood. She mentioned that although she did not realize it at the time, buying a house signaled to the people she wanted to work with that she was serious about staying in Mississippi, that she was not, like so many before her, just there for a short time, only to leave and return to the North. What is perhaps most striking about her is her rich and beautiful contralto voice, which animates her conversation and shines through her singing and poetry readings.

Hill's circuitous route to Mississippi was an interesting one. She graduated from high school in 1967 and went on to attain her bachelor's degree from Central State University, a historically black university located in Wilberforce, Ohio. She came of age a little after the height of the 1960s civil rights movement. However, she says that her "comeuppance" in the movement was in response to the Orangeburg Massacre, which occurred on the campus of South Carolina State University (also an HBCU) on February 8, 1968. Three students were killed and twenty-seven were shot or beaten with billy clubs by the police for protesting segregation. It was at that point that Hill became politically committed to the Black liberation movement. After graduation from college, she worked for five years with the Committee for Unified Newark, which would later become the Congress of African People under the leadership of Amiri Baraka in Newark, New Jersey. There she was engaged in organizing and in community and cultural work, and along the way, she also taught high school English.

Hill describes herself as a cultural worker, because in addition to her sociopolitical endeavors, she is also a poet, songwriter, and singer. She subscribes to Amílcar Cabral's assertion that culture is a weapon and further that "culture is simultaneously the fruit of a people's history and a determinant of history."[51] She began singing as a youngster in a Baptist church, but whenever she makes speeches she always includes a cultural piece such as poetry or a song, for example, either before or after the speech so that she "integrates the culture with the words."

Hill also defines herself as a labor organizer, and she has provided training for workers and for other trainers from New York to Mississippi. The center actually builds upon her previous activism and advocacy for laborers at the New York Committee for Occupational Safety and Health (NYCOSH). NYCOSH, founded in 1979, is a coalition of workers, unions, grassroots organizations, and safety and health advocates. It aims to establish better safety and working conditions for workers, specifically public service workers. Thus, many of Hill's earlier endeavors were centered on health and safety issues as she dealt with employers who were in violation of OSHA and other laws that had been designed to protect workers. From that work, her understanding of segregation expanded in a visceral manner that acknowledged that segregation was not just was an issue about schools but also impacted neighborhoods and the work environment. She was specifically concerned about the problems of Black laborers being steered toward the most dangerous and dirtiest jobs, which were also the lowest paying. Further, she became aware that these issues were not confined to any particular region but were widespread nationally.

NYCOSH founded both a conference and the People of Color and Low Wage Worker Network. It convened three conferences in which workers were encouraged to speak publicly about their issues, including toiling in the dirtiest and most dangerous jobs. They also testified before the New York State legislature and before the Environmental Protection Agency on segregated workplaces and pollution, which overwhelmingly impacts workers of color and poor white workers, who often have no choice about the places in which they are forced to work.

Hill attained a law degree from the City University of New York so that she could specifically address the issue of police brutality as an attorney. While in law school, she was part of the civil rights clinic Equality Concentration, where she learned about Title VII and section 1983, both of which would have a profound impact upon her work.[52]

Awarded a Skadden Foundation fellowship after law school, Hill went to work in Oxford, in the northern part of Mississippi, immediately following graduation. The Skadden Foundation provides support for law school graduates who are committed to developing careers focused on providing services to the poor and working poor. Fellows receive the necessary financial support so that they can pursue public interest work.[53] While she was in Oxford, from 1995 through 1998, she also worked with Amnesty International on behalf of mentally challenged death row inmates.

From Oxford, Hill moved to the town of Greenville, in the poorest region of the country, the Mississippi Delta. At that time, almost half of its population, 43 percent, lived below the poverty line, yet only 5 percent of workers in the state of Mississippi were unionized.[54] At first, she worked for the Southern Regional Office of the Center for Constitutional Rights while working part time for the Mississippi Workers' Center for Human Rights, which she established in 1996. The two organizations shared an office; however, when she resigned from the Center for Constitutional Rights to work full time for the workers' center, the Center for Constitutional Rights decided that it was no longer able to sustain an office in Mississippi and closed it down. The workers' center was then able to take over their office space.

In 1996 Jaribu Hill convened the first biannual Southern Human Rights Organizers' Conference, and it was immediately following that meeting that she founded the Mississippi Workers' Center for Human Rights. During the conference, one of the panels focused on workers' rights in the Deep South, especially focusing on "slave plantation workplaces and modern-day forms of slavery and oppression that black workers experience here in the Deep South and certainly in the slave state of Mississippi." In founding the workers' center, Hill explained, "we want not only to address wages and human rights violations in the workplace but we want to address other ways that working-class people are accosted, condemned, and mistreated by the system. So of course police misconduct is another layer of it. But the center was founded basically to provide education, advocacy, and solidarity for workers who are at the very bottom of the workforce." The workers, more often than not, do not have the recourse of unions to uphold and protect their rights. They seek the assistance of the center because they also do not have the necessary funds to file lawsuits and because there is very little union organizing in Mississippi, so they have no other place to go. At that time, only a few poultry and catfish plants were organized, so most people worked in small, nonunionized shops. Few people had access to information about their rights, and most were unaware that they even had any rights.

Hill passionately asserted that all people from birth have rights

> because they are living and breathing, and they survived poverty, they survived bad prenatal care, and everything else, and they were born into this world, and so they are entitled to basic rights and privileges. Workers are entitled to basic things like a clean, safe workplace. Not to be discriminated against. If you are the most qualified and most senior person, you should get the job, as opposed to someone with white skin getting it because of white skin privileges. So those are the kinds of human rights violations we address, and the issues crisscross.

She is committed to "actually doing work that addresses the misery and suffering of people who cannot easily climb out of their predicament and need support, need to know what they can do in the legal arena, and otherwise to rid themselves of the abuses that they are facing." She insists that the center is a human rights institution because the people who work there know that "workers' rights are human rights."

Hill is unequivocal in her belief that although the center's job is to help the workers with their struggles, the workers themselves were the ones who would make change happen. Through her work, she upholds the radical "inclusive democratic style of leadership" practiced by the legendary civil rights worker Ella Baker. Baker, who was once described as "Fundi" (the Swahili word for "teacher" or "facilitator") in a filmed documentary of her work, was an intense and politically effective social movement force. According to her biographer, Barbara Ransby, Baker "sought to empower those she taught and regarded learning as reciprocal. Baker's message was that oppressed people, whatever their level of formal education, had the ability to understand and interpret the world around them, to see that world for what it was and to move to transform it."[55] Rather than leader-centered groups, Baker advocated for and ably assisted in the development of group-centered grassroots leadership wherever she went.

Hill highly respects Baker's life work, as well as the work of other Black "sheroes" whose roots are deeply embedded in Mississippi history, including Ida B. Wells and Fannie Lou Hamer. She declares simply that she admires them because they resisted: "They threw off the yoke of slavery and oppression and risked their lives to do that. And so that's the tradition that I want to bring to the table."

Honoring Ella Baker's tradition of resistance, the Mississippi Workers' Center for Human Rights works in solidarity alongside laborers through organizing and providing education and legal representation. It is a center for human rights because its members work simultaneously with the civil and political rights that address individual rights, as well as within the realm of social, economic, and cultural rights. The center's mission is to provide service and support to its clients, although Hill is reluctant to being cast as a service provider. However, she cites a not uncommon example of an extremely impoverished client who needed to attend a hearing but who had no food in the home. Recognizing that need means that part of the center's work includes someone dropping off a bag of groceries for the family when picking up the individual to take them to their hearing. Such realities leave Hill exasperated by the theoretical debates around human rights that are unattached to real grassroots work with the people. She observes that as a person who has attained a law degree, it would be hypocritical of her not to recognize the importance of scholarship; however, she insists that human rights must be rooted in reality—in the issues of the day.

Organizing requires center workers to listen carefully to the concerns that people express and the struggles that they are involved in. She cited an important meeting with a group of laborers who worked for the city of Leland, Mississippi. She observed that they were the victims of so many human rights violations and atrocities that she was just almost amazed that they could go in to work every day. One egregious and even dangerous example was that they routinely worked with chemicals and other kinds of hazardous substances, yet they did not have the proper safety attire or access to showers on the premises. The bathrooms were unacceptable, but even so, the workers were not "privileged" to use them, which meant that many were forced to go home at lunchtime to use the bathroom. Additionally, their boss watched them carefully to track how much time they spent away from working. Outraged, Hill insisted that those employees of the city of Leland were basically being treated as if they were slaves.

Unlike some others who have been frightened to go to a public meeting, the Leland workers were so highly motivated that they immediately signed up when they were invited to dialogue around the possibility of organizing. They quickly identified a church for their meeting place and set a time so that they could strategize on how best to address the very serious problems that they encountered on their jobs.

Hill has no illusions about the fact that people who work at the center have to deal with hate crimes in the workplace and that those crimes crisscross "between civil and political and social, economic and cultural rights because of the nature of the discrimination." For example, center members have collected pictures of the racist graffiti they have found in workplaces. One of the starkest representations of graffiti scrawled across the wall of a workplace read "Kill all niggers. Fact. Crime will drop 98 percent." That was recognized for what it was—a very serious death threat that affected the entire group of workers, not just one individual. Hill insisted that such graffiti affects not only workers' civil and political rights but also their right to work in a safe and secure environment. Further, if they were forced to leave such an environment because they were being terrorized, they would certainly make less money. She noted that those shipyard laborers commanded upward of fifteen dollars an hour, an excellent salary in comparison to other workers who were making minimum wage and lower if, for example, they were in food service. If workers were forced to leave their jobs because of the harassment and the terror they faced, that situation would most certainly have a serious impact upon their economic and social rights. Hill firmly insisted that "scholarship that does that kind of crisscrossing and sees the interrelatedness of the bundle of rights that we're talking about, I think that's real important. Not to just simply look at those rights individually or say, 'Oh, you're working on civil and political rights, Jaribu, because you're working with individuals and their rights.' But I'm working with workers, so how can I not be working on social and economic and cultural rights at the same time? So I think it's real important that there is an integration in the work and theory."

At the time of our interview, the center was engaged in two campaigns. One was called "Terror on the Plant Floor" and specifically addressed hate crimes in the workplace. The second campaign, "Dying to Make a Living," concentrated on "segregated workplaces and the unhealthy and unsafe conditions that workers of color find themselves in. And how to address those issues."

Hill explained that a typical training for the center provides workers with information about their rights to equality. Center employees begin by telling workers about their rights under the Thirteenth Amendment to the Constitution, which abolished slavery.[56] They discuss the fact that the amendment was meant to abolish not only the physical condition of slavery but also the badges and incidents of slavery—modern day de facto slavery, so to speak. They then move on to discuss the quality of life issues enumerated particularly in article 23 of the Universal Declaration of Human Rights.[57] At that point they use an overhead projector with transparencies of the Thirteenth Amendment and article 23 laid side by side so that people can gain a sense that they are embroiled in both a national and an international struggle, not just a local struggle. In fact, they share information with workers about how migrant workers, for example, or commercial workers in Zimbabwe deal with similar issues.

Typically, a training session also includes an organizing component, which is why it is called an organizing session. Workers specifically brainstorm about strategies to address issues that have been raised during the workers' speak-out time. Other workers are invited, and they will step up to say, "I tried this, and this worked. Why don't you try this?" So, for example, workers who were not employed by the city of Leland were invited to come and help the Leland workers develop their strategies.

Hill insisted that her work is not limited to Black people. She recalled a training session in Indianola a few weeks before the center began to work with the Leland workers. She was asked by one worker what the center was going to do about the Mexican workers taking their jobs. Another worker chimed in to say that they had been required to do a drug test, to pee in a cup, but forty-three Mexican workers who had been hired didn't have to pee in a cup. Hill explained to them:

> First of all, [the Mexican workers] don't have to pee in a cup. Blame the boss for trying to divide and conquer. It is not those workers who make the policy. . . . It's not their fault. And secondly, those workers are despised, just as you are. They fled from oppression in their country, coming here to the so-called land of milk and honey. So, if anything, they are worse off, because they had illusions about how they were going to be treated fairly, and you never had those illusions. Unless you are psychotic, you never had those illusions. So to blame brown-skinned people because they don't speak like you, because they look a little different from you, is a problem.

Although it would have been easy to just agree with these workers that someone ought to make the Mexicans pee in a cup, Hill was compelled to help them understand that they, the Black workers, were allowing themselves to be used to oppress other workers, to question or challenge other people's rights. They then went on to have a very healthy discussion, Hill observed. She insisted that such frank discussions were a big part of what differentiated their training sessions from other sessions.

Hill laughingly attributed her ability to look younger than she is and her capacity to keep going to the fact that she knows who she is. Becoming serious, she went on to declare:

> It's because I know who the enemy is. I'm never unclear about that. I know it's not poor white folks. I know it's not Mexicans. I know it's not people who happen to be middle class now, and it wasn't when I was growing up. I know who the real enemy is. The enemy is a system of white supremacy and class oppression. Those are the enemies of people who don't have a

way out. It's governments, it's structures and institutions that decide who will be a "have" and who definitely has to be a "have not."

She passionately insisted:

So long as you are focused, you don't blame yourself. If you lose a lawsuit, you don't blame yourself. If you lose a struggle, you don't blame yourself. When someone hangs himself in jail before you can get help for him, you don't blame yourself. You understand that it is the system that creates the atmosphere and the climate through which certain things occur without your making, without your being able to stop it from happening. All you can do is, when it happens, give definition to it so the people know why this thing happened.

Hill describes herself as the primary trainer, who in turn trains others. As a licensed lawyer in the state of Mississippi, she is able to provide legal representation to people, which means that she is also able to provide them with information regarding what they are specifically entitled to under the law: "The representation I provide for people also involves explaining how the system does not work and why it doesn't work so people don't continue to blame themselves for the ways in which they are victimized."

Based on Hill's profound interest in women's international human rights, in 2000 the center sponsored an event in Zimbabwe that members called the Black Women's International Roundtable, which addressed the challenges of working women. Sarah White, board president of the Mississippi Workers' Center for Human Right, was a coconvener of this session. A worker in the catfish industry, she had become an organizer of catfish workers and later went on to organize in other industries across the South. I will return to Sarah White's story, which is worth more than a digression. Her story is representative of Jaribu Hill's commitment to Ella Baker's legendary legacy of fostering a community's innate leadership.

The Black Women's International Roundtable focused on the plight of women who were experiencing the intersections of race, class, and gender oppression. Participants included a woman who had fled from Kenya because as a labor organizer she had been threatened with persecution and death. A Nigerian woman spoke about workers' rights in Nigeria. A woman from Canada and another from Ethiopia were also among some thirty women who sat at the roundtable. As they discussed their respective experiences, they realized how connected they were, because their struggles were so similar. All were firmly committed to attaining their rights and affirming their dignity as human beings who were laborers.

Although I have not had the honor of meeting Sarah White in person (she was unavailable when I was in Mississippi), I cherish the opportunity I had to hear her speak on a panel titled "Voices of Victims" at the UN World Conference against Racism, Racial Discrimination, Xenophobia and Related Intolerance in Durban, South Africa, August 31–September 7, 2001.[58]

She prefaced her speech by forcefully expressing her absolute anger with President George W. Bush and his administration for refusing to participate in the conference. (Then secretary of state Colin Powell did not attend this UN conference. Instead, the US government sent "low-level" representation, as if the United States did not have a problem with race and racism!)

White testified as an organizer with the United Food and Commercial Workers Union Local 1529, and her presentation was riveting. Everyone in that cavernous hall seemed to be holding their breath as she spoke. She told us how she and the other Black female workers had to stand on their feet for twelve hours a day, ankle-deep in water that was so contaminated with chlorine and other harmful chemicals that many women suffered from serious skin rashes and other physical ailments. The white male supervisors who forced them to work ever more quickly on the assembly line to maximize profits for the owner constantly harangued them to "speed it up or lose your job." The bosses, she insisted, did not care about the health and well-being of their workers; furthermore, the women were sexually and racially harassed on a daily basis.

> We were denied bathroom privileges. Even when we were allowed to go [to] the bathroom, we were forced to wait long periods of time and as a result many of the elderly workers wore pampers (disposable baby diapers) to keep from soiling their clothes. Many times, white male supervisors would come into the women's bathrooms which had no doors on the stalls. They would stand over us and look at us while we actually sat on the toilet. They would shout, "hurry up and get up and go back to work." These are some of the conditions workers encountered every day in catfish and poultry plants across the Mississippi Delta. These indignities were suffered by us as workers because of our skin color and economic class. At that time, workers at Delta Pride were given six (6) bathrooms breaks a week. . . . workers in catfish and poultry plants in the Delta, are forced to clock out and go to the bathroom. In other words, they lose money when they go to the bathroom.[59]

White said that the workers came together to fight Delta Pride for justice and human rights. For three months, Black women led the largest labor strike in the state of Mississippi. Despite their bosses' efforts to either intimidate them or "buy them off" with things such as televisions, the women persevered (and took the televisions) and won that battle. White stated, "We as African American women had to show the bosses that we were proud, beautiful Black women who would never again tolerate that type of abuse."[60] Following that victory, they began a workers' rights movement, organizing all across the state. Although they have won many battles, Sarah and her colleagues are clear that the struggle continues. Jim Crow continues to exist to this day—workplaces are still racially segregated, and Black workers are still assigned to the dirtiest and most dangerous jobs.

After unionizing Delta Pride, Sarah White was assigned to organize in "hog farm country," Tarheel, North Carolina, to support the Smithfield Farm workers, who were also suffering from a wide range of inhumane treatments. They too were working twelve-to-fourteen-hour shifts while being harassed and denied bathroom breaks. (At one point during our interview, horrified, incredulous, and naive, I asked Jaribu, "What *is* it about these bathrooms and white men watching Black workers use the toilet!" She patiently explained to my dense self that it is one aspect of the power that white people used to control Black people. That it is a form of humiliation and intimidation coupled with a complete lack of respect for poor Black workers.) According to White, the Smithfield workers were virtually held as prisoners during the workday. Their bosses even set up makeshift health stations to keep the workers from going outside the plant to take care of their personal medical needs. They were denied time off and would even be terminated if they took their sick children to see a doctor. Additionally, the bosses pitted the Black and Latino workers against each other in the age-old strategy of divide and conquer.

White also observed that the hog farms caused "tremendous environmental hazards for local residents. The stench is horrible. The exposure to chemicals caused eye infections, skin rashes, and serious chronic illnesses, including cancer."[61] Furthermore, White found that many of the residents were forced to stay inside their un-air-conditioned homes regardless of 90–100-degree heat in order to try to mitigate breathing in the harsh chemicals and awful smell that permeated the air.

In her work as an organizer, White learned to become a part of the community through, in part, seeking the support of religious leaders and other community leaders for the union and for the human rights of workers. She encouraged Black women to be courageous and take a stand. Although many were fearful, they gained strength through their efforts to challenge the conditions at Smithfield. Finally, after many years of struggles, the workers won their right to unionize. Although it was clearly a victory for the union, White was certain that, more importantly, it was an inspirational victory for the community. "This inspired me as a Black woman who worked in slave plantation–like conditions in the Mississippi Delta. This fight was my fight and the fight of all those who believe in justice."[62]

With uncompromising fortitude, Sarah White explained to those of us in Durban and to others listening around the world why she does this work:

> The reason I do this work is because as a Black woman I was put down, forced to fight for my dignity. I was humiliated and subjected to inhumane treatment. Today I know, as an organizer, my story will inspire other Black women. I know that we are now in a better position to fight because we have a center—a human rights organization in the delta. We can help all women workers rise up and have a better chance for fairness and human rights in the work environment. On a personal note, I am a grandmother of six, and I want my grandchildren to know they can grow up in a world where fairness and justice exist, and they must raise their voices to be heard.[63]

The light of charisma shines through Sarah White. Jaribu Hill, who exudes her own form of charisma, recognized White's powerful potential, provided some support and guidance, then moved out of the way so that White could unleash the power of her grassroots leadership.

Hill also mentors and trains high school students and law students who are funded to come each summer to spend time at the center. The students learn about practicing law from a human rights perspective, including how to be an advocate and an organizer. She observed that the center's location in Mississippi defines what she referred to as "the shape" of what they do and how they do it in a way that is different from what happens in New York. Being on site and working with members of the local community who have been systematically estranged from their rights provide students with an acute sense of the struggle for human rights.

Hill is also profoundly concerned about women's human rights because she understands sexism to be the twin sister of racism. She grew up in what she described as "concrete poverty, not grass poverty or dirt poverty, but in segregated inner cities." She also understands and recognizes the United States as a patriarchal society. Thus sexism, according to Hill, "has to always be attacked in a frontal way as opposed to a behind-the-scenes, back-door way. It constantly has to be addressed in progressive circles and in reactionary circles." She further argued that the struggle against sexism must not be dominated by any white middle-class women's movements or any other movements of privilege. She insists that the voices of grassroots poor women must be heard as they grapple with a wide array of issues and layers of oppression, from finding milk for their babies to female genital mutilation.

Hill declared that we must recognize how race and class issues affect women in order to have a full understanding of the layers of oppression that affect women.

> Our work comes at it from the issue of how women of the working class, women who work, who are forced into some of the most undignified forms of work and how that affects their psyche and their spirt and their sense of themselves. And we don't, I don't purport to be somebody who is whole. I know that I am damaged goods just like everyone else. But I have had the benefit of being around strong women and had the benefit of knowing about posthumous mentors who have helped me to understand why we hurt so much and what needs to be done about it. And so I think that all of our work focuses on women's international human rights because most of the people we help and most of the people who help us are women. And they are women who are not rich. They are women who are not white. And they have no privileged standing in this society. And so if human rights struggles cannot address their issues, then it seems to me that those struggles are not relevant to the largest amount of people in the world . . . women who hurt. And who are abused. And if anything came out at that roundtable [in Zimbabwe] it was the length and breadth of abuse that women experience.

Hill wrote "Haunting Mirrors," the poem that appears at the beginning of this chapter, about women who are abused and oppressed. In December 2000 she was an artist in residence at the Women's International War Crimes Tribunal in Tokyo, where she wrote and performed this piece. When she received a copy of the judgment from the tribunal, she unexpectedly found this poem included in the report. For Hill, then, the questions of international human rights are large and all consuming. She wants the Workers' Center in Mississippi to become more internationalized, and to that end she founded the roundtable forum so people could participate in conversations around the world about the issues: "I want to be one of the catalysts for having the dialogue across the globe about these issues."

Conclusion

Lee Ann Banaszak observed a rise in the number of local organizations and groups that have developed relationships with groups in other countries without relying upon the US government or other national organizations to act as their intermediaries.[64] Her observations are characteristic of the endeavors of the three center women who are the subject of this chapter.

Passionate, innovative, and charismatic, Linda Burnham, Dazon Dixon Diallo, and Jaribu Hill are unheralded champions in early twenty-first-century struggles for social justice. As the sociopolitical progeny of twentieth-century activists in the long civil rights movement in the United States, they are respectfully building upon that legacy as they expand upon and imbed international human rights in different corners of the United States in ways that reflect their specific concerns.

5

Weaving Together
Global Tapestries

My feminist consciousness was formed around racial justice.

Barbara Phillips, interview with the author, 2004

But I think that the international feminist agenda will always be a dilemma for women because women have different priorities based on their national origin and social location.

Filomina Chioma Steady, interview with the author, 2002

In previous chapters, I have explored Black women's human rights work in law schools and within the international criminal tribunals at The Hague. I have examined women's struggles to build their own grassroots organizations to address the concerns that challenged aspects of the multiple oppressions experienced by women. In this chapter, I examine the human rights endeavors of Filomina Chioma Steady and Barbara Phillips. One has positioned her efforts to secure human rights within the United Nations system, while the other has pursued a human rights agenda from the Ford Foundation, a more conventional and robustly funded nongovernmental organization (NGO). Both are well educated in the formal university sense, having acquired impressive academic credentials. Building upon their educational accomplishments and activist skills, as well as their capacity to construct strategic advantageous alliances, they developed the requisite expertise and dexterity to negotiate the chambers and halls of the United Nations and the Ford Foundation. From those mainstream vantage points, they were able to contribute significantly to the continuing struggles to define and refine human rights in a manner that both affirms and actualizes its promise.

Filomina Chioma Steady

I had known Filomina Chioma Steady for a number of years by the time we met for our formal interview on a warm summer day in 2002 in my office overlooking Lake Mendota in Helen C. White Hall at the University of Wisconsin–Madison. We were friendly in the way of academic colleagues who shared similar intellectual interests, as she was chairing the Department of Africana Studies at Wellesley College, and I was chair of the Department of Afro-American Studies at UW–Madison. We occasionally encountered each other at academic conferences or around Madison. She and her husband, Dr. Henry Steady, shared a home in Madison, where he had a medical practice, while she commuted between Madison and her work on the East Coast and around the world. We were and continue to be deeply committed to the critical task of developing our scholarship around Black women through our respective lens of Black and African feminisms. Filomina Chioma Steady edited the groundbreaking anthology *The Black Woman Cross Culturally* (1981), which ascended to a place of honor within the transgressive renaissance of Black women's literature in the last quarter of the twentieth century.[1] We were both engrossed, albeit in very different ways, in the field of international human rights.

Prior to our formal interview we had traveled together to Durban, South Africa, representing her NGO at the UN World Conference against Racism, Racial Discrimination, Xenophobia and Related Intolerance in 2001. Steady had registered her NGO with the UN in Geneva, Switzerland, so our official badges indicated that we were representatives from Switzerland. Two Black women, she with her soft and precise Sierra Leonean accent and me with my midwestern American accent, earned many perplexed looks at that conference!

Noticing that her home country was not represented at the official UN governmental conference, Steady contacted a government office in Sierra Leone and offered to represent the country. (I was stunned to learn that someone could just "call up" their government and offer their services for such a task and then be given the necessary credentials and clearance so effortlessly!) As she participated in the formal governmental meetings with other governmental representatives, I was given a pass to sit in on those sessions as the only other member of her NGO in Durban.[2] It was a fascinating opportunity to watch, up close, the controlled yet chaotic and painstaking final process of constructing the necessary international consensus to produce the Durban Declaration and Programme of Action.

Filomina Chioma Steady shared her remarkable story with me in a long interview on August 20, 2002.[3] Filomina was born and raised in Sierra Leone, where she began her formal education attending primary school, passing through the fifth form, and moving on through secondary school to complete the sixth form.[4] Students like Filomina who successfully completed the Higher School Certificate Examination could go abroad for further study. She had planned to attend a British university; however, because the academic schedules of Sierra Leone and Britain were not in sync, she had a long waiting period. The school year in Sierra Leone ends in December; thus, students planning to study in Britain had to wait until the following October to start college. Filomina spent her waiting period teaching school in her country. She traveled to England, where she had been accepted at both Leeds University and Durham University, but before she could decide which school to attend, she received an opportunity to come to the United States to study that included a scholarship.

Filomina admitted that she was "not too crazy about coming to the US. I had heard all kinds of stuff about the States, and the image we got in Africa was that it was full of crime, cowboys and Indians, and racism, which bothered me a lot." Despite those concerns, she finally decided to come to the United States to study government and anthropology at Smith College. She went on to attain a master of arts degree in anthropology from Boston University. Following that, she married in 1966, and she and her husband moved to England so that he could study medicine at Oxford University. She too studied at Oxford, pursuing the British B. Litt. degree (bachelor of letters), which was comparable to our American master of arts, in anthropology. The degree required a thesis based on library research, and since she had always had an interest in women, she titled her paper "The Social Position of Women— Selected West African Societies," including Nigeria, Cameroon, and Sierra Leone. For her doctorate degree, which required fieldwork, she chose to study women's associations in Sierra Leone as part of the process of urbanization. By this time, she had two children, one two and a half years old and the other five months old. She brought them with her when she did her fieldwork: "Looking back now, I think I must have been crazy. At the same time, I taught sociology at the University of Sierra Leone for a year. In fact, the sociology department was just being started, and another faculty member and I got it established. There was no anthropology department, but that was combined with sociology. I taught at the university and carried on my field research at the same time. My children and I were living with my parents in Freetown. It was a very productive time." Although she had lots of help with her children, her son became dangerously ill with malaria when he was barely six months old. Fortunately, he recovered. They later returned to Oxford so that she could write her dissertation. By the time she completed her doctoral degree at St. Anne's

College, Oxford, her husband had attained a medical residency in Boston, so they returned to the United States in 1974.

Upon their return to the United States, Steady taught first at Yale University for one semester, then at Boston University for two years, and then later at Wesleyan University. At Yale, she taught courses on Africa and African America and on African sociology through literature. At Wesleyan and Boston Universities, she taught medical anthropology, sex roles in cross-cultural context, and courses on Africa. Her teaching repertoire also included courses on women's movements, urban development, Third World urbanization, anthropological theory and methodology, and environmental studies. She would later help launch a major in environmental studies at Wellesley College. Interestingly, she has never taught a course specifically on human rights, although she included a human rights perspective in all her courses. Through her research and teaching, she has always maintained her interest in women's issues and rights.

In 1977 the Association of African Women for Research and Development (AAWORD) was established in Dakar, Senegal, with Filomina as one of its founding members.[5] Thus, early on in her career, she was cultivating an international network of academics. It was somewhere around 1979, through her AAWORD connection, that she began her work with the UN.

Among the women included in this book, Filomina Chioma Steady has one of the more versatile records of participation in United Nations activities. Beginning with her participation in the 1975 UN World Conference on Women, held in Mexico City, she has served in a number of capacities with the UN. In 1972 the UN General Assembly voted to proclaim 1975 the International Women's Year (IWY) as part of the Second United Nations Development Decade. The purpose of the IWY was "the encouragement of the full integration of women in the total development effort," and to that end the UN Commission on the Status of Women was asked to develop a program for the year.[6]

Generally and theoretically, United Nations world conferences are designed to develop a global consensus that governments will commit to in order to address what has been deemed an urgent problem. The process brings together the international community of member states, UN experts, and nongovernmental representatives in national and then regional preparatory conferences (often referred to as "prep cons") prior to the international conference to develop shared values and goals and the strategies to achieve them. This preliminary document is presented at the governmental conference, where the delegates representing state parties proceed to negotiate the language of international consensus. By the time each conference has ended, an agreement has been forged around the issue, and governments have committed to address the urgent problem. Their agreement is then presented to the world in the form of a platform or programme of action.[7]

Filomina's first encounter with the UN was the result of an invitation to AAWORD to send a representative to the 1975 conference in Mexico City. During our interview, she chuckled and admitted that she was kind of young and not quite involved with the whole process. After this historic initial conference in Mexico City, the UN declared 1976–85 the Decade for Women and held the mid-decade UN World Conference in Copenhagen in 1980 and the end-of-decade conference in Nairobi in 1985.

From 1979 to 1980, Filomina was a consultant to the secretariat working on the 1980 UN World Conference on Women in Copenhagen.[8] At the same time, she was also a professor at Wesleyan University in Middleton, Connecticut. From 1984 to 1986, she served as a director of the Branch for the Advancement of Women (later known as the Division for the Advancement of Women) in Vienna, Austria, which was responsible for preparing the third UN World Conference on Women in Nairobi in 1985. For that conference, she served as a member of the executive committee, which collected data, prepared documentation, organized prep cons, and consulted with various governments and NGOs, and within the UN system. As a director, she helped supervise the executive committee team that developed the draft of the Nairobi "Forward-Looking Strategies," based on its research and policy analysis. The team developed the recommendations and options for governmental consideration in the prep cons and at the conference itself.

Filomina's UN endeavors are grounded in her belief that women's rights are and should be deeply embedded in ever more comprehensive human rights. She therefore characterized her work as multidimensional: "If you include women's rights, which broadly speaking is a part of human rights, I have worked quite a bit at the international level for the United Nations in different capacities. However, working for the advancement of women is multidimensional and cannot be completely subsumed under rights." In her third assignment at the UN, she was special advisor to Maurice Strong, secretary-general of the UN Conference on Environment and Development, dubbed the "Earth Summit" and held in Rio de Janeiro in 1992. As a special advisor, she lived and worked at the UN secretariat based in Geneva, Switzerland, from 1990 to 1993. Her title was the Special Advisor on Women, Environment, and Development, and her assignment was to mainstream gender issues in all areas of the work of the Earth Summit, particularly as they pertained to documentation. Her work, then, involved research, gender analysis, policy analysis, and gender-sensitive policy development. Although this was critical work in and of itself, it was also groundbreaking in another very important sense, because this was the first general conference to mainstream gender issues in an extensive way. Filomina recalled that prior to this world conference, "women's issues were dealt with at conferences on women and at population conferences." The pioneering aspect of this conference was evident in the Plan of Action, "Agenda 21," adopted by the Earth Summit. The plan included a chapter on women as part of the section on the role of major groups in environment and development. According to Filomina, "a pattern of action was established that encouraged conferences to mainstream women's agenda and gender issues. Because of the 1992 Earth Summit experience, all major conferences since that were not specifically on women have followed suit and mainstreamed gender issues." She argued that the emphasis on "women's rights are human rights" so prevalent at the 1994 Vienna Conference on Human Rights developed out of this work at the Earth Summit. Filomina described what she calls the "rights approach," which is based on the premise that however we came to be in unequal situations, women are entitled to certain opportunities, benefits, and rewards "because it is their right. So one should not waste time arguing anymore. One should simply say that women have a right to equality, development, and peace." Even though problems continue to exist, this approach, according to Filomina, avoids having to waste precious time trying to prove certain things. She likened this global issue of gender oppression to the problem of race and racism in the United States: "All Americans have certain rights, and there should be no obstacles to their enjoyment of these rights. But we know the reality. We know that we still have to work on the de facto realities of inequalities and injustices or racism that persist."

Steady would go on to work with the UN on the Fourth World Conference on Women, held in Beijing in 1995.[9] During this time and afterward, she served as special advisor to the United Nations Industrial Development Organization (UNIDO), based in Vienna, from 1994 to 1995. She recalled that most of her assignments involved extensive traveling to New York to participate in meetings of the conference secretariat, held at the UN headquarters. The meetings often lasted anywhere from six weeks to two months, and they provided her with opportunities to spend precious time with her husband and family, who remained in Madison. After UNIDO, she continued to work with the UN through short-term consultancies with UN organizations working on programs, field missions, and advisory boards or helping with some aspects of the implementation of plans of action and programs.

Although, as previously mentioned, Steady was introduced to the UN through her attendance at the IWY conference in Mexico City, it was in the preparation for the Copenhagen conference that she became more fully immersed. The UN Secretariat for Copenhagen was seeking someone from

AAWORD to be involved in the preparation of documents for the prep cons and the conference itself. The secretariat was specifically seeking someone to work on a women and health document who could focus on the social and cultural dimensions of health. At the time, Steady happened to be teaching medical anthropology at Wesleyan University, so AAWORD felt that she was the best candidate to recommend for the consultancy. While other people, including medical doctors, were brought onto the team, the secretariat was specifically seeking an anthropologist.

The UN Decade for Women promoted three themes: equality, development, and peace. There were also three subthemes under development: education, employment, and health. Although health was one of the areas emphasized at the Mexico conference, it was necessary to conduct additional research specifically on the health subtheme, and the Copenhagen conference was tasked with monitoring and evaluating the progress made since 1975. Filomena came to work in 1979 to help develop the questionnaires that were sent out to governments requesting information on women's health in their respective countries. They asked questions such as "What were the problems? What were the obstacles? And what did they plan to do? The governments completed them and returned them, and we analyzed them." She recalled: "Certain areas featured prominently, such as the basic health statistics of life expectancy, infant mortality and morbidity, and questions such as what diseases were most prevalent in women. . . . And then governments also had to answer questions about health services, including, What are the services available to women? How accessible are they? How affordable are they? . . . How are women themselves participating in the delivery of health care as doctors, nurses, and so on?" Although those were the main questions, Steady felt that from a sociological perspective "we needed to look more extensively at issues of nutrition, women's workload, and what impact did these have on women's health." And it was at this point that "violence against women was introduced as a health issue."

While Dr. Lucille Mair, the secretary-general of the conference and the secretariat, appreciated the new focus on violence as a health issue, Filomina then had to present this work to a team composed of people from UN agencies, including the World Health Organization (WHO). She recalled that the WHO representative at the meeting "was not at all disposed toward all the social indicators I was examining that she thought had nothing to do with health." She remembered arguing with the WHO representative and, finally, exasperated, saying, "Well, are you trying to tell me that violence is only a health issue when a woman collapses in the hospital emergency room? The problem starts long before that!" Fortunately, she had the full support of the secretariat, and WHO did eventually support the report. In fact, the document WHO prepared for the conference included information on violence.

Filomena is justifiably proud of the role she played in bringing violence against women as a health issue to global attention. She acknowledged that while violence against women had already garnered attention from a legal point of view, this was the first time that a link was drawn between women's health and violence against women. Filomina insisted: "Coming in with a health perspective actually made it much more urgent, and people took it more seriously because they realized this went beyond the law. People could get sick, people could be maimed, and people could die even before the law stepped in. So it is, in a way, gratifying to see that it has become a central issue in human rights today." She noted that the UN responded to the issue in 1979 by preparing the Declaration on Violence against Women and appointing a special rapporteur on violence against women in the UN Office of the High Commissioner for Human Rights in Geneva, Switzerland. Filomina was also deeply involved in developing the secretariat draft of the Nairobi "Forward-Looking Strategies," in which violence was included in the "areas of special concern." But by the 1995 Beijing conference, the issue of violence against women had evolved sufficiently to merit a chapter of its own.

Filomina provided an intriguing analysis of the controversial aspects of the issue of violence against women and how it evolved from Copenhagen to Nairobi. She opined that the divisiveness of the Cold War conflict played a dramatic role in the manner in which violence was framed, especially at the Nairobi conference. In fact, she chuckled ruefully, "A couple of times one forgot that the discussions were about women." As previously mentioned, equality, development, and peace comprised the themes of the Decade for Women; however, Filomina observed that each regional political bloc emphasized one specific theme over the others. Thus, the central issue for the Eastern European bloc was peace, the United States seemed more concerned with equality, while the countries of the Global South stressed development.

The issue of peace for the Eastern Bloc was related to actually fighting wars, so achieving peace for them meant putting an end to such wars. Steady's assessment was that "the Soviet Union did not want to dilute the agenda for peace by bringing in domestic violence. And, of course," she opined, "the United States did not want peace to be dominant, because at the time the US was much more involved in the arms buildup, nuclear weapons, and all that." She found the impact of this political polarization regrettable, because it meant violence was put out of what she felt was its proper place: "It became a health factor and the legal factor and not so much part of war and global security. Of course, there is violence where women are raped during war and stuff like that.

But domestic violence became the issue that had to be central to peace, and that I think was unfortunate." Although the issue of domestic violence attained prominence, at the same time, Filomina argued, "it also diluted the whole question of weapons and war." It also deflected attention away from "the macroeconomic issues that were creating major global imbalances and impoverishing countries of the Global South to the advantage of countries of the Global North," critical concerns to women subsisting in the Global South.

Steady insisted that the economic crisis of debt stemming from structural adjustment programs encumbered the Global South during the 1980s and therefore became a critical issue at the 1985 Nairobi conference. Clearly, for Filomina the issue of violence against women was caught up in the complications of the global political economy, and she maintained that this must be recognized as the West wrested control of the agenda from other countries by restricting the broader topic of violence to the private domain and to private injustice. According to her, "People feel that domestic violence can be surmounted, whereas the more challenging problems are underdevelopment and poverty that require interventions with a much higher level of involvement through international financial institutions to bring about change. Dealing with the debt burden and the way economies are dominated and tuned to make profits for corporations and financial institutions are problems of a completely different magnitude." She went on to clarify that "although most people feel it is important that domestic violence must be ended, they also feel that it must not take our attention away from other issues like the negative impact of global economic forces." Despite her involvement in efforts to put domestic violence on the global agenda, she was also "a little disturbed that we may not be putting enough emphasis on the global economic issues."

For too long, violence against women was relegated to the private sphere. The call to acknowledge that "Women's Rights Are Human Rights" that rang out at the 1994 UN Conference on Human Rights in Vienna was to ensure that violations in the area defined as the private sphere were also "brought to justice as human rights violations." The fact that violence that occurs in the private domain is finally recognized for what it is, a violation of human rights, is a considerable achievement. Steady recognized that it was no longer as easy to isolate women in domestic settings characterized by secrecy because of this acknowledgment. However, she is yet to be mollified, because she is aware that we still lack the institutions and mechanisms that are effective in really eliminating domestic violence: "There ought to be better laws and greater awareness, because what happens is a lot of complicity between the law enforcement and domestic partners. One can see that in India, in Africa, and here in the United States." She pointed out that in the United States, for example, "we are now finding out . . . that police and army officers are among the worst offenders when it comes to domestic violence. So the institutions here apparently do not work very well either."

Steady noted that some exasperated women in Africa and other parts of the Global South were suggesting that it might be appropriate to resurrect some of the traditional mechanisms that had been used to prevent violence against women. She recalled the systems that were in place in Sierra Leone when she was growing up. Male members of the family played very important roles in the negotiations when a woman's hand was sought in marriage. The groom was accompanied by a delegation when he went to the home of the prospective bride, and the woman's family would also have male representatives present, although often the mother of the bride had the final word, because she had to agree to the marriage. "But during the negotiations one very important aspect of the proceedings was that the woman's brothers would warn the prospective in-laws against mistreatment of the future wife, saying 'If your son does not treat our sister (or our daughter) right, we will beat him up. If he lays a hand on our sister, we will do the same thing.'" Thus women "not only had advocates but also her own defenders and protectors. In a way, that protected her."

In Sierra Leone, Sande, a secret women's society, initiated young girls and prepared them for their roles as women in the society. Each age grade of initiates had a special relationship with each other for the rest of their lives. According to Filomina, the Sande was also available to help settle domestic disputes, functioning as a kind of support group. If a woman was being oppressed at home, she could always call upon her sisters for help, and they in turn had ways of putting pressure on the man, including physical violence, to conform. This was an example of "the society putting on this pressure. Kinfolk and neighbors could interfere in domestic disputes. So there were ways a woman could maneuver, either turn things around or leave."

Some women at the UN Commission on the Status of Women argued that often women could not rely upon the police for protection against domestic violence and, further, that some women did not know their rights. Although Filomina acknowledged that she had not seen much research on this issue, she thought that it might be an area worth exploring: "It may not prevent all domestic violence but certainly seems to have more force as a deterrent than do some of the laws." Such customs may be effective in areas where marriage is understood to be a family affair rather than in relationships built upon Western notions of romance between two individuals and on individual rights. At best, such thinking may be understood as pragmatic. That is, because the world continues to be more or less dominated by a range of patriarchal traditions and institutions, it is perhaps expedient to rely upon those few mechanisms of patriarchy that seem to protect women as the struggle to advance the development and implementation of women's human rights continues.

When asked about her preference for terminology, Filomina provided a nuanced approach to notions of social justice and human rights. She was somewhat reticent about using the term "social justice" because, although it is applicable, she felt it also presented a problem because of the complication of culture: "How people define culture and 'justice' or what could be 'just' in one culture could be seen as 'injustice' in another culture." She noted that this debate played out in the 1994 UN World Conference on Human Rights in Vienna and was reflected in the tension between China and the United States or the West generally in how human rights should be defined:

> The United States and the West were looking primarily at the human rights of the individual in the absence of cultural concerns rather than human rights of the group, which was stressed by China and some countries of the Global South that focused on cultural rights. China argued that they were more interested in the human rights of the group. And in the human sense, some countries argued that they were more concerned about people being fed, clothed, and sheltered, having the right to work, and having certain cultural protections obtained by advancing and protecting the group rather than just an individual. So when we say "social justice," that evokes the whole question of cultural and group rights vis-à-vis individual rights.

This has been and continues to be an argument characteristic of international human rights since the 1940s, when it was enshrined in the Universal Declaration of Human Rights. Filomina went on to confirm that as an anthropologist she was more inclined toward what she referred to as the cultural/social approach. While she was comfortable with the term "social justice," she felt it was necessary to understand that it must also include political and cultural justice; furthermore, for her, it had to also incorporate economic rights. She expressed concern that the human rights agenda seemed to be obscuring the kinds of concerns that relate to what she calls economic justice: "It is often implied that Third World governments are the violators of human rights. But what about the human rights violated all over the world by multinational corporations, international financial institutions, and so forth that are institutions of the Global North, especially Western countries?" She declared:

> These are among the worst violations of human rights in the world. Yet emphasis is not placed on that type of violation. How can one justify the

kind of human rights terms that countries have to enter into in order to obtain financial loans? The debt "conditionalities" literally destroy the economies of poor countries. And then many countries of the Global South are being forced more and more to grow crops for export to pay off debt interest rather than for food consumption by their people. In order to pay back these debts, which carry high interest, there are many ways in which the banks can use what they call "provisions" to rewrite these loans as losses to themselves and so obtain tax breaks from the governments and the US. But the countries of the Global South need to repay these loans at high rates of interest. So how do we define human rights?

For those reasons, Filomina found herself "quite uncomfortable at times with the term 'human rights'" and therefore actually preferred the term "social justice," which for her also incorporates "economic justice." She did acknowledge that it was probably necessary to use both terms, "human rights" and "social justice." It is only by using both terms that "one can then capture some of the violations of human rights that the large corporations perpetuate." Large corporations move their factories to the Global South so they can exploit laborers who are unable to unionize around such critical issues as low wages, and to make matters worse, corporations also receive concessions such as tax holidays from the governments of the countries where they locate. She argued that many corporations exploit these countries' resources, both human and natural, and then leave behind devastation and underdevelopment.

Just as she was intent upon providing nuance to notions of social justice, Filomina was also careful in her definition of feminism. For her, feminism is a broad concept based upon a vision for a different kind of society. "Oppression," Filomina insisted, "is not just seen as what men do to women but also what one race does to another, and what one economic class does to another, and what rich countries do to poor countries." Thus, feminism as she conceptualizes it "should transform the oppressive divisions of human societies. It is an idealistic vision where there would not be oppression or exploitation." She described herself as an African feminist and notes that when this wave of feminism appeared early in the 1970s, it envisioned "fewer hierarchies, less competition, less materialism, and less exploitation of one group by another." The hope was that women would develop alternatives from a different vision. Filomina questioned whether feminists were really committed to this. Instead, she noted that feminists seemed to be more committed to seeking equality with men, replacing men getting "their" jobs and positions and so on: "I do not define feminism like that, because I think that would mean accepting the status quo, that we accept some of the structural inequalities in the system. And I think that the feminists should try to make more fundamental changes in the system rather than simply try to adapt to it or be like men. Because what happens then is that women who get into the position [of authority or power] would be just as oppressive as the men." She insisted that "unless we change the systems and our paradigms we will not move forward as human society. We need some qualitative changes in our power relations. Economic control does confer power on people who have resources, money, and opportunities. Cultural patterns develop to maintain these positions of dominance that are then transmitted to people in the group and their offspring. So we have a situation where cultural imperatives reinforce economic domination and, subsequently, political domination." This situation must change, and such change is much more profound than simply having women replace men, because that will inevitably fail to alter the relationships of domination and subordination.

Steady is also uncomfortable with the term "humanism" because she feels it is so easily dismissed based on its liberal connotations and idealism. However, she feels that it is what comes closest to her understanding of feminism. Although she also hesitates to use the terms "revolutionary" and "radical," because, as she put it, people have such "naive reactions" to them, she argues that they are useful terms, as they recognize the necessity for major changes that could institutionalize this humanistic vision. She insisted that her feminism is a more robust type that embraces ending racial discrimination, ending extreme forms of class exploitation, ending exploitation based on religious differences and nationalities, and so on. She stated, "I am proudly feminist, but not just to be equal to men or to be like men."

When asked what she brings to the international movement for human rights she replied that working at the United Nations has provided her with opportunities to contribute to the women's movement at an international level in a manner that enhances the concept of feminism and makes it more inclusive. She noted that the women's movement has also made socioeconomic development central. It is her considered opinion that "if one has development as a main goal, it would be much easier to achieve equality." Furthermore, she argued that it would also be much easier to achieve peace: "All of these goals are interrelated, and women pushed the idea of integrating these three themes of the UN Decade for Women, but for me, development is central. One cannot fight for equality and peace on an empty stomach."

Filomina was certain that development is a priority for the Global South. Much like Jaribu Hill in Mississippi, Filomina also questioned "how one could fight for equality if one does not have the means to even get to the court, or the means to hire a lawyer, or even know what one's rights are." She noted that this is particularly true if one is unable to read. "So," she argued, "there are certain basic and fundamental aspects of development that also mean human development: education, literacy, training, and all of those things that are necessary preconditions to equality and peace."

In addition to her feminist efforts, in concert with many of her colleagues, Filomina also struggles to bring a racial dimension to the work in the UN. She briefly traced this difficult task of fostering an intersectional perspective through the UN Decade of Women. The decade began with emphasis on slogans such as the "sisterhood of women" and "sisterhood is global"; however, some people at the 1980 Copenhagen conference were uncomfortable with what they considered to be a rather token solidarity with those who were known to be oppressors in terms of racial domination and discrimination. In fact, she recalled that one French delegate observed that there was much hypocrisy, because even as the women had come together to discuss female solidarity, the conversation was occurring in a world that continued to be unequal, unfair, and unjust. Despite the fact that the United States had, grudgingly, apologized for its indiscriminate sterilization of women of color in the past, the conference was regarded as being dominated by Western neocolonialists and ex-colonialists: "They were acting in solidarity with African and Asian women whom they had colonized and women of color in the United States." It was also at the Copenhagen conference that the United States not only refused to denounce racism but also failed to support the Convention on the Elimination of All Forms of Discrimination Against Women. By the 1980 conference in Nairobi, Filomina was among those who were influential in focusing attention on women of color and on problems of minority women and Indigenous women, including Native American and Aboriginal women, whose lands had been taken from them.

Filomina articulated an understanding of human rights that was honed by her years of engagement within the United Nations. Indeed, she described human rights as a technical term applied to a type of legal instrument that is designed to rectify wrongs. Early on, those wrongs were public wrongs and sometimes wrongs against individuals; however, now the term "human rights" is also applied more and more to private wrongs and wrongs against groups, including women. "But," she asserted, "I do not see human rights as the main agenda leading the UN." Because the UN was established after World War II with the clear understanding that another world war would be even more catastrophic, the emphasis was essentially on trying to win some sort of global security; thus, peace was the priority. Over time, human rights evolved to encompass decolonization and humanitarian endeavors, followed by a focus on the environment. But Filomina observed that the Office of the Commissioner for Human Rights is a small one and located in Geneva, essentially away from the center of UN action in New York, where the Security Council is housed.

While the Geneva office certainly handles some conventions, it must be noted that equality is a major theme within the UN system. However, Filomina noted that the theme of equality is certainly not limited to human rights. It is found, for example, in UNESCO for education and in the International Labour Organization (ILO) for labor, both of which have adopted different terminology to reflect their concerns. Thus, the ILO focuses on discrimination against workers and their rights, while UNESCO concentrates on rights to education. To Filomina, "the term 'human rights' . . . borders on being a moral code." And while the agenda of human rights continues to expand, she doubts that it has reached a point where the ordinary person sees problems as human rights violations—that, she declared, will take a while.

Because of her extensive involvement in the UN, Filomina acknowledged that "it is now almost impossible for me to think on the national level. My perspective is global and cross-cultural." She went on to assert that "at the UN one sees a diversity of possibilities and come[s] to value all of them. . . . One is an international civil servant and does not really have a home country while there. One almost sheds one's country and slides into this glorious international identity. It's great!"

Barbara Phillips

I met Barbara Phillips on May 24, 2004, in her office at the Ford Foundation in New York City. At that time, she was the program officer for the area of peace and social justice with a focus on women's rights and gender equity. Prior to this meeting, I had sent a proposal to Ford seeking funding to do the interviews and research necessary for this book. Perhaps a year or more had passed when one day, as I was sitting in my office, the phone rang. Barbara Phillips identified herself and told me she was very interested in the proposal. She asked me to send her a budget for what I wanted to do, and after consultation with a dear friend and colleague who writes many grant proposals that attract funding, I did so. Barbara approved the budget, and that in turn allowed me to identify the smart, strong, visionary, committed, and ultimately fascinating women whom I wanted to interview for this project and to go and meet them in person. Along the way, I learned that a number of the women I interviewed had received funding from Barbara during her tenure at the Ford Foundation. Thus, it was perfectly clear to me that she too must be interviewed for her critical interventions in support of women's international human rights. I was very excited to finally meet this professional woman with the engaging smile in her comfortable and airy office at "the Ford."

Barbara, who worked at the Ford Foundation from 1999 to 2005, described her work as "trying to understand what is needed to advance the field of women's rights."[10] This she did through careful listening at various convenings that were organized by other people or that she organized at the foundation or through the foundation elsewhere. From time to time, she also engaged consultants to delve deeper into a "perceived area of concern to advise me on the kind of grant making and kind of work that need to be supported." Globally, she relied upon collaboration with program offices overseas so that she could gain a better understanding of the work women were engaged in in their respective countries. She was informed in her work by women's assessment of the work that needed to be supported in order to advance the rights of women. "And," she laughed, "I read a lot . . . a wonderful necessary luxury!"

Before she went to Ford, Barbara described herself as being "involved in social justice work but not through a human rights framework," nor did she work in the international arena. Rather, she was deeply involved in her profession as a civil rights attorney addressing issues of sex discrimination, sexual harassment, employment discrimination, and democracy and political participation, specifically regarding issues of race and gender. Outside her legal endeavors, she was involved in the women's movement from the early 1970s, and she was also a community organizer.

Phillips's route to the Ford Foundation was also a circuitous one and was, of course, a product of her upbringing and early experiences. Both of her parents were from Virginia, where she was born. Her family lived in Virginia until she was about five years old and then moved to Memphis, Tennessee, so she grew up in the segregated South. After she finished the ninth grade in Memphis, her father took a teaching position at the HBCU Winston-Salem State College for two years; the family lived there while Barbara was in the tenth and eleventh grades. In the tenth grade, she attended the neighborhood Black school, but the next year a "freedom of choice" plan was offered to desegregate the R. J. Reynolds High School. So when she was in the eleventh grade, her parents decided that she should attend that school. With droll humor, she mentioned that she did not recall having participated in that decision, but she did remember that her parents were the only Black parents in Winston-Salem, North Carolina, who thought that their child needed to desegregate the eleventh grade at that high school. Her parents were joined in that decision by parents of two Black children in the tenth grade and one Black child in the twelfth grade who also determined that their children should participate in the desegregation program. So there were four Black children attending a high school with three thousand white children in 1965. During that entire year, only three white students bothered to speak to her, but she stayed on the honor roll despite that alienation. Perhaps it helped her to think of school as her job: "It wasn't where I went to have fun. It was where I went to do this job. . . . This was my part of being in the [civil rights] movement." She recalled, "I didn't go to school to have fun, [so] I wasn't miserable, but it was not fun. It was being challenged every day about my right to be there." After she completed the eleventh grade, her family returned to Memphis, where she completed the twelfth grade. In the ninth and twelfth grades, she attended the segregated Black Catholic school in Memphis, so she was essentially well versed in both segregated and desegregated education in the South by the time she graduated from high school.

Both her parents and her grandparents were involved in the civil rights movement, and they, along with their family friends, expressed a great deal of pride. "Black people would say to each other, we're so proud of you. The idea of being a credit to your race wasn't a joke. . . . We were a collective, we were a group." One example of such pride was evident later when Willie Herenton was elected the first Black mayor of Memphis in 1991. Barbara laughingly suggested that you would have thought that her parents' other child had won the election.

After graduation in 1967, Barbara went to Macalester College in St. Paul, Minnesota, where she was one of about ten Black students. In 1968 she returned home to Memphis for spring break immediately following the assassination of Martin Luther King Jr. She and her father decided to participate in the march after the assassination. Horrified by the assassination and also by what happened at the march, she felt as if they were in a foreign country, with soldiers, armed with bayonets on top of their rifles, standing along both sides of the streets on which they marched.[11] By this time the civil rights movement was morphing into Black Power. Macalester, a small private liberal arts college, had a biracial organization called Student Action for Human Rights, but when Barbara returned to school after the King assassination, students who were aligned with the Black Power movement separated from the organization to start their own group, the Black Liberation Affairs Committee. Chuckling, she stated, "You know, we were just so radical!"

Also during that fateful freshman year, Fannie Lou Hamer came to speak at the college, and Barbara was profoundly impressed by her: "There she stood this short, dark, oh-so-country Black woman emanating power. She talked about the civil rights movement, the Freedom Democratic Party, the 1968 Democratic Convention. In those early days at Macalester, her words sustained my own sense of self in this overwhelmingly white environment and stayed with me as I attempted to make myself relevant to the world in which I lived. Here was an opportunity to learn first-hand something about her world in Mississippi."[12]

In Barbara's senior year, students were provided with opportunities to do independent study. Majoring in history, she decided to take advantage of the opportunity and went to Fayette, Mississippi, for a month in 1970 to do an oral history project with Charles Evers and to explore the Fayette civil rights movement.[13] Her parents drove her to Fayette, where she stayed in the home of a lovely Black woman who was a staunch supporter of the movement and who had shotguns leaning up against some of her windows. Barbara's parents pretended not to notice them.[14]

Barbara was totally captivated by the "local folk of the civil rights movement" and the time she was able to spend with them. There was to be an election in 1971, and Charles Evers had decided to run for governor of Mississippi along with one hundred Blacks, including Hamer, who were running for election to local offices. In a kind of preemptive retaliation, the white people of Mississippi moved to purge the voter registration rolls of people who had not voted within the past three years. It therefore became necessary to reregister thousands of Black voters if they were going to have any impact on the fall election of 1971. With the help of the newly formed student-based Minnesota Public Interest Group, Barbara organized two hundred students in Minnesota to go with her to Mississippi over spring break. They went wherever people would have them to register voters, and then they brought students from Tougaloo College (a small private HBCU) to register voters in Minnesota. Although she received her bachelor of arts in history from Macalester and had planned to go to graduate school to study history, Barbara's plans evaporated as she became determined to become a community organizer.

The summer after graduation from college in 1971, Barbara completed a summer training program with the Industrial Areas Foundation and became part of a cohort of new organizers.[15] Founded in 1940, the Industrial Areas Foundation describes itself as "the nation's largest and longest-standing network of local faith and community-based organizations."[16] After her training, she returned to what she referred to as the "finishing school" of Mississippi to be "raised" by the people there. While she volunteered in Charles Evers's 1971 campaign for governor, she was educated by the people who had gone to Mississippi to be part of the civil rights movement and stayed and the local people who were the foundation of the movement. They took her under their wing and schooled her in the local politics and in activism. It was at this point that she forged a lasting relationship with Hamer, who helped ground her in the movement and social justice work.

When asked about her relationship with Hamer, Barbara reminisced that she admired her tremendously and at the same time was amazed at how accessible she was. She recalled that Hamer lived in a little brick house that was part of a development that she had founded for people who, like herself, had been evicted from the plantations they worked on for having the audacity to register to vote. Although she lived in the middle of the community, she always made herself available and invited Barbara to come and visit her whenever she was in the delta. Barbara recalled that Hamer always seemed to have a pot of green beans on the stove whenever she went to visit her and that she was willing to mentor her: "She would take the time to kind of explain things." Mrs. Hamer was still very involved in what she called the "Loyalist Democratic Party."[17] The Mississippi Freedom Democratic Party had ceased to exist by 1971, so the Loyalist Democratic Party under the leadership of Charles Evers and Aaron Henry (the chairperson) was formed out of a merger of the MFDP and the Democratic Party. At that time, it included a few white liberals but was mostly comprised of Black people. Although Hamer was involved in the negotiations to bring the two groups together, she was eventually frozen out of the party because she was steadfast in upholding her principles.

Barbara insisted that one of the most important things that she learned from Hamer was to know where you are "in the sense of place, in terms of power dynamics going on around you, in terms of time, in terms of appreciating where you are now as opposed to where you were a year ago or five years ago. She meant that. That phrase meant knowing a lot of things. And keeping a lot of things on your radar screen. Knowing where you are. Just meant a whole lot. And she would explain things like that to me." Hamer was adamant that the cause of social justice meant that a person needed to evaluate the work that they were doing: "She explained that some people never evaluated the impact of the work they were doing. Wrong! To be effective one had to periodically lift one's head out of the trenches, pause and actually assess the political landscape in which one was laboring and whether the work being done was what was needed to move forward."[18]

That time with Hamer was wonderful for Barbara, and she admitted that "as a young person I . . . knew every damn thing, . . . and everything needed to happen as of yesterday." She admitted that she would visit Hamer feeling "just discouraged" and would leave there "just wanting to slap myself, you know how in the world could I be discouraged when this woman has faced, has come up with a vision of the future that she had no right to even hold in her head. . . . Where did she even get this vision of justice and equality? . . . She has that, and she wasn't discouraged. So it was really a wonderful experience."

Hamer was many things, but, Barbara insisted, she was not sweet, "she was not just some 'This Little Light of Mine' song-singing, sweet woman." Rather, much like Ida B. Wells, another uncompromising woman from Mississippi who fought against lynching at the end of the nineteenth century, Hamer was very clear about her values and about what strategies were consistent with those value and what strategies were not, even if they were viewed as pragmatic by some because they might get you where you wanted to go in the short term. To her, "principles mattered. Expediency would never get you to the Promised Land."[19] In that respect, Hamer was not the person whom one would want to have at a meeting if one was trying to figure out how to compromise. She was uncompromising, and because of that the Loyalist Party did horrible things to her, according to Barbara. For example, Hamer would attend a meeting, and the chair, Aaron Henry, would refuse to recognize her, refuse to allow her to speak. Barbara felt strongly that this was a lesson in how things in a movement could go astray. As she reflected on what she learned, she continues to adhere to one critical lesson to this day. She has found that she is very uncomfortable if everyone in a meeting is agreeable: "I know that somebody is missing. You know, if we're all just so happy to see each other and we are just all on the same page, something is wrong!"

As mentioned previously, Barbara was involved in various forms of activism and advocacy in the women's rights movement from the early 1970s. In 1971, for example, she was a founding member of the Women's Coalition in Jackson, Mississippi, a biracial group of women who were engaged in social justice work. They met weekly in each other's homes for potluck dinners and consciousness-raising. They read and discussed books and wrote papers analyzing various issues and critiqued them. Barbara recalled that they devoured *Our Bodies, Ourselves* in isolated Jackson, for example, and when Judy Chicago's exhibition *The Dinner Party* was installed in San Francisco, they found pictures in magazines that represented Chicago's vision of famous women's vulvas, and each member chose one for herself. At a special potluck dinner in honor of Chicago, they placed their pictures at their place settings and then walked around, examining what each had chosen and engaging in lively discussion. (Barbara, of course, chose Sojourner Truth.) Later, she would serve as president of the Northern California Black Women's Lawyers Association. Still later, when she became a law professor, she created and taught a seminar on gender, race, and the law.

From 1971 to 1973, Phillips worked in Claiborne County, in southwestern Mississippi, where she was involved in the political struggles of the area. After passage of the 1965 voting rights bill, Mississippi began electing a significant number of Black people to political offices for the first time since the era of Reconstruction. In Claiborne County particularly, Black politicians held the majority of elected offices, although only one Black person held a seat on the powerful county governing board. They also elected a Black tax assessor and collector, who discovered that Black people were paying more taxes on two-bedroom houses than whites were paying on antebellum mansions. Despite the new tax rolls based upon the evidence collected by the Black assessor and tax collector, the county board of supervisors refused to accept those changes. It was at this point that Barbara learned a very valuable and difficult lesson:

> In Mississippi I met some of the most courageous Black folk I'd ever known; I also met Black folk who believed themselves and other Black folk to be actually inferior to whites. . . . I developed a much deeper and more profound understanding of white supremacy and the harm it visits upon Black folk and their ability to participate in democracy. A devastating legacy of slavery, lynching, and segregation was the belief among some Black folk that there is such a thing as "white folk's business," with which Black folks should not be involved and are not capable of mastering. And the assessor and tax collector were running into that dark place in the minds of some Black folk in Claiborne County.

White people mounted a very effective disinformation campaign that insinuated that the Black elected tax officials were incompetent. This in turn fed into Black people's political inexperience and their inferiority complex. While they knew that they wanted social change, the people were unsure about what to do and whom to trust to bring about change.

Barbara was employed by the Black Economic Research Center, which was founded by Black economist Robert S. Brown and had offices in New York and Mississippi. She and Jesse Morris, the local director, staffed the two-person office in Claiborne. She also worked with its sister organization, the Emergency Land Fund, which focused on the loss of Black-owned land in the South.[20] Their examination of the racial injustices of the property tax system in Claiborne County was designed to support the idea of putting in place an equitable property tax system. Such a system could, in turn, provide the county with the resources it needed to address the social conditions that were having a disparate impact on the Black community. Ultimately, their intention was to empower the Black community to reallocate public resources. Unfortunately, the county supervisors (four white and one Black) rejected the changes they were trying to make with the tax system.

Barbara and Jesse Morris decided that they needed to counteract the misinformation and obstruction, and they felt that the most effective way to do so was through a lawsuit. They asked the Lawyers' Committee for Civil Rights Under Law to file a suit on behalf of Evan Doss, the tax assessor. Barbara admits that they knew nothing about the law, but they felt that such a lawsuit would help the Black people in Claiborne understand that Doss was right: "We saw a lawsuit as a community organizing tool regardless of whether it was legally frivolous."[21] But because lawyers do not think that way, the Lawyers' Committee declined their pleas to mount a lawsuit. Barbara was so infuriated over the lawyers' apparent ignorance about how to serve the community that she decided to go to law school to show them how it should be done.

In 1973 she was accepted into Northwestern University School of Law. Like Judge Gabrielle Kirk McDonald, Phillips too wanted to go to law school in order to become a civil rights lawyer. She returned to Mississippi the summer after her first year at law school to work again in Claiborne County, and she also volunteered with the Mississippi Council on Human Relations. The council, under the leadership of Michael Raff, had released a report in 1974 that found that all state agencies were routinely refusing to hire any Black workers in clerical or professional positions, indeed, in any positions above menial ones. In order to document this problem, Barbara bought a dress and shoes and went off to apply for positions that required a college education in about ten state agencies, including the offices of the secretary of state and the attorney general: "There was quite a fluster when I showed up at these places, résumé in hand, and announced my desire to be employed." She recalled that she created such a stir that Heber Ladner, the secretary of state himself, interviewed her. He asked a long list of questions to determine whether she was qualified to work in a professional position. She assured him that she was capable of doing all he asked, until he finally asked her if she could take shorthand. When she admitted that was the one thing she could not do, "the relief on his face was palpable, and he began to return to normal coloring as he exclaimed with great exuberance, 'Well, EVERYBODY here takes shorthand.' And he most graciously and with much apparent relief concluded the interview."[22]

After graduating in 1976, Phillips went to work in the Office of the Solicitor General of the Minnesota Attorney General to, as she put it, learn how to be a lawyer. Her plan was to spend two years in the office and then, still angry about the Claiborne County situation, return to Mississippi as a staff attorney with the Lawyers' Committee for Civil Rights Under Law so that she could teach them how to practice law in service to the community. She learned that a staff attorney for the committee was leaving, so she applied for the position but heard nothing for weeks. Learning that she was not their first choice and that the job had been offered to someone else and that they were awaiting the reply, she called them every week for a month to find out what was happening with the position. Finally, she had had enough, so she tracked down the number one candidate and called him. She told him that it was obvious he was not interested in the job and asked him to call the committee to decline the offer and get out of her way, because she did want the job. He did so, and in the summer of 1978 she became a staff attorney for the committee in the Mississippi office, where she handled a variety of civil rights cases, including housing discrimination, voting rights litigation, and prison conditions.[23]

One of Phillips's favorite cases was a First Amendment case that challenged the state of Mississippi for its refusal to permit the use of a particular history textbook in the public schools. The history book, *Mississippi: Conflict and Change*, had been written collaboratively by faculty and students at the HBCU Tougaloo College and at Millsaps College, a historically white institution (HWI) in Jackson.[24] Appalled by the inaccuracies that permeated his students' historical knowledge, James Loewen, a Tougaloo professor, obtained a grant from the Southern Education Foundation and recruited faculty and students from Tougaloo College and Millsaps College. With his Millsaps colleague Charles Sallis and their students, they researched and wrote an accurate history of Mississippi for ninth graders. The book received the Lillian Smith Book Award for best nonfiction in 1975. Unfortunately, it was not universally appreciated because it did not advance the ideology of white supremacy. It was subsequently not approved by the State Textbook Commission, so it could not be purchased by local school districts. That decision was challenged in federal court in *Loewen* et al. *v. Turnipseed, Mississippi State Textbook Purchasing Board* et al. (1980) on First Amendment grounds of the rights of students to learn and the rights of teachers to teach. This decision, according to Barbara, had a critical impact on "what students learned about the realities of slavery, about the realities of Reconstruction, the realities of the civil rights movement." Recently, a book was published by "Ole Miss" historian Charles Eagles titled *Civil Rights, Culture Wars: The Fight over a Mississippi Textbook*, recounting this story and the court case.[25]

In 1980 Barbara moved to the national office of the Lawyers' Committee on Civil Rights Under Law in Washington, DC, to work on its National Voting Rights Project. While there, she worked on an amendment to extend the Voting Rights Act and was also engaged in voting rights litigation around the country. In about mid-1982, she moved to San Francisco to become a partner in the law firm that would subsequently be named Rosin and Phillips. About 60 percent of their practice was civil rights law, and the other portion was representing small to medium-size corporations. Sometimes they also represented large corporations in litigation and governmental entities, including foreign governments. At one point they were appointed by a court to supervise a consent decree around discrimination in hiring, promotion, and conditions of employment for the San Francisco Fire Department. The case would bring the first women into and add more people of color to the Fire Department.

About that time, Phillips had a baby and took three months' maternity leave. The child totally changed her priorities about the law. Her friend Shana

Marshall, who would later become dean of the Hastings Law School, had received a fellowship at Stanford Law School designed for minority lawyers who were interested in transitioning their careers into the academy. Barbara was accepted for the two-year fellowship, which included teaching while pursuing an advanced degree. From 1992 to 1994, she cotaught a course on constitutional law while she pursued a doctor of law degree in the science of law. When she completed the program, she joined the faculty at the University of Mississippi Law School. At the end of the twentieth century, she was the first Black female tenure-track professor at the University of Mississippi Law School. She taught there from 1994 to 1999, when she joined the Ford Foundation.

As previously mentioned, when Barbara went to the Ford Foundation in 1999, she had very little international experience; however, she brought to the position her profound understanding of racism and sexism and her commitment to social justice. Indeed, she declared that her "feminist consciousness was formed around racial justice." When I asked her what she thought Black women bring to international human rights work, she responded that they bring a layered perspective of race, class, and gender, "and then understanding of living subordination that grows out of all three layers." She mused that Black women's perspective was like color television compared to the black-and-white television perspective of elite white women. She argued that "they just can't see. Or they have to work at seeing, or they have to study or . . . But this is how we live. . . . We have a deeper understanding of what we are experiencing not just personally, but we have a deeper understanding of . . . how subordination in society works." She went on to suggest that "living in this multidimensional way gives us a much more complex perch, a much more complex understanding of the rules. So, I think we have appreciation for complexity and multiple things going on at one time." She also agreed that US Black women's historical knowledge and experiences with multiple oppressions had an impact upon the way that they understand international human rights.

> [What] it brings to my understanding . . . is the ability to see where it [knowledge and experience of multiple oppressions] is impoverished by the absence of taking complexities, by where it is absent in taking into account the various cultural, class, race, group realities around the world. It allows me to see those instances in which it is really speaking about a particular context and attempting to make that particular context universal. It becomes visible . . . that this . . . context of the description is really not universal. The content comes from a particular context, which is fine, it's just that it should be identified as being content from a particular context. . . . [It] then makes space for the concept to be enriched from other contexts.

As Barbara reflected upon the work of Black women in the international arena, she noted that we are often not prepared to recognize that Black women are also viewed as privileged Americans: "We still need to do a lot of work in understanding that position and where [and] how we want to respond to the accusation of it but appreciate where we are. . . . As Fannie Lou Hamer would say, 'I think we need to work on our deeper appreciation for where we are.'" Women in developing countries have often shocked US women who have been so dominant in the international arena training women in developing countries about how to hold their governments accountable. They are pushing back by asking US women, including Black women, "What are you doing to hold your government accountable?" They are asking, "Why should these US-based women's international organizations still be roaming the world, training people to hold their governments accountable when clearly there's some work that needs to be done here at home? And progressive women of color who get out there are also being met with the same challenge. . . . To say you didn't do it and you're progressive is no longer letting people off the hook anywhere on the globe. So I think those are important conversations to be had. And challenges that are healthy."

Phillips has seen coalitions developing within the African diaspora and beyond, particularly exemplified by a working coalition between INCITE! Women of Color against Violence and a women's movement in India called Creating Resources for Empowerment in Action (CREA). INCITE!, founded by Beth Richey, describes itself as a national organization of radical feminists of color who are working to end violence against women of color and their communities. Their methods include direct action, critical dialogue, and grassroots organizing.[26] CREA, a feminist human rights organization based in New Delhi, partners with a range of human rights movements and networks to advance the rights of women and girls and sexual reproductive freedoms of all people.[27] CREA intersects with INCITE! in their commitment to prevent violence against women and to enhance women's security. Both are also working to increase the voice and visibility of marginalized women, including the transgendered, especially in the United States. Barbara notes that such coalitions are moving beyond sharing information to the strategic idea of working together to advance a shared agenda. Dazon Dixon Diallo's work in both South Africa and Atlanta, discussed in chapter 4, also exemplifies this new phase in international human rights development.

Barbara considers the reciprocal relationship between Black feminist thought and international human rights to be a useful one. Harking back to Fannie Lou Hamer once again, she suggests that the international women's rights movement brings to Black women an intellectual conceptualization of knowing where they are within a larger global perspective. "And knowing that we are not as women of color a minority. As people of color, we're not a minority. And secondly, the international movement brings to us an appreciation for the possibility of legal frameworks beyond the Constitution." She sees, then, a "potential for new strategies, new ways of linking issues together. New points of entry to leverage change. . . . The possibility that international instruments can have the potential to bring about some different outcomes. To address the limitations of our Constitution, to ameliorate the limitations."

As we were ending our conversation, I asked Barbara what was the most important, critical, specific information or knowledge that she has obtained from her work in the field of international human rights. Here is her profound response:

> I think actually the most important thing I've learned is that comfort, by those who benefit from the status quo, is highly valued. And that from the perspective of those who are comfortable in the status quo, the biggest sin you can commit is to make them uncomfortable. This is presented in a way that makes it seem commonsensical that, one, the language of the advocate must be shaped to maintain the comfort of those to whom one advocates. If your language is not soothing, if your language introduces discomfort, those who are in power are incredibly privileged to stop the conversation. They will not listen. But not only will they not listen, but it is your fault that they are not listening, because you are using inappropriate language. You are using language that is too sharp, you are using language that is too raw, you are using language that is too confrontational. And I have been astounded at how powerful that privilege is to be comfortable. How it is used to stop conversations, how it is used to silence people.

She observed that the privilege of comfort means that those who lack privilege or are marginalized are then supposed to, for example, set up focus groups to learn how to say what they need to say in a manner that the focus group likes. So if they don't like words such as "rights" and "discrimination" and "race," then we have to stop using those words. Barbara argued that this is a contribution to the ideology of the Right when we are forced to say that race is not an issue, that there is no discrimination, and that somehow we are all playing on a level field: "Since we had stopped using those words because focus groups said we were not supposed to use those words, we created a landscape where that seemed to be the case. So that has been just how powerful this thing is about comfort."

This notion of comfort is so pervasive and powerful that it not only serves to silence people but also forces them to go back to the drawing board to figure out some new language: "I mean we really want to communicate, so it's our job to find something that makes people comfortable. Well, there is a certain idiocy in that!" She recalled speaking with a friend about this critical issue and, fully exasperated, stating crudely, "You know, white men are the only people in the world who think they have the right to screw you up one side and down the other and then tell you how to complain about it!" She finds that there is something very wrong with our acquiescence to this privilege of comfort and that, furthermore, "as a woman of color, I don't—I have never experienced the privilege of being comfortable. And demanding that people make me comfortable." She notes that, generally, white people not only do not make her comfortable, but they are not even about the business of trying to make her comfortable: "It is very powerful. And to feel, I just, I wonder what it is like to wake up in the morning, and the world is supposed to make you comfortable. And if the world doesn't make you comfortable, you get to shut it down!"

As I found with all the interviews for this book, it was difficult for me to end the conversation. Phillips responded to my question about whether human rights really exist, and if so, are they ineffective? She observed that the rights embedded in international human rights and those embedded in the US Constitution and the federal laws prohibiting discrimination are all aspiration. Indeed, she argues that "the concept of rights is something that remains aspirational in this world for everyone." Continuing with her previous thoughts about privilege and comfort, she suggested that even for those who feel that their lives have not been impacted by discrimination, "it may be that their status in life has benefited from their being the recipients of unearned privilege. So their lives are impacted. Just as much but not as detrimentally as their lives are impacted positively by privilege. And therefore, that privilege is a violation of the aspiration." She further opined that "the person who is affected detrimentally by being denied rights is of course also impacted by the failure of society to live up to the aspiration of these rights." In her considered opinion, "the concept of international human rights is no more ephemeral to me than the rights that are assured to Blacks by the US Constitution." She reminds us that those rights remain ephemeral to her and to millions of other Black people in this country. So, she says with a laugh, if she couldn't see those rights as aspirational, "we could all just stay in bed, because none of us have any of them. To the extent that makes them a reality." We agreed that this was an ongoing reality and that we do not have the luxury of just being tired and giving up because the problems cannot be solved tomorrow. Furthermore, even when we have "solved" one problem, we discover that there is yet another injustice underneath it that also needs to be ameliorated, so the work continues.

Bringing International Human Rights Home

Our government has repeatedly blocked attempts to bring these rights home to America's own racial minorities, and that hypocrisy lurks at the core of our moral identity as a nation, undermining our claims to global leadership.

Gay McDougall, interview with the author, 2002

I n this chapter, I explore the impressive and multifaceted endeavors of Gay McDougall. Her work has spanned the US civil rights movement to the South Africa antiapartheid movement into the chambers of the United Nations, radiating out from there across the globe. Thus, her quintessential endeavors are emblematic of the human rights endeavors of all women in this book and beyond.

I asked each respondent after our interview whom they thought I should interview for this book, and almost to a woman, everyone asked me, "Have you interviewed Gay yet?" So it was with curiosity and excitement that I made my way to Gay McDougall's office in Washington, DC. As we sat down for our first interview on June 13, 2002, she was in the midst of her fourteen-year tenure as the executive director of the International Human Rights Law Group (1994–2008).

Like the other women in this book, Gay's pathway into international human rights seemed inevitable. She grew up in segregated Atlanta, marinating in what historians refer to as "the long civil rights movement," that is, beyond the tenure of Martin Luther King Jr.'s civil rights endeavors. In fact, her family lived around the corner from the King family, and her mother and King's mother were good friends. Gay described her schoolteacher mother as her central role model, but she was also influenced by her aunt, her mother's sister, who was deeply involved in the mid-twentieth-century civil rights movement.

In the 1950s her aunt was active in the YWCA movement, which was "dedicated to breaking down the barriers between white and Black communities" throughout the South.[1] When the four students from North Carolina A&T State University decided to "sit in" at a lunch counter in Greensboro, North Carolina, in 1960, McDougall's sister, who was four years older than Gay and at that time a student at Bennett College in Greensboro (one of the two Black women's colleges in the country), joined the demonstrations and was arrested.

Gay also found ways to participate in the movement through demonstrating in picket lines, as she lived through the consequential Atlanta boycotts. The Black community in Atlanta was characterized by a complex social hierarchy that included a comfortable elite component. Atlanta was economically stratified not only by class but also by color, with many fair-skinned Black residents occupying the top of the hierarchy. Atlanta had made limited progress toward desegregation in the 1950s because residents had little interest in causing trouble through struggles to desegregate. The Georgia state legislature had even less interest in desegregation. In fact, acting proactively about two weeks after the 1961 sit-ins at Greensboro, the legislature passed a law making it a misdemeanor to refuse to leave a place of business when ordered to do so by the management.

Meanwhile, Morehouse College student Lonnie King, who had secured support from the presidents of the six colleges that comprised what, at that time, was referred to as the Atlanta University Center, was already organizing student leaders within the historically Black colleges and universities.[2] The coalition they formed, the Committee on Appeal for Human Rights (COAHR), wrote a manifesto called "An Appeal for Human Rights." With financial support from the college presidents, the appeal was published as a full-page newspaper advertisement in both of the mainstream white Atlanta newspapers, as well as in the newspaper that served the Black community.

On March 15, 1961, COAHR launched its direct-action campaign, with two hundred students participating in sit-ins in ten different locations in downtown Atlanta, including the state capitol, the county courthouse, the city hall, and bus and railway stations. Some seventy-seven students were arrested; however, the NAACP arranged legal assistance for them. Two days later in a closed meeting, students decided to temporarily cancel the sit-ins so that white and Black business leaders could engage in negotiations. After those negotiations fell apart, Lonnie King, in an address to the Georgia NAACP, announced a march on the state capitol for May 17. The governor responded by encircling the building with state troopers and dogs. Meanwhile, rumors circulated that violent racist white people were coming to attack the marchers. Not to be dissuaded, several thousand students prepared to march even as Lonnie King was informed by the highly respected Morehouse College president, Benjamin E. Mays, that the city police had decided that they could not protect the students against the state police or against any enraged white people who might act out on state property. Students were advised not to march if they felt they were unable to adhere to nonviolent principles. No one backed down. However, despite their intentions, the students were diverted from marching on the state capitol by the city police.

The KKK had already staged a rally of some five hundred people on May 29 to intimidate the students. This action in turn led members of the Black community, including the Negro Voters' League, the Baptist Ministers' Union, the AME Ministers' Union, and the NAACP, among other community organizations, to join the students in signing the appeal. Because the Black newspaper refused to print students' perspectives on the unfolding events, COAHR began publishing its own newsletter, edited by Julian Bond, and distributed twenty thousand copies via the Black churches. The slogan for the boycott launched in June was "Close down your account with segregation; Open up your account with freedom." Its focus was the venerable, long-established Rich's Department Store in downtown Atlanta. Students, who at that time comprised about one-third of the Black population of Atlanta, sought the support of Black churches to participate in the boycott. Lonnie King estimated that Rich's lost some $10 million because of the boycott. In August some students also began "pray-in" demonstrations at local white churches on Sunday but soon abandoned that particular form of protest. A decision was made to postpone further action until the students returned to classes in the fall and the Student Nonviolent Coordinating Committee (SNCC) conference in Atlanta in October.

Returning to full strength when classes resumed after the summer hiatus, students organized mass sit-ins in two department stores and eight variety stores and picketed four other stores. Dr. Martin Luther King Jr. joined their demonstrations and was arrested, capturing national attention for the struggle. Meanwhile, the downtown stores retaliated by closing down the store lunch counters when the protesters arrived and then reopening them when they left. As soon as the lunch counters reopened, COAHR "spotters" in the stores would alert their headquarters to send in more demonstrators. More and more students were arrested, but the stores continued to refuse to desegregate. The students' persistence finally led to the closure of all the downtown lunch counters by the end of November. Protests continued for the next three months, bringing sales figures down by some 13 percent. Store owners finally agreed to meet with the traditional leaders of the Black community rather than the student demonstrators to discuss a plan for desegregation. On March 7, 1961, they reached an agreement to desegregate the following fall. Not surprisingly, the students and many others were unhappy with the delay and with the alliance between the Black and white business owners. Nonetheless, they accepted the agreement, and in the fall of 1961 the city of Atlanta ended the formal practice of segregation in public facilities.[3]

Gay stood in many of those demonstration lines, picketing during the Atlanta boycotts. After passage of the Voting Rights Act of 1965, she participated in the voter registration and community organizing projects in southern Georgia, South Carolina, and Alabama that were organized by different groups, including the Southern Christian Leadership Conference (SCLC) and SNCC. A few years later, in about 1967, she worked for the US Commission on Civil Rights as an investigator attached to the Office of the General Counsel. Her work was particularly focused on Alabama and Texas, where she interacted with the local population and where hearings were held.

Gay's K–12 education had occurred within the segregated public school system of Atlanta. Although she had other options, she chose to attend Booker T. Washington High School, a segregated school that served middle- and lower-class Black students. After high school, Gay was chosen to be the first Black student to integrate Agnes Scott College, a small Presbyterian white women's liberal arts college in Decatur, Georgia. She recalled a meeting with the college president before she moved into the dorm, during which she was told that she would not have a roommate "because the school couldn't spring *that* on a white girl. 'You understand' he said."[4] Daily subjected to subtle forms of racism, she described her time at Agnes Scott as "very difficult and very lonely." While there were no Klan rallies on campus, for example, she was certain that "they weren't ready for me and I wasn't ready for them."[5] After two years, she felt that she "had served her time" and transferred to Bennington College in Vermont.[6]

Although Bennington might seem an odd choice, Gay chose it for two reasons. First, she had an interest in dance, and at that time Bennington was the home of avant-garde modern dance. Second, she had perused a map in order to find a place that was as far away from Georgia as she could go, and Bennington seemed to meet that requirement. At that time, Bennington had perhaps three hundred students, and about twelve of that number were American Negroes (as they would have been called at that time). Laughingly, Gay stated, "That sounded like a bunch of folks compared to Agnes Scott!" More seriously, she described herself as always being very self-directed, and Bennington was a school that supported that characteristic. She thought there were only two or three majors at that time, and she remembered that students were not required to take specific subjects and that there were neither exams nor grades. Thus, students were encouraged and able to design their own course of studies, a situation that suited her perfectly.

When one reads about students desegregating public schools, particularly in the South, one is often left with one-dimensional depictions of stoic heroes and "sheroes" who were the "firsts." Gay McDougall and Barbara Phillips provided a small glimpse into both the fortitude required to desegregate a school day after day and the emotional and psychological trauma of assuming the role of students in the vanguard of school desegregation struggles. These students faced environments that not only were overtly and covertly hostile but always held the dangerous potential of bubbling over into virulent and even violent racism.

After graduating from Bennington, Gay determined that her ongoing interest in civil rights would best be served by pursuing a law degree so that she could, like Gabrielle Kirk McDonald, become a civil rights attorney. With that in mind, she went on to attain a law degree from Yale Law School. Like the law school professors featured elsewhere in this volume, she too felt it necessary to first venture into corporate law to supplement her legal training. Subsequently, she joined the New York law firm Debevoise, Plimpton, Lyons & Gates, where she was the only African American and one of very few women. She felt that "it was very important for human rights lawyers to understand 'the other side.'"[7] Despite feeling marginalized because of her race and gender, she spent two years in the firm studying that other side. These experiences at the law firm and at Agnes Scott pushed her further along the path of understanding the critical need for rights.

When she left Debevoise, Gay joined the National Conference of Black Lawyers (NCBL). Often described as the progressive arm of the Black law community, the NCBL was interested in linking the US civil rights movement to the decolonization and liberation struggles primarily in Africa. In chapter 1, Adrien Wing described her work with the NCBL, as she too supported African liberation struggles and the Palestinian liberation movement. Those priorities led the NCBL to attain nongovernmental status at the United Nations, and Gay became the NCBL's representative to the UN. It was during this early tenure at the United Nations that she "began to see that there was actually a profession that was sort of connected with this [notion of human rights]. I started to work with people at the UN on these issues. . . . That's what eventually made me decide to go back to school and further my skills in international law, particularly human rights law."[8] She returned to law school to pursue the next level of training beyond the law degree, the master of laws, in international public law with a focus on human rights at the London School of Economics and Political Science (LSE). While in London, she also established a relationship with an arm of the South African liberation movement that was headquartered there.

"The thing is, though," she mused, "formal education doesn't teach you anything about doing this kind of work." She noticed that international human rights "for a good little while existed basically . . . on the conceptual level. Mostly it was a subject for academic discourse that experts taught in law schools and wrote articles about." The practice of human rights, she observed, was preceded by its introduction into law school curriculums. McDougall attributes her informal training in the practice of human rights to her early participation in civil rights projects in the 1960s. Even then she was drawing connections to other international human rights struggles, as she had come to understand the US civil rights movement as a struggle against American apartheid. While in college, she had also raised money for liberation movements; thus, her involvement in the antiapartheid movement was of long-standing interest and, for her, a logical progression into the arena of international human rights.

In 1980 Gay moved to Washington, DC, to work with the Lawyers' Committee for Civil Rights Under Law directing the Southern Africa Project (SAP). SAP was founded as a response to the South African government's adoption of the 1967 Terrorism Act. This particular legislation was used by the government to detain political activists and lawyers indefinitely without trial or legal representation. "A lot was happening," McDougall recalled. "The first couple of months after I moved to Washington when I would speak about apartheid, nobody knew what I was talking about, nobody cared. By the end of that year, the townships were being burned, people were rioting in the streets of South Africa. Everybody cared."[9] South African lawyers were recruited to defend political prisoners in South Africa. They developed legal defense strategies that would ultimately result in the freeing of thousands of political prisoners.

Gay collaborated with South African lawyers through helping with research, providing resources, and raising money from around the world for the struggle. She found herself faced with an unexpected problem: how to smuggle that money into South Africa. For years she was banned from South Africa by the government. In fact, it was not until the mid-1980s that she actually visited South Africa for the first time, and then she had to sneak across the Botswanan border in the trunk of a car.[10]

When Namibia, located on the South Atlantic coast of Africa and bordering South Africa, was in the early stages of its struggles to be liberated from South Africa, Gay sought to test whether a Namibian visa would allow her to travel through South Africa to get to that country. She flew from Zimbabwe to Namibia, but because there were no direct flights to Namibia, she had to pass through Johannesburg. South Africa treated such flights as if they were a domestic transfer (i.e., as if one was flying from Georgia to Alabama). When her plane landed in the Johannesburg airport, she was escorted by a policeman to the Namibian departure gate. Although her plane was not scheduled to depart until the following morning, McDougall was detained in the airport all night with a policeman who had been instructed to stay with her the entire time she was in South Africa. He informed her that "they told me that I should not leave you until you are strapped into the seat." And then he asked her, "Lady, what have you done?"[11]

Since she was banned by the government from stepping foot into South Africa, McDougall focused her attention on raising money and helping design critical legal defenses from a distance. Strategically, while this was a necessity, it also meant she was not there on the ground with her friends and comrades— the people she struggled with for the liberation of South Africa: "When people would get out of jail in South Africa and they would have a party, I was not there. When things went wrong . . . I was not there."[12]

It was especially traumatic when the African National Congress (ANC) implemented a dangerous defense strategy that McDougall had devised. The strategy called upon ANC members who were arrested and had to appear before a judge to declare that they did not recognize the jurisdiction of South African courts because they were in fact prisoners of war. When this risky strategy was first implemented, judges sent them straight to jail, where they were summarily executed. Finally, in 1990 McDougall was granted a visa to visit South Africa after Nelson Mandela was released from prison. Upon her arrival, she learned that she and her work were well known by the governmental authorities as well as by those activists on the ground who were involved in the struggle to liberate their country. When she presented her passport to the immigration officer at the airport, he exclaimed, "*You're* Ms. McDougall. Your file is *gigantic!*"[13]

Because she had been so effective with her work in the struggle to liberate the country, soon afterward she was appointed to the South African Independent Electoral Commission. Gay McDougall was the only American among the five non–South African appointees to the sixteen-member international body responsible for overseeing the first all-race South African election, ensuring that it was free and fair. Such a monumental endeavor required her to move to South Africa during the year leading up to the historic event. The commissioners, McDougall explained during our interview, "decided everything about the election: how it would be conducted, where the polling stations would be, training people to be poll officers—the whole thing." She worked feverishly around the clock "putting out fires, including getting ballots to key townships where they were missing." She also provided political assistance to those parties that were negotiating with the South African government for a peaceful transition to a postapartheid democratic government. She provided "analyses of comparative constitutional arrangements. She also facilitated a detailed examination of constitutional options under consideration by organizing a series of consultations with experts from other countries with practical experience implementing similar systems in their own countries."[14]

The election was held on April 26–29, 1994. On April 27 Gay McDougall stood next to Nelson Mandela as he cast his first ballot in the election that would confer upon him the office of president of South Africa after the demise of apartheid. There is an iconic picture of that moment, but McDougall, chuckling about that day, declared that she was "*comatose*" when it was taken because she had forgone any sleep, literally working around the clock for the three days prior to the election.

Not only was Gay deeply involved with the South African struggles for liberation, but she also found time to work with the Namibia liberation struggles. South West Africa had become a German colony during the European scramble for Africa in the 1880s. When Germany was defeated in World War I, the League of Nations appointed South Africa to administer the South West Africa territory as a mandate in a manner that was supposed to eventually result in its independence. This mandate arrangement lasted until after World War II, when South Africa unilaterally annexed South West Africa and extended apartheid into the territory. Finally, in 1966 the United Nations General Assembly voted to terminate South Africa's right to administer the territory. Then in 1969 the UN Security Council also called upon South Africa to withdraw its administration from the territory; however, South Africa ignored those international admonitions to forsake its illegal involvement in South West Africa. Ultimately, the UN sued South Africa in the International Court of Justice, objecting to its continued presence in the territory. In an advisory opinion issued on June 21, 1971, the court found that the continued presence of South Africa in South West Africa was illegal and that it was obligated to immediately terminate its occupation of the territory. Despite this judgment, South Africa maintained its obdurate refusal to withdraw. Meanwhile, in 1966 the South West African People's Organization (SWAPO) launched guerrilla warfare to attain the country's independence. The struggle continued for some twenty years, until 1988, when South Africa finally agreed to end its administration of the territory in accordance with a UN peace plan for the region. Namibia, the people's name for the former South West Africa, would finally attain its independence in 1990.

In 1989 Gay founded the Commission of Independence for Namibia. This was a thirty-one-member bipartisan group of distinguished Americans who

Gay McDougall's antiapartheid endeavors followed by her membership on the South African Independent Electoral Commission culminated in watching Nelson Mandela cast his vote in the first all-race election, April 1, 1994. He, of course, became the first African president of South Africa. (UN Photo / Chris Sattlberger)

were responsible for carefully monitoring the nine-month process to independence mandated by the UN: "The Commission successfully intervened to force modifications in critical legislation, such as the voter registration and election laws, which as drafted, threatened the fairness of the election process."[15]

Had her participation in the South African and South West African liberation struggles been her only accomplishments in the field of international human rights, the career of Gay McDougall would have been noteworthy. However, after fourteen years, she stepped away from her position as director of the SAP in 1994 and returned to the United States.

Upon her return, Gay accepted the position of executive director of the International Human Rights Law Group (IHRLG), an NGO founded in Washington, DC, in 1978, and she remained in that position until 2006. Early on in her tenure, the IHRLG described its challenge as finding "the most effective ways to support human rights movements and the individuals who comprise[d] them." With their local partners, they sought "to give voice to human rights concerns; press for justice and accountability from the ground up; and set the international agenda for human rights norms."[16]

When I first interviewed Gay in 2002, the IHRLG was about to celebrate its twenty-fifth anniversary the following year. She had come to work with an organization that she felt "had at least slightly turned in a direction where it had more of a focus on people in other countries and interacting with them than Human Rights Watch did."[17] She noted that in the late 1980s, after the fall of the Berlin Wall, there was an emphasis among American human rights NGOs on going out to other countries to help them write their constitutions and to monitor their elections, in some ways similar to the work she had done in South Africa and Namibia. The IHRLG had established contacts on the ground in various countries around the world; however, when she accepted the position of executive director, the IHRLG was an all-white organization. She was determined to apply the expertise that she had attained from her work with people in southern Africa "helping them to gain the capacity to tear down the walls from the inside" even as she recognized that her work with the IHRLG would be unlike the work she had done in southern Africa.

She was, however, intrigued by the idea of learning whether the model that she had been instrumental in developing could, in some manner, be useful to in-country liberation movements in other parts of the world.

> So I set about refocusing this organization on actually going into countries that . . . we have an interest in and concern about and setting up shop there, to work directly with . . . fledgling human rights movements in those countries. And to help them in their efforts to define what human rights

means to them. And then to help them gain the organizational capacity to carry out their vision, whether it be bringing down a dictator like [Sani] Abacha in Nigeria or building . . . structures to protect rights in countries where all the institutions have been decimated, like they were in Cambodia. Or working with . . . Afro-Brazilian groups to help them figure out how to first spread a sort of progressive consciousness about race and then to challenge racial discrimination in the courts or in policy.

Over the years, McDougall labored to transform the IHRLG into a capacity-building organization; that is, the IHRLG's work in these countries emerged out of what people inside the countries determined that they needed and wanted. Based on those evaluations, the IHRLG tried to support the fledgling human rights groups with whatever resources it could, including training, expertise, and technical assistance. The IHRLG supported people in their efforts to envision human rights, and then it worked with them to develop the organizational capacity to carry out their visions: "In all cases we bring an access to the international community and particularly the institutions at the UN or the Organization of American States or the Organization of African Unity" (more recently, the African Union). The IHRLG helped people learn how to use those resources appropriately, "how to lobby and maneuver and to focus world attention through those institutions on their issues and their problems." When we spoke in 2002, the IHRLG was operating in a dozen countries with long-term staff on the ground that was working every day with local human rights groups. Thus, the mission of the IHRLG was transformed even as its name was changed in 2003 to Global Rights: Partners for Justice to reflect the expansive mission.

Global Rights was committed to increasing access to justice for poor and marginalized groups, to promoting women's rights and gender equality, and to advancing racial and ethnic equality. It also developed special initiatives for the rights of LGBT and intersex people. Global Rights was convinced that long-term systemic change would, and could, only happen when stakeholders were deeply involved in the transformational processes. It was committed to transferring knowledge and skills to local partners to ensure that the work would continue after the training Global Rights provided was completed and it left.

Even as she has engaged in these international endeavors, McDougall has also attempted to build America's consciousness about major issues in the world in areas such as Latin America. She pointed out that the International Human Rights Law Group, much like other "aggressive, largely white organizations" formed in the 1970s in the United States, "had spent a lot of time working in Latin America helping to get rid of the dictators in Latin America." Certainly, that was a critical endeavor; however, when Gay arrived to work with the IHRLG, she reminded them that the dictators were gone, so the question had become, "What are the current cutting-edge human rights issues . . . in Latin America?" She felt that there were two or three critical issues, the most prominent being race, and not just in the most likely countries hosting large African-descended communities such as Brazil and Panama but in other countries where this issue had been neglected, including Colombia, Chile, Paraguay, and Uruguay. The IHRLG deployed many resources to help those communities gain international visibility and construct additional strategies to challenge the structures that supported racism.

The IHRLG also focused on women in Latin America who were enduring very difficult conditions. When I spoke with Gay in 2002, she had just returned from Peru, where she had been working with a group that was committed to educating girls. According to the people she was working with, girls, particularly in rural areas, were frequently attacked, often sexually assaulted, as a way of dissuading them from pursuing an education. In order to ensure that girls could attend school, it was necessary to provide security protection to ensure their safety. Gay also insisted that gender and the rights of indigenous peoples were two interrelated issues requiring sustained attention. Thus, the IHRLG's mission included supporting the development of gender equity laws along with the development of indigenous leaders who understood and supported gender equity.

The IHRLG sponsored numerous programs throughout Africa, including Burundi, DRC, Nigeria, Sierra Leone, and Morocco. It also had a project in Yemen; was working in Cambodia, Bosnia, Sarajevo, Nicaragua, and Brazil; and was planning to establish projects in Mongolia and East Timor.

Additionally, Gay was deeply committed to "bringing human rights home" to the United States. In her article "Shame in Our Own House," Gay revisited the United States' fraught relationship with the international human rights movement: "In its relations with the rest of the world, America struggles with a profound contradiction. On the one hand our country has been a pioneer in the human rights movement, providing much of the language and inspiration for international efforts to win equality for all. On the other hand, our government has repeatedly blocked attempts to bring these rights home to America's own racial minorities, and that hypocrisy lurks at the core of our moral identity as a nation, undermining our claims to global leadership."[18]

As she engaged in the project of bringing human rights home, Gay set about supporting initiatives that focused on racism in the United States, a topic she insists was of little interest to traditional American human rights scholars and activists. According to Gay, American NGOs were negligent in recognizing that there were serious human rights issues within the borders of the United States that required the attention of international human rights practitioners. She observed, "At least within the US, the international human rights label has been traditionally applied to a limited group of organizations and individuals that have primarily been concerned with foreign policy issues—issues of rights outside of the United States. And [they] have been almost totally and uniformly white." So, for example, although she brought to the field of human rights twenty years of experiences in southern African liberation struggles, she learned that those people involved in what she termed "the international human rights club" did not believe that the "community of people who were involved in African liberation were properly within the definition of human rights."

Meanwhile, and perhaps at least partially because of such perceptions, American civil rights attorneys and activists did not seriously view themselves as being members of the larger community of the international human rights movement. According to Gay, American civil rights practitioners usually limited any engagement in the international human rights arena to race and racism, with, at best, limited attention to the UN Convention on the Elimination of Racial Discrimination (CERD). Gay insists that "this lack of connection between the civil rights movement in America and the global human rights movement is a tremendous loss. Even our understanding of what justice is about has been narrowed and clouded by it."[19]

The Council on Civil Rights exemplified this resistance to the broader movement of international human rights. Established in 1950 by A. Philip Randolph, founder of the Brotherhood of Sleeping Car Porters; Roy Wilkins, longtime executive director of the NAACP; and Arnold Aronson, a leader of the National Jewish Community Relations Advisory Board, the Leadership Conference on Civil Rights was an umbrella organization that was established with thirty civil rights and labor movement organizations. Committed to liberation and social justice through focusing on civil rights, they were certain that only through alliances and coalitions would they be able to lobby successfully to pass the necessary legislation to extend and protect civil rights. Throughout the 1950s and 1960s as activists demonstrated in the streets, their influential contribution to the movement was to lobby diligently for passage of the Civil Rights Acts of 1957, 1960, and 1964, the Voting Rights Act of 1965, and the Fair Housing Act of 1968. Over the years, membership in the conference has grown to more than two hundred organizations, and in 2010 the name was finally changed to the Leadership Conference on Civil and Human Rights.

From behind the scenes, Gay encouraged the ongoing transition from the limited civil rights agenda to a more expansive emphasis on the broader human rights perspective. For example, she found money to finance representatives from the Leadership Conference to attend the 2001 UN World Conference against Racism, Racial Discrimination, Xenophobia and Related Intolerance (WCAR) in Durban, South Africa. In addition to supporting grassroots organizations from around the world, she also financially supported representatives of American grassroots organizations, including Sarah White from the Mississippi Workers' Center for Human Rights, to attend the conference. "It is good news that American civil-rights organizations have recently begun to examine the relevance and meaning of international human-rights norms to our struggle here at home."[20]

Acknowledging that while much work has been done to build bridges between the human rights and civil rights communities, Gay recognized a need for continued diligence "on a wide array of other issues. You know, our community still doesn't see itself as part of the global movement and doesn't see that those issues are, you know, of the same content, character, nature, etc., and that it benefits us here to use these systems of international human rights language. You know? Claim those rights, raise our issues, and be participants in the processes and in the arena [of] international human rights!" She observed that the problem of the disconnect between the two communities persists and, further, that "of course the [international human rights] club still exists. But as far as I'm concerned, clubs exist until the excluded group decides it's worth tearing down the walls. And I think that we have not fully decided that—yet. So the club goes on and exists."

McDougall confirmed in our more recent interview in 2018 that the point of her current and future endeavors is to address this serious shortcoming: "A bridge has to be built between the white human rights movement in this country and the civil rights work in this country." She insisted that "all those people who are working on the ground on local issues need to be elevated and connected to the global movement." For too long they have been ignored by white groups, and she is committed to building the necessary bridges between these groups. To that end, early in the 1990s she initiated a focus on race issues in the United States at the IHRLG. Just as the IHRLG had been working to empower human rights groups in nations around the world, it began working to empower the endeavors of grassroots organizations in the United States and to see that they were enabled to establish relationships with other groups around the world.[21]

Even as she engaged in the process of transforming the IHRLG into Global Rights: Partners for Justice, Gay, a master multitasker, was simultaneously forging ahead with crucial initiatives in different capacities at the UN. For example, she was elected in 1995 by the UN Commission on Human Rights to a four-year term as an alternate member of the Subcommission on the Prevention of Discrimination and Protection of Minorities. While serving in that capacity, she was appointed a special rapporteur (1995–99) to investigate the issues of systematic rape, sexual slavery, and slavery-like practices in armed conflict. She was originally commissioned to serve as a special rapporteur in response to shocking revelations concerning more than two hundred thousand women enslaved by the Japanese military during World War II at "comfort stations," but she was not limited to investigating only that issue. Based on her careful research, she produced a wide-ranging, groundbreaking, highly regarded study, which was presented to the Subcommission on Human Rights. It called for the development of international legal standards for prosecuting acts of systematic rape and sexual slavery committed during armed conflict. The International Criminal Tribunal for the former Yugoslavia, discussed in chapter 2, cited this report as an authorized statement of international criminal law that in turn informed the decisions rendered in the Bosnia and Herzegovina trials. As the special rapporteur, she also toured Sierra Leone with the UN high commissioner for human rights to assess the devastating impact of civil war on the civilian population.

In 1998 she became the first American elected to serve as an independent expert on the UN committee that oversees compliance with the CERD, an eighteen-member body of experts. In that capacity, she was deeply involved in the preparation of General Recommendation 25: Gender-Related Dimensions of Racial Discrimination. UN recommendations might be understood as comparable to amendments to the US Constitution in that they seek to address a problem that may have been overlooked or even unknown at the time of promulgation. In this case, Recommendation 25 sought to remedy a lacuna in both CERD and CEDAW (Convention on the Elimination of All Forms of Discrimination Against Women). At the time they came into existence, neither convention addressed the complexity of discrimination and therefore failed to address the ways in which racism reverberates through gender and how sexism can and does further distort the social construction of race. In this recommendation, the Committee on the Elimination of Racial Discrimination "notes that racial discrimination does not always affect women and men equally or in the same way. There are circumstances in which racial discrimination only or primarily affects women. Or affects women in a different way, or [to] a different degree than men. Such racial discrimination will often escape detection if there is no explicit recognition or acknowledgement of the different life experiences of women and men, in areas of both public and private life." The recommendation acknowledges that women have often been the target of certain forms of discrimination because of their gender. It specifically highlights "the sexual violence that is committed against women because of their membership in particular racial or ethnic groups in detention or armed conflict, the coerced sterilization of indigenous women; abuse of women workers in the informal sector or domestic workers employed abroad by their employers."[22]

From 2005 to 2011, Gay was the first UN independent expert on minority issues under a mandate that was established by what was then the UN Commission on Human Rights. This appointment was later reviewed and confirmed by the new Human Rights Council in 2008. She felt strongly that this position was a "tremendous opportunity to shape a vehicle that would bridge the gap between the process of norm-setting and the realities on the ground for millions of people who would never visit the chambers of the United Nations." Furthermore, she understood this was an "opportunity to inform the norm-making process, to infuse into it the realities of the lives of minorities in remote places around the world."[23]

The UN Declaration on the Rights of Persons Belonging to National or Ethnic, Religious and Linguistic Minorities was, according to Gay, very narrowly focused on "problems that arose out of mid-twentieth-century European wars."[24] Furthermore, she observed that the United Nations established parallel and separate definitions, legal instruments, and mechanisms for persons belonging to minorities and indigenous persons: "The rights of indigenous persons are recognized in the United Nations Declaration on the Rights of Indigenous Peoples adopted by the General Assembly on 13 September 2007 and the International Labor Organization's Indigenous and Tribal Peoples Convention. Indigenous persons fall outside the mandate of the Independent Expert on Minority Issues." Despite this discrepancy, as the independent expert she was provided with an unprecedented opportunity to move beyond the limitations of a European perspective to bestow a twenty-first-century global face upon the issue of minority rights. As she examined minority populations around the world, it became clear to her that there were pronounced linkages between discrimination and poverty; "extreme measures of exclusion like denationalization sometimes resulting in statelessness; and an international industry of conflict prevention that appeared to not be sufficiently mindful of the relationship between conflict and the denial of the rights of minorities." Further, she felt very strongly that "the UN as an institution had an appalling lack of minority voices across all of its institutional mechanisms. The voices of oppressed minorities were generally presented to describe the problems and sufferings, not to be experts in developing solutions."[25]

Once she began her work with the mandate, McDougall quickly became cognizant of the relative lack of knowledge about the declaration outside of "academic circles, European regional bodies and the Organization for Security and Co-operation in Europe (OSCE)."[26] At the level of civil society, Gay observed that knowledge about the declaration was virtually nonexistent, with the exception of the fortunate few who were able to participate in the Office of the High Commissioner for Human Rights Fellows Program or who had been invited to make a presentation before the UN Working Group on Minorities.[27]

UN global norm-setting is a gradual process that evolves over time to bring countries to consensus around a particular international concern. In the mid-twentieth century, the focus on the evolution of a norm on the elimination of racial discrimination culminated in the 1965 adoption of the Convention on the Elimination of All Forms of Racial Discrimination by the UN General Assembly. Soon afterward, the rights of minorities were briefly addressed in the 1966 International Covenant on Civil and Political Rights. Article 27 states that persons belonging to ethnic, religious, or linguistic minorities should not be denied their rights to "enjoy their own culture, to profess and practice their own religion or to use their own language."[28] Later, in 1989, the Convention on the Rights of the Child provided in article 30 that indigenous children or children with ethnic, religious, or linguistic origins had the right to live in a community with other members of their group, to practice their religion, and to use their own language.

The world was confronted by a wide array of appalling situations during the late 1980s and early 1990s, including ethnic cleansing in Bosnia, genocides in Rwanda and Darfur, and conflicts in Chechnya and Kosovo. Building on the provisions of the earlier instruments and in response to these crises, the UN General Assembly adopted in 1992 the Declaration on the Rights of Persons Belonging to National or Ethnic, Religious and Linguistic Minorities, which at that time was the only UN instrument solely devoted to the rights of minorities. The Human Rights Committee would later adopt general comment no. 23 to provide an authoritative interpretation of article 27 of the Covenant on Civil and Political Rights on minority rights.

Th Working Group on Minorities, a subcommission of the Promotion and Protection of Human Rights, was established in 1995 by an Economic and Social Council resolution. Between 1995 and 2005, that working group met five days each year in Geneva, Switzerland, to develop a deeper understanding of minority issues and to create solutions to the problems that minorities were experiencing. According to Gay, however, the most comprehensive document that reviews the legal obligations and makes recommendations as to racial discrimination and the situation of minorities is the 2001 Declaration and Programme of Action of the World Conference against Racism, Racial Discrimination, Xenophobia and Related Intolerance, and as such it informed her mandate as the independent expert on minority affairs.

As the independent expert, McDougall's voluminous portfolio included:

a. Promot[ing] the implementation of the Declaration on the Rights of Persons Belonging to National or Ethnic, Religious and Linguistic Minorities, including through consultation with Governments, taking into account existing international standards and national legislation concerning minorities;
b. Identify[ing] best practices and possibilities for technical cooperation by the Office of the United Nations High Commissioner for Human Rights at the request of Governments;
c. Apply[ing] a gender perspective in . . . her work;
d. Cooperat[ing] closely, while avoiding duplication with existing relevant United Nations bodies, mandates, mechanisms as well as regional organizations; and
e. Tak[ing] into account the views of non-governmental organizations on matters pertaining to . . . her mandate.[29]

Charged by both the Human Rights Commission and the high commissioner on human rights, Gay began carefully articulating her understanding of the term "minority" and developing the broad areas of concern that she intended to address. Drawing from her previous endeavors in South Africa and Namibia, she was determined to move beyond the notion that minority status was defined only by numerical factors. Instead, "the focus would be on groups that are disproportionately disadvantaged because of discrimination and that are otherwise denied the power to protect their rights."[30] On this basis, she developed the four broad areas of concern relating to minorities that would serve to guide her work as the independent expert:

a. Protecting a minority's existence including through protection of their physical integrity and the prevention of genocide;
b. Protecting and promoting cultural and social identity, including the right of individuals to choose which ethnic, linguistic, or religious groups they wish to be identified with, and the right of those groups to affirm and protect their collective identity and to reject forced assimilation;
c. Ensuring effective non-discrimination and equality, including ending structural or systemic discrimination;
d. Ensuring effective participation of members of minorities in public life, especially with regard to decisions that affect them.[31]

McDougall used those critical concerns to form a framework for evaluating the situations she encountered in the countries that she visited.[32]

During the first six years of her mandate, she was able to make twelve official country visits. Although she had planned to make thirteen additional visits, the governments of those countries deployed the sacrosanct UN tradition of protecting national sovereignty to ignore her requests for an invitation. Their refusal to welcome her to conduct the mandate in their specific country suggests their extreme reluctance to invite international scrutiny of their treatment of minorities. She described her visit to five additional countries as activities designed to promote greater awareness of the declaration. She communicated with governments through official letters regarding violations and failures to fulfill the rights of members of minority groups. She also held three expert seminars, including one that was cosponsored by the Inter-American Commission on Human Rights. During this seminar, experts worked on what was then a draft of their regional convention on racial discrimination.[33] Additionally, she organized three forums on minority issues. The theme of the first forum was "Minorities and the Equal Right to Quality Education," the second was "Minorities and the Right to Equal Participation in Economic Life," and the third was "Minority Rights and Conflict Prevention." Three thematic reports were produced from these forums, one of which was presented to the UN General Assembly.[34]

Gay assessed the mandate in the following manner: "[It] proved to be an unparalleled mechanism to extend the reach of the Declaration out of the elite chambers of international norm setting and into the real world where exclusion and marginalization are daily facts on the ground. The high-level access given to cabinet ministers and even heads of state during my country visits created an opportunity to bring the Declaration to the attention of national governments as never before." Her country visits provided her with an unprecedented opportunity to build relationships with members of civil societies, many of whom were often unaware of the declaration and of existing UN mechanisms that they could use to strengthen and further their work at the local level. But most important to Gay was that the country visits afforded her with opportunities to interact directly with minority communities. "Often that meant traveling far outside of the major urban centers, to areas where infrastructure was poor to non-existent. That is where the promise of the Declaration were most meaningful."[35]

Gay McDougall has garnered numerous prestigious awards throughout her multifaceted career. For example, in 1999 she was awarded a MacArthur Fellowship—known more colloquially as the "Genius Award"—for her groundbreaking work in the field of human rights. The American Society of International Law awarded the Goler T. Butcher Medal to Gay in 2011 for a lifetime of leadership in human rights advocacy. Incidentally, she and Butcher were close colleagues who worked together for twenty years on international human rights projects. Thus this award was quite appropriate because it recognized that she, much like Butcher, was fiercely committed to the general advancement of international human rights. In 2015 she was also the recipient of the Order of the Companions of O. R. Tambo, which is awarded to "eminent foreigner persons" for their "friendship to South Africa." It was given to her for her "excellent contribution in the fight against apartheid or injustices meted out on the Black majority."[36]

As she contemplated her long career in the field of international human rights, Gay insisted, "I can't imagine that I could have had a more exciting and satisfying career. This has taken me right to the front lines of a lot of human dramas. I've learned that there is a lot of suffering in the world but right there is where you find all of the people who have an amazing wherewithal to overcome suffering, so you walk away with a net gain in terms of inspiration and hope."[37]

Conclusion

Remember, we are not fighting for the freedom of the Negro alone, but for the freedom of the human spirit, a larger freedom that encompasses all mankind.

Ella Baker, speech in Hattiesburg, 1964

We are caught in an inescapable network of mutuality tied in a single knot of destiny. Whatever affects one directly, affects all indirectly.

Dr. Martin Luther King Jr., *Letter from a Birmingham Jail*, 1963

Expediency won't get you to the promised land.

Fannie Lou Hamer, as told to Barbara Phillips

Appalled, infuriated, provoked, and, perhaps most important, determined at the dawn of the second millennium, many Black women found that they were still, in the words of Fannie Lou Hamer, "sick and tired" of carrying the burden of destructive multiple and interrelated human abuses. Disheartened that the promise of the long civil rights movement had not realized its full potential and indeed that many of those gains were faltering under the onslaught of a wicked backlash, many women felt obliged to seek stronger and better solutions to the complexities of oppressions. This book has explored some of the innovative interventions of capable and visionary Black women who were and still are determined to contribute to the improbable task of building a better world.

Women—especially Black and other women of color—have, more often than not, been omitted from formal written history, or if they are included, their stories have been poorly told. For years, for example, the story of Rosa Parks sparking the Montgomery bus boycott focused upon the mythology of her so-called tired feet but omitted the crucial years she spent laboring in the dangerous trenches of antiracism and antisexism work in the Deep South.[1] Not only were the many years she spent fighting against segregation and seeking legal remedies for many Black women who had been sexually abused by white men in Alabama overlooked, but the stories of the critical contributions of other Black women, the unsung "sheroes" and foot soldiers of the revolution, were also neglected.

Also neglected by scholars until recently are the stories of those who move through the pages of this book, those who are endeavoring to construct a world that honors the vision of human rights from conceptualization to implementation. This book, then, is an intervention that sets about the task of retrieving the modern history of Black women's contributions to the development of contemporary international human rights. The fourteen women who are featured here can be characterized as exemplars of Goler Teal Butcher's legacy of impassioned human rights scholarship and activism. They are contributing to a contemporary tradition of visionary yet practical audacity. That is, they are realistic, constructive, pragmatic, and capable, yet at the same time they are also boldly intrepid and courageous. They are quite willing and able to challenge and transgress the imposed boundaries of norms that have not protected their humanity, and they do so in order to shepherd societies toward an encompassing vision and practice of human rights.

The work of these women is sophisticated and complicated and therefore does not easily lend itself to categorization. While many have attained law degrees, the way they have chosen to wield those degrees varies from researching, writing, and teaching about international law in law schools around this country to practicing law in international tribunals and courts as judges and prosecutors. Because the United States consistently refuses to ratify international human rights treaties, at least one of the law professors has worked with city governments to implement CEDAW and/or DEVAW into their local ordinances. As a student, she had helped prepare the legal briefs that moved through the legal system challenging the imprisonment of Haitians in Guantánamo Bay rather than extending asylum to them in the United States.

Yet human rights do not reside solely in law schools, nor are they the exclusive property of international lawyers working at the UN in New York or its global ancillary offices. Others without formal legal backgrounds have brought their considerable skills to the task of implementing human rights through leading small local nongovernmental organizations (NGOs) in the seemingly unlikely outlying venues of Greenview, Mississippi, Berkeley, California, and Atlanta, Georgia, for example. Still others serve in larger and more robustly funded organizations in the more cosmopolitan venues of Washington, DC, and New York City. Some acquired degrees in disciplines such as anthropology, English, sociology, and public health to, as one respondent quipped, "put some theory in her practice." All, however, have been careful to ensure that their formal educations do not overshadow their unwavering commitment to transformative activism; instead, those educations enhance that commitment.

Each woman has focused upon the particular issue that she has identified as critical, from providing support for workers' rights; to addressing the impact of HIV/AIDS on the lives of Black women, their families, and their communities; to expanding reproductive rights into a movement for reproductive justice. One has sought to (re)claim progressive visions of women's rights under the auspices of Islam, while at least one has had a profound impact on the antiapartheid struggles of South Africa, and another was deeply involved in drafting a Palestinian constitution that incorporated a human rights perspective. Some learned to negotiate the inner sanctum of the United Nations in order to contribute to the critical processes of forging global consensus around the development of international norms of nondiscrimination. They understood that forging consensus is, in turn, absolutely crucial to the expansion of the human rights corpus.

It is important to acknowledge that these fourteen women are certainly not alone in either their visions or their endeavors. Although I was only able to include fourteen of the eighteen women I originally interviewed for this book, I would be remiss if I did not also call attention to the important work of Julianne Cartwright Traylor and Barbara Arnwine. An independent human rights practitioner, Traylor has taken leadership roles in a variety of human rights organization, including, most notably, serving as chair of the Amnesty International USA board of directors. She is an international human rights educator, consultant, researcher, and grassroots organizer and was a founding member of the Human Rights Advocates, based in Berkeley and recognized by the UN Economic and Social Council. This organization advises and assists US lawyers involved in lawsuits that could effectively incorporate international human rights law into their cases. Traylor resided in Oslo, Norway, for five years as a fellow at the International Peace Research Center, where, like Goler Butcher, she researched the idea of food as a human right. She also studied in Geneva, Switzerland, as an intern in the Ford Foundation Human Rights Internship Program. She is a highly sought-after speaker and human rights educator for schools, universities, law schools, and civic organizations. She too has attended and brought groups to important UN world conferences on gender and racism.

Barbara Arnwine served as the national executive director of the Lawyers' Committee for Civil Rights Under Law from 1989 until 2015. Thus, her human rights initiatives were filtered through her advocacy of civil rights. From that perspective, she served as the head of the electoral observers' delegation for the South African election in 1994. That same year she also went to Guantánamo

Bay to investigate the conditions of the Haitian refugees. In 1995 she assembled a large delegation of US Black women attorneys and brought them to the NGO Forum for the Fourth World Conference on Women in Beijing.

Within the context of their dedication to bringing to fruition the promise of human rights, each of these women has honed her human rights expertise and dexterity through education and practice, even as she has also fostered creative alliances. As these human rights scholar-practitioners have toiled away at these seemingly disjointed endeavors in far-flung venues, they have felt compelled to establish supportive relationships with one another and with others who share their commitment to creating and embodying visions of an expansive network of international human rights. Emerging from the affinity of their varied interests, they have also created mutually beneficial alliances in which they share expertise, encouragement, and support. Some, for example, are members of the US Human Rights Network. Sixty of the most prominent individual and influential social and human rights activists met together in 2003, and from that meeting the US Human Rights Network was established to "strengthen a human rights movement and culture in the United States." Today it boasts a membership of three hundred partner organizations and individual memberships, with Lisa Crooms (Robinson) currently serving on its board of directors.

Although all women featured in this book are leaders in their own right in this complicated and all-consuming work, they have also come to rely upon each other, to learn from each other, to mentor each other, and to share information about funding resources informally but also often through the Human Rights Network. Much like Women Living under Muslim Laws, the network essentially operates in parallel yet frequently intertwined relationships with one another. Together and with other colleagues elsewhere beyond this book, they are constructing both national and international networks of human rights practitioners who are intent upon and committed to contributing to the evolving, innovative, fascinating, yet sometimes tedious and radical vision of social justice offered by the global movement of international human rights.

Notes

Introduction

1. Audrey Thomas McCluskey and Elaine M. Smith, eds., *Mary McLeod Bethune: Building a Better World* (Bloomington: Indiana University Press, 1999). See also "Biography: Mary McLeod Bethune," PBS, *American Experience*, accessed February 13, 2017, www.pbs.org/wgbn/americanexperience/features/biography/eleanor-bethune/.

2. Hanes Walton Jr., *Black Women at the United Nations: The Politics, a Theoretical Model and the Documents*, edited by Paul David Seldis and Mary A. Burgess (San Bernardino, CA: Borgo Press, 1995), 8.

3. Shelby Lewis, "Black Women at the Founding Conference," in Walton, *Black Women at the United Nations*, 20, 21.

4. The center of the International Bill of Rights is the Universal Declaration of Human Rights, flanked on either side by the Covenant on Civil and Political Rights and the Covenant on Economic, Social, and Cultural Rights.

5. Race men and women were devoted to improving the lives of Black people. They consistently confronted and challenged political, economic, and social threats to the well-being of Black people and their organizations, institutions, and ideas.

6. Lewis, "Black Women," 17.

7. This chapter's opening epigraph is Butcher's paraphrasing of Reinhold Niebuhr's quote "Nothing that is worth doing can be achieved in a lifetime; therefore, we must be saved by hope."

8. J. Clay Smith Jr., "Tribute: United States Foreign Policy and Goler Teal Butcher," *Howard Law Journal* 37, no. 139 (1994): 6.

9. Ibid., 55, 22.

10. Henry J. Richardson III, "Tribute: African Americans and International Law: For Professor Goler Teal Butcher, with Appreciation," *Howard Law Journal* 37, no. 217 (1994): 7.

11. Smith, "Tribute," 20.

12. Richardson, "Tribute," 6.

13. Paul Gordon Lauren, *The Evolution of International Human Rights: Visions Seen* (Philadelphia: University of Pennsylvania Press, 2011), 1.

14. Lee Ann Banaszak, *The US Women's Movement in Global Perspective* (Lanham, MD: Rowman & Littlefield, 2006), 20, 320.

Chapter 1. A Global Feminist "Jurisprudence of Resistance"

1. For information about the development of critical race theory, see Kimberlé Crenshaw, Neil Gotanda, Gary Peller, and Kendall Thomas, eds., *Critical Race Theory: The Key Writings That Formed the Movement* (New York: New Press, 1995); Richard Delgado and Jean Stefancic, *Critical Race Theory: The Cutting Edge*, 2nd ed. (Philadelphia: Temple University Press, 2000). See also Kimberlé Williams Crenshaw, "The First Decade: Critical Reflections, or 'a Foot in the Closing Door,'" *UCLA Law Review* 49, no. 1343 (June 2002): 1343–72; and Athena D. Mutua, "The Rise, Development and Future Directions of Critical Race Theory and Related Scholarship," *Denver University Law Review* 84, no. 2 (December 2006): 329–94.

2. Derick Bell, *Race, Racism and American Law* (Boston: Little, Brown, 1973).

3. The Howard University Law School was often referred to as the laboratory for civil rights. Throughout the 1930s and 1940s, Howard trained many of the lawyers and developed innovative strategies that were deployed in the struggle to legally dismantle de jure segregation—a struggle that was highlighted by, and culminated in, the 1954 Supreme Court decision of *Brown v. Board of Education*.

4. Crenshaw, "The First Decade," 14.

5. Ibid., 16.

6. As described in Mutua, "Rise, Development and Future Directions," 347.

7. Adrien Katherine Wing, ed., *Critical Race Feminism: A Reader* (New York: New York University Press, 1997), 2.

8. Cheryl I. Harris, "Law Professors of Color and the Academy: Of Poets and Kings," in Wing, *Critical Race Feminism*, 101.

9. Ibid., 102. The quotation in my chapter title is a modification of this quotation.

10. Unless otherwise indicated, the information on Adrien Wing is compiled from my phone interview with her on July 28, 2004. At that time, she was in Iowa City, Iowa, while I was in Madison, Wisconsin.

11. Constance Baker Motley was the first African American woman accepted at the Columbia Law School, the first to be elected to the New York Senate, the first woman and the first Black to hold the position of Manhattan borough president, and the first Black woman appointed to serve as a federal district judge. President Lyndon Johnson appointed her to the US District Court for the Southern District of New York. For sixteen years she was an attorney with the NAACP LDF and litigated many cases during the civil rights era. She was the only woman on the legal team in the landmark *Brown v. Board of Education* Supreme Court case. She won nine of the ten cases she tried before the Supreme Court. See "The National Women's History Project," accessed May 27, 2013, www.nwph.org/whm/motley_bio.phy.

12. See David M. Mastio, "Wing Nut," *Weekly Standard*, May 27, 1996.

13. The first woman of color appointed to a tenured professorship at Harvard Law School, Lani Guinier is a theorist who specializes in American civil rights jurisprudence. In 1993 President Bill Clinton nominated her for the position of Assistant Attorney General for Civil Rights. Her scholarship and writings were unfairly characterized and came under blistering attack from conservatives (many would argue in retaliation for the Supreme Court hearings on Robert Bork). She was never provided with an opportunity by the Clinton administration to meet with senators or to testify in front of the judiciary committee. Instead her nomination was withdrawn by President Clinton.

14. Dr. Ralph Bunche, the first African American Nobel Peace Prize winner, had an illustrious career in education, at the US State Department, and with the UN. He was principal secretary of the UN Palestine Commission. He became an acting UN mediator in 1948 and after months of ceaseless negotiations was eventually able to attain signatures on armistice agreements between Israel and the Arab States.

15. The nine components of the Amer-I-Can program are motivation, conditioning, attitudes, and habits; goal setting; problem-solving and decision-making; emotional control; family relationships; financial stability; effective communication; job search and retention; and drug and alcohol abuse. "Program Components," accessed May 27, 2013, www.amer-i-can.org/program/program.html.

16. Michael O'Keeffe, "Former NFl Legend Jim Brown Teaches through 25-Year-Old Program Amer-I-Can Foundation," *New York Daily News*, November 6, 2011.

17. See Adrien Wing and Christine Willis, "Critical Race Feminism: Black Women and Gangs," *Journal of Gender, Race & Justice* 1, no. 141 (1997). A condensed version of the article, titled "Sisters in the Hood: Beyond Bloods and Crips," is in Wing, *Critical Race Feminism* 243–54. See also Adrien K. Wing and Christine A. Willis, "From Theory to Praxis: Black Women, Gangs, and Critical Race Feminism," *La Raza Law Journal* 11, no. 1 (1999): 1–15; and Adrien K. Wing, "Black Women and Gangs," in *States of Confinement: Policing, Detention and Prisons*, ed. Joy James (New York: St Martin's, 2000), 94–105.

18. While the term "polygamy" refers to various kinds of multiple marriages, the technical term for this variation would be "polygyny." Wing has written about cross-cultural polygamy. See "Polygamy from Southern Africa to Black Britannia to Black America: Global Critical Race Feminism as Legal Reform for the Twenty-First Century," *Journal of Contemporary Legal Issues* 12, no. 137 (2001): 811–80. See also "Polygamy in Black America," in *Critical Race Feminism: A Reader*, 2nd ed., ed. Adrien Wing (New York: New York University Press, 2003), 186–94.

19. bell hooks, *Feminist Theory: From Margin to Center* (Boston: South End, 1984), 24–25.

20. Unless otherwise indicated, the information in this chapter, including quotations, is a compilation of my interview with Professor Lisa Crooms on October 17, 2003.

21. In 1987 Tawana Brawley was the center of an extremely controversial case in which the teenager claimed that she had been abducted by six white law enforcement

officers who raped her, wrote racist epithets on her body, and smeared her body with feces.

22. The Wilmington Ten—nine Black men and one white woman—were wrongfully convicted in 1972 of firebombing a grocery store during an intense struggle for civil rights in Wilmington, North Carolina. Over the next forty years, their convictions, tainted by racism, were eventually reduced in 1978. Later the convictions were overturned, and group members were finally pardoned by then outgoing governor Beverly Perdue.

23. UN General Assembly, Declaration on the Elimination of Violence against Women, Article 1, A/RES/48/104, December 20, 1993.

24. Lisa Crooms, "Using a Multi-tiered Analysis to Reconceptualize Gender-Based Violence against Women as a Matter of International Human Rights," *New England Law Review* 33, no. 4 (Summer 1999): 887–88.

25. Ibid., 881, 882, 883.

26. Ibid., 884.

27. Ibid., 889, 890.

28. Ibid., 892, 893, 896.

29. Unless otherwise indicated, information on Professor Hope Lewis was compiled from my interview with her on July 14, 2003, at Northeastern University in Boston. Sadly, Dr. Lewis passed away on December 6, 2016, at the age of fifty-four after a long illness. She was an extraordinary scholar and activist who cofounded Northeastern Univesity Law School's program on Human Rights and the Global Economy, and served as the faculty director of the law school's Global Legal Studies Program. She was a prolific writer who produced many scholarly articles and op ed pieces for newspapers. She coauthored with Jeanne M. Woods the seminal textbook *Human Rights and the Global Market Place: Economic, Social and Cultural Dimensions* (2005). She also co-drafted and compiled the "Boston Principles on the Economic, Social and Cultural Rights of Non-citizens." She was a brilliant and gracious scholar activist even as she adroitly negotiated her issues with blindness. She, so appropriately, signed her correspondence "Peace, Hope" and is fondly remembered and sorely missed.

30. David Hall would later become dean of the law school and still later provost at Northeastern.

31. Hope Lewis, "Lionheart Gals Facing the Dragon: The Human Rights of Inter/national Black Women in the United States," *Oregon Law Review* 76 (1997): 625–26.

32. Ibid., 574, 576. According to Lewis, in Jamaican dialect "lionheart gals" refers to "courageous women" (567).

33. Ibid., 602–3, 604, 605–6.

34. Ibid., 606.

35. Ibid., 607.

36. Ibid., 608–9.

37. Ibid., 618.

38. Ibid., 613–14.

39. Ibid., 618, 621, 624.

40. Unless otherwise indicated, the information compiled on Professor Catherine Powell was obtained from my interview with her on May 25, 2004, at Fordham University in New York City.

41. It was called the Ford Fellowship in Public and International Law.

42. Attorney Zoë Baird was also nominated by President Bill Clinton in 1993 to serve as the first female Attorney General of the United States. She was forced to withdraw from consideration when it was discovered that she had hired undocumented immigrants and failed to pay social security taxes for them. This unfortunate incident was dubbed the "Nannygate matter."

43. Catherine Powell, "Dialogic Federalism: Constitutional Possibilities for Incorporation of Human Rights Law in the United States," *University of Pennsylvania Law Review* 150, no. 1 (November 2001): 245.

44. Ibid., 249, quoting Robert M. Cover and T. Alexander Aleinikoff, "Dialectical Federalism: Habeas Corpus and the Court," *Yale Law Journal* 86 (1977): 1035, 1047.

45. Ibid., 250, quoting Karen Knop, "Here and There: International Law in Domestic Courts," *New York University Journal International Law and Politics* 32, no. 2 (2000): 501, 504–5.

46. Ibid., 251.

47. Ibid., 255, 256, 260.

48. The US government has managed to ratify the Covenant on Civil and Political Rights but not the Covent on Economic, Social and Cultural Rights. It finally ratified the Convention on the Elimination of All Forms of Racial Discrimination, although it has yet to ratify CEDAW or CRC, the Convention on the Rights of the Child.

49. Powell, "Dialogic Federalism," 261–62.

50. Ibid., 254, 260.

51. Ibid., 253.

52. The second approach involves state and local efforts to implement international obligations that the federal government has adopted through ratification but not fully implemented. The third approach, while hypothetical, might be possible. In this case, state and local governments could attempt to apply those human rights principles that the US government filed reservations to when ratifying a treaty. Ibid., 274.

53. Ibid., 277–78.

54. Mark Sappenfield, "In One US City, Life under a UN Treaty on Women," *Christian Science Monitor*, January 30, 2003. Krishanti Dharmaraj and Wennie Kusma had attended the conference in Beijing and were determined "to bring Beijing home." They did so by cofounding WILD in San Francisco.

55. Powell, "Dialogic Federalism," 279.

56. New York City Human Rights Initiative, accessed May 30, 2013, www.ACLU.org/hrc/NYC_initiative.pdf.

57. Lisa Crooms, "To Establish My Legitimate Name inside the Consciousness of Strangers: Critical Race Praxis, Progressive Women-of-Color-Theorizing and Human Rights," *Howard Law Journal* 46, no. 2 (Winter 2003): 242.

58. Sally Engle Merry, *Human Rights and Gender Violence: Translating International Law into Local Justice* (Chicago: University of Chicago Press, 2006), 1–2.

Chapter 2. Humanitarian Human Rights

1. The idea of "generations" of rights acknowledges the historical order in which rights developed. Thus, political and civil rights are the oldest and most well-developed rights, while third-generation rights to peace and development are the youngest and least developed rights. The concept does not imply that each generation replaces the previous generation. Rather, the concept is meant to suggest that human rights are expansive and evolving.

2. See Paul Gordon Lauren, *The Evolution of Human Rights: Visions Seen*, 3rd ed. (Philadelphia: University of Pennsylvania Press, 2011), 67–71, for a summary of these early efforts in the development of humanitarian law.

3. Ibid., 68, 69.

4. "100 Years of the Red Cross," *Daily Telegraph*, December 29, 1962, as quoted in ibid., 70.

5. Convention (I) for the Amelioration of the Condition of the Wounded and Sick in Armed Forces in the Fields, Geneva, August 12, 1949.

6. Convention (II) for the Amelioration of the Condition of the Wounded, Sick and Shipwrecked Members of Armed Forces at Sea, Geneva, August 12, 1949.

7. Convention (III) Relative to the Treatment of Prisoners of War.

8. Convention (IV) Relative to the Protection of Civilian Persons in Time of War.

9. Protocol Additional to the Geneva Conventions of 12 August 1949, and Relating to the Protection of Victims of International Armed Conflict (Protocol I), of 8 June 1977.

10. Protocol Additional to the Geneva Conventions of 12 August 1949, and Relating to the Protection of Victims of Non-International Armed Conflicts (Protocol II), of 8 June 1977. Conventions and Protocols of Humanitarian Law can be found at "Geneva Conventions of 1949 and Additional Protocols, and Their Commentaries," International Committee of the Red Cross, accessed December 3, 2020, www.ICRC.org/ihl.nsf/TOPICS?OPENVIW.

11. UN Convention on the Elimination of All Forms of Discrimination Against Women, "General Recommendations Made by the Committee on the Elimination of All Forms of Discrimination Against Women," 11th session, 1992, https://www.un.org/womenwatch/daw/cedaw/.

12. Patricia Viseur Sellers, "The Prosecution of Sexual Violence in Conflict: The Importance of Human Rights as Means of Interpretation," Office of the High Commissioner for Human Rights, n.d., 7, http://www.2.ohchr.org/english/issues/women/docs/Paper_Prosecution_of Sexual_Violence.pdf.

13. Unless otherwise indicated, the information that follows is a compilation from my interview with Judge Gabrielle Kirk McDonald in Houston, Texas, March 12, 2004.

14. Although Kirk did attain a law degree from Howard in the 1960s, her time did not overlap with Goler Teal Butcher's time at the law school. They in fact never met, although McDonald would later be awarded the Goler Teal Butcher Award by the American Society of International Law.

15. Gabrielle Kirk McDonald, "Reflections on My Journey for Justice," in *Black Women and International Law: Deliberate Interactions, Movements and Actions*, ed. Jeremy I. Levitt (New York: Cambridge University Press, 2015), 13.

16. Vietnamese Fishermen's Association v. Knights of the Ku Klux Klan, 518 F. Supp. 993, 1010 (S.D. Tex. 1981).

17. Morris Dees of the Southern Poverty Law Center was one of the lawyers representing the fishermen in this case.

18. See Andrew Chin, "The KKK and Vietnamese Fisherman," University of North Carolina School of Law, accessed December 3, 2020, www.unclaw/chin/scholarship/fishermen.htm.

19. As quoted in Sally J. Kenney, *Gender & Justice: Why Women in the Judiciary Really Matter* (New York: Routledge, 2013), 144.

20. Secretary of State Madeleine K. Albright, remarks at a dinner hosted by the American Bar Association in honor of Gabrielle Kirk McDonald, on the occasion of receiving the ABA CEELI Leadership Award, Supreme Court Great Hall, Washington, DC, April 5, 1999, as released by the Office of the Spokesman, US Department of State. The chapter epigraph by McDonald is from this speech, which included the Albright quote used as this chapter's second epigraph.

21. See UN Doc. 2/25704 at 36, annex (1993), and S/25704/Add.1 (1993), adopted by the Security Council on 25 May 1993, UN Doc. S/Res/827 (1993).

22. Article 1 of the Statute of the International Tribunal for the Prosecution of Persons Responsible for Serious Violations of the International Humanitarian Law Committed in the Territory of the Former Yugoslavia since 1991, UN Doc. S/25704 at 36 annex (1993) and S/25704/Add.1 (1993) adopted by the Security Council on 25 May 1993, UN Doc. S/Res/827 (1993).

23. See article 2 for the complete list of the grave breaches.

24. Gabrielle Kirk McDonald, "Problems, Obstacles and Achievements of the ICTY," *Journal of International Criminal Justice* 2 (2004): 558–71, 558.

25. Elizabeth Neuffer, *The Key to My Neighbor's House: Seeking Justice in Bosnia and Rwanda* (New York: Picador USA, 2001), 80.

26. Ibid., 168.

27. McDonald, "Problems," 559. See also Christopher Greenwood, "The Development of International Humanitarian Law by the International Criminal Tribunal for the Former Yugoslavia," in *Max Planck Yearbook of United Nations Law*, ed. Armin von Bosdandy and Rudiger Wolfrum, vol. 2 (Berlin: Max Planck Institute for Comparative Public Law and International Law, 1998), 100.

28. Greenwood, "The Development," 101–2.

29. McDonald, "Problems," 559–60.

30. Ibid., 563.

31. Greenwood, "The Development," 113.

32. McDonald, "Problems," 561–62.

33. Ibid., 563.

34. Neuffer, *Key to My Neighbor's House*, 180.

35. Ibid., 181.

36. Ibid., 302.

37. James Walsh, "'I'm Kind of a Crusader': With the First War-Crimes Sentence, Judge Gabrielle McDonald Vents Her Passion for Justice," *Time* (Europe), July 28, 1997.

38. Ibid.

39. Greenwood, "The Development," 98.

40. McDonald, "Problems," 564.

41. Ibid., 569.

42. Unless otherwise indicated, the information about Patricia Viseur Sellers is from this interview, July 31, 2002, The Hague, the Netherlands.

43. K. Alexa Koenig, Ryan Lincoln, and Lauren Groth, "The Jurisprudence of Sexual Violence," 9, Sexual Violence and Accountability Project Working Paper Series, Human Rights Center, University of California Berkeley, May 2011.

44. Sellers, "The Prosecution," 7. See also Koenig, Lincoln, and Groth, "The Jurisprudence."

45. Koenig, Lincoln, and Groth, "The Jurisprudence," 10.

46. As quoted in ibid., 11.

47. Ibid.

48. Ibid., 21, 12.

49. As quoted in Sellers, "The Prosecution," 21.

50. Ibid., 3.

51. Koenig, Lincoln, and Groth, "The Jurisprudence," 14.

52. Sellers, "The Prosecution."

53. Koenig, Lincoln, and Groth, "The Jurisprudence," 2.

54. Christine M. Chinkin, "Women's International Tribunal on Japanese Military Sexual Slavery," *American Journal of International Law* 95, no. 2 (April 2001): 335–41, 335.

55. Patricia Sellers, "Wartime Female Slavery: Enslavement?," *Cornell International Law Journal* 44 (2011): 115–42, 117, 118.

56. Ibid., 118.

57. Chinkin, "Women's International Tribunal."

58. Rumi Sakamoto, "The Women's International War Crimes Tribunal on Japan's Military Sexual Slavery: A Legal and Feminist Approach to the 'Comfort Women' Issue," *New Zealand Journal of Asian Studies* 3, no. 1 (June 2001): 49–58.

59. See Chinkin, "Women's International Tribunal"; and Sakamoto, "Women's International War Crimes Tribunal."

60. Sakamoto, "Women's International War Crimes Tribunal," 55.

61. Chinkin, "Women's International Tribunal," 337.

62. Ibid., 338.

63. Ibid., 339.

64. Sakamoto, "Women's International War Crimes Tribunal," 57.

Chapter 3. Localizing International Human Rights

1. Charter of Feminist Principles for African Feminists, adopted at the African Feminist Forum, November 15–19, 2006, Accra, Ghana, http://awdflibrary.org/handle/123456789/119. See also Stanlie James, "Remarks for a Roundtable on Feminism," NWSA, Baltimore, MD, 2017, repr. in *Meridians: Feminism, Race, Transnationalism* 18, no. 2 (October 2019): 471–79.

2. Charter of Feminist Principles, 5.

3. Ibid., 8–9.

4. Ibid., 8.

5. "A Black Feminist Statement: The Combahee River Collective 1978," in *Still Brave: The Evolution of Black Women's Studies*, ed. Stanlie M. James, Frances Smith Foster, and Beverly Guy Sheftall (New York: Feminist Press, 2009), 5.

6. Ibid., 6.

7. hooks, *Feminist Theory*, 24.

8. Universal Declaration of Human Rights, adopted by the UN General Assembly, December 10, 1948, GA Res 217A, https://www.un.org/en/universal-declaration-human-rights/index.html.

9. Richard Pierre Claude, "The Right to Education and Human Rights Education," in *Human Rights in the World Community: Issues and Actions*, ed. Richard Pierre Claude and Burns H. Weston (Philadelphia: University of Pennsylvania Press, 2006), 211.

10. United Nations, Human Rights, Office of the High Commissioner, "Human Rights Education and Training," accessed July 8, 2015, www.ohchr.org/EN/Issues/Education/Training/Pages/HREducationTrainingIndex.aspx.

11. Claude, "Right to Education," 215.

12. Eleanor Roosevelt, 1948 speech, as quoted in ibid., 220.

13. Merry, *Human Rights and Gender Violence*, 1.

14. Ayesha Imam, "An Acceptance Speech on Islam and Women's Rights," for the John Humphrey Freedom Award, December 2002.

15. Unless otherwise indicated, all quotes are from my interview with Ayesha Imam, May 25, 2004, New York.

16. Ayesha Imam, personal correspondence to the author, August 18, 2015.

17. For more information on the impact of SAP, see, for example, Eucharia Nwabugo Nwagbara, "The Story of Structural Adjustment Programme in Nigeria from the Perspective of the Organized Labour," *Australian Journal of Business and Management Research* 1, no. 7 (October 2011): 30–41. See also Pamela Sparr, "What Is Structural Adjustment," in *Mortgaging Women's Lives: Feminist Critiques of Structural Adjustment*, ed. Pamela Sparr (London: Zed Books, 1994).

18. Each year WIN would select a broad theme for its national focus, although local chapters also retained the options of focusing on local concerns and continuing work on issues from the previous year(s).

19. Imam, personal correspondence, August 18, 2015.

20. Women Living under Muslim Laws, *Knowing Our Rights: Women, Family, Laws and Customs in the Muslim World* (New Delhi: Zubaan Books, 2006).

21. Imam, "An Acceptance Speech," 2.

22. Known as the Oputa Panel, this commission was established by President Olugegun Obasanjo to investigate gross human rights violations in Nigeria between January 15, 1966, the day that a military coup took control of the government of Nigeria, until May 28, 1999, when Obasanjo became president. The panel was charged with identifying persons and institutions responsible for human rights violations and to recommend appropriate measures to redress past injustices and prevent future violations. See Hakeem O. Yuseuf, "Human Rights Violations Investigation Commission, the Oputa Panel (Nigeria)," in *Encyclopedia of Transitional Justice*, ed. Lavinia Stan and Nadya Nedelsky (New York: Cambridge University Press, 2013), 161–65.

23. The Mock Tribunal was held in Abuja, the capital city, on March 14, 2002. A high-powered panel of judges was selected to listen to the testimony of thirty-three women, and after the judges' deliberations they produced a public policy proclamation on the issue. See "A Mock Tribunal to Advance Changes: The National Tribunal on Violence against Women in Nigeria," by Mufuliat Fijabi, edited by Liam Mahoney, and published in 2004 by the Center for Victims of Torture, accessed June 17, 2015, www.cvt.org. www.newtactics.org.

24. Imam, "An Acceptance Speech," 2.

25. Ibid.

26. Ibid., 3.

27. Ibid.

28. Ibid.

29. Ibid., 4–5.

30. Ibid., 5.

31. Ibid.

32. Unless otherwise indicated, all quotes are from my interview with Loretta Ross, July 8, 2002, Atlanta, Georgia.

33. Zakiya Luna interview of Loretta Ross for the Global Feminisms Comparative Case Studies of Women's Activism and Scholarship, University of Michigan, Ann Arbor, May 22, 2006, 6–7.

34. Ibid., 7.

35. On May 4, 1970, the Ohio National Guard fired on students at Kent State who were protesting the Vietnam War and troops also being sent into Cambodia. Four students were killed and nine were injured. Ten days later, on May 14, 1970, a peaceful demonstration on the Jackson State Campus, a historically Black college in Mississippi, escalated into violence. The police came and shot hundreds of rounds into a women's dormitory on campus. Two men were killed and many others were injured. This incident did not receive the nationwide attention that was focused on Kent State.

36. *The Autobiography of Malcolm X: As Told to Alex Haley* (New York: Ballantine, 1965); Toni Cade (Bambara), ed., *The Black Woman: An Anthology* (1970; repr., New-York: Simon & Schuster 2005).

37. Luna interview of Ross.

38. Ibid., 8.

39. Loretta J. Ross, "African American Women and Abortion: 1800–1970," in *Theorizing Black Feminisms: The Visionary Pragmatism of Black Women*, ed. Stanlie M. James and Abena P. A. Busia (New York: Routledge, 1993).

40. Ibid., 143.

41. Ibid., 142.

42. Luna interview of Ross, 11.

43. bell hooks, *Ain't I a Woman? Black Women and Feminism* (Boston: South End, 1981).

44. Paula J. Giddings, *When and Where I Enter . . . : The Impact of Black Women on Race and Sex in America* (New York: William Morrow, 1984).

45. Luna interview of Ross, 12.

46. Longtime civil rights activist C. T. Vivian was a close friend and confidant of Martin Luther King Jr. In 1963 he was appointed the director of the Southern Christian Leadership Conference.

47. Thomas F. Jackson, *From Civil Rights to Human Rights: Martin Luther King Jr. and the Struggle for Economic Justice* (Philadelphia: University of Pennsylvania Press, 2007), 8. See also Taylor Branch's epic two-volume, Pulitzer Prize–winning biography of King and the civil rights movement: *Parting the Waters: America in the King Years, 1954–63* (New York: Simon & Schuster, 1988) and *At Canaan's Edge: America in the King Years, 1965–68* (New York: Simon & Schuster, 2006).

48. Sally Helgesen, *The Female Advantage: Women's Ways of Leadership* (New York: Currency Doubleday, 1990).

49. At the time of the interview, the Affordable Care Act (Obamacare) had not been enacted.

Chapter 4. Grassroots Praxis

1. Martha F. Davis, "Introduction to Part 1," in *Bringing Human Rights Home: A History of Human Rights in the United States*, ed. Cynthia Soohoo, Catherine Albisa, and Martha F. Davis (Philadelphia: University of Pennsylvania Press, 2007), 4.

2. As quoted in Belinda Robnett, *How Long? How Long? African-American Women in the Struggle for Civil Rights* (New York: Oxford University Press, 1997), 18.

3. Ibid., 20, 13.

4. Other characteristics are that these women become bridge leaders because of the social construction of exclusion rather than because they lack leadership experience; often they are more visible before an organization is formalized because they have initiated an organization and done the groundwork; they operate in the free spaces of movements and organizations and are thus allowed to make connections that formal leaders are unable to make; even though they may hold formal leadership positions in social movements organizations they may still be considered outside the circle of formal leaders. See ibid., 30.

5. Ibid., 21.

6. Loretta J. Ross interview of Linda Burnham, March 18, 2005, for the Voices of Feminism Oral History Project, Sophia Smith Collection, Smith College, Northampton, Massachusetts.

7. Robnett, *How Long?*, 28.

8. For a detailed history of Black women's awakening feminist and Black feminist consciousness, see Kristen Anderson-Bricker, "'Triple Jeopardy': Black Women and the Growth of Feminist Consciousness in SNCC, 1964–75," in *Still Lifting, Still Climbing: African American Women's Contemporary Activism*, ed. Kimberly Springer (New York: New York University Press, 1999), 55.

9. Frances Beale, "Double Jeopardy: To Be Black and Female," in *The Black Woman: An Anthology*, ed. Toni Cade (New York: Washington Square Press, 1969), 121. The essay was reprinted in *Sisterhood Is Powerful: An Anthology of Writings from the Women's Liberation Movement*, ed. Robin Morgan (New York: Vintage Books, 1970).

10. See Anderson-Bricker, "'Triple Jeopardy,'" esp. 60.

11. Ibid., 61.

12. Ibid.

13. Ross interview of Burnham, 19, 22, 21.

14. Ibid., 21–22.

15. Ibid., 21, 29.

16. Ibid., 30.

17. Ibid.

18. Ibid., 31.

19. Unless otherwise indicated, information and quotations are from my interview with Linda Burnham, June 18, 2002, Berkeley, California.

20. Ross interview of Burnham, 38.

21. TANF was a block grant program created by Congress through the Personal Responsibility and Work Opportunity Reconciliation Act of 1996.

22. Ross interview of Burnham, 31, 32.

23. Ibid.

24. Unless otherwise indicated, all the information on Dixon Diallo is from my interview with Dazon Dixon Diallo, July 9, 2002, in Atlanta, Georgia. Dixon felt as if a class divide among Black students at HBCUs may have been a factor in "who participated in the movement and what was on the minds of the really poor 'totally responsible for everybody back home' kind of students who have the same ideology, who have the same fierceness, who have the same need for change but had a different sense of how to be involved in that."

25. Charityt Nebbie, "Byllye Avery: Advocate for African-American Women's Health," *Talk of Iowa*, Iowa Public Radio, September 23, 2015.

26. The final quote in this paragraph is from the Dazon Dixon Diallo interview by Loretta Ross, tape 1, video recording, April 4, 2009, Voices of Feminism Oral History Project.

27. Stina Soderling and Alison R. Bernstein, "Dazon Dixon Diallo: Feminism and the Fight to Combat HIV/AIDS," in *Junctures in Women's Leadership: Social Movements*,

ed. Mary K. Trigg and Alison R. Bernstein (New Brunswick, NJ: Rutgers University Press, 2016), 164–65.

28. Randall Terry founded Operation Rescue, an anti abortion group, in 1986. It was the most aggressive antiabortion group during the 1980s and 1990s. Members demonstrated outside clinics and often incited violence against the doctors and other staff who worked in the clinics. They were frequently arrested. "Operation Rescue," accessed January 25, 2021, https://www.encyclopedia.com/politics/legal-and-political-magazines/operation-rescue.

29. Ross interview of Dixon Diallo, 8.

30. Ibid.

31. Ibid.

32. For a good comprehensive discussion of the Black Women's Health Project and self-help projects, see Evan Hart, "Building a More Inclusive Women's Health Movement: Byllye Avery and the Development of the National Black Women's Health Movement, 1981–1990" (PhD diss., University of Cincinnati, 2012).

33. Ross interview of Dixon Diallo, 24.

34. Ibid.

35. Ibid., 25.

36. Ibid., 24–25.

37. Ibid., 27.

38. See Soderling and Bernstein, "Dazon Dixon Diallo," 173.

39. Ibid.

40. As quoted in ibid., 174.

41. Ross interview of Dixon Diallo.

42. SisterSong is a national collective of sixteen women of color organizations that work on reproductive health issues. With the support of a Ford Foundation grant, they structured a collaborative umbrella organization to collect reproductive health data, to share their experiences in treatment and prevention, and to address the societal factors that impact the reproductive health of women of color. Loretta Ross served as Sister-Song's national coordinator and Dazon Dixon Diallo as SisterLove's president/CEO. SisterLove serves as one of the anchors of the four primary ethnic groups represented in the collective. See Loretta J. Ross, Sarah L. Brownlee, Dazon Dixon Diallo, and Luz Rodriquez, "The 'SisterSong Collective': Women of Color, Reproductive Health and Human Rights," in "The Health of Women of Color," special issue, *American Journal of Health Studies* 17, no. 2 (2001).

43. Loretta Ross, "Understanding Reproductive Justice," November 2006 (updated March 2011), accessed October 21, 2016, www.trustblackwomen.org/our-work/what-is-reproductivejustice.

44. Zakiya Luna and Kristin Luker, "Reproductive Justice," *Annual Review of Law and Social Science*, September 2013, 328, 329, http://lawsocsi.annualreviews.org. See also Dorothy Roberts, "Privatization and Punishment in the New Age of Reprogenetics," *Emory Law Journal* 54 (2005): 1343–60.

45. Ross, "Understanding Reproductive Justice."

46. Asian Communities for Reproductive Justice discussion paper, 2005, quoted in ibid.

47. Ibid.

48. Asian Communities for Reproductive Justice, quoted in ibid.

49. Ibid.

50. Unless otherwise indicated, all information about Jaribu Hill is from my interview with her on June 24, 2002, in Greenville, Mississippi. The chapter epigraph is from "Haunting Mirrors," written and performed by Jaribu Hill on the Asian Culture Night after the third day of hearings at the Women's International War Crimes Tribunal on Japan's Military Sexual Slavery, December 20, 2000, Tokyo, Japan, and included in the final judgment, delivered in The Hague, December 4, 2001.

51. Amílcar Cabral was a leader in the liberation movement in Guinea-Bissau and Cape Verde. The quote is from his speech "History Is a Weapon: National Liberation Culture," February 20, 1970.

52. Title VII of the 1964 Civil Rights Act prohibits employers from discriminating against their employees on the basis of sex, race, color, national origin, and religion. Section 1983 was passed after the Civil War to protect the rights of those people who are deprived of their rights either under the Constitution or under federal laws by persons who are acting "under color of state law." More recently, it has been applied to public sector employees who allege claims of employment discrimination.

53. See the Skadden Fellowship Foundation website, https://www.skaddenfellow ships.org/.

54. Sarah White summary of her remarks from her speech "Voices of Victims," given at the UN World Conference against Racism, Racial Discrimination, Xenophobia and Related Intolerance, Durban, South Africa, August 31–September 7, 2001, and presented at a Durban Review Conference, Geneva, Switzerland, April 20, 2009, https://www.un.org/en/durbanreview2009/pdf/Sarah%20White.pdf.

55. Barbara Ransby, *Ella Baker and the Black Freedom Movement: A Radical Democratic Vision* (Chapel Hill: University of North Carolina Press, 2003), 7.

56. Article 1 of the Thirteenth Amendment to the US Constitution states, "Neither slavery nor involuntary servitude, except as a punishment for crime whereof the party shall have been convicted, shall exist within the United States, or any place subject to their jurisdiction."

57. Article 23 of the Universal Declaration of Human Rights states: "1. Everyone has the right to work, to free choice of employment, to just and favorable conditions of work and to protection against unemployment. 2. Everyone, without any discrimination, has the right to equal pay for equal work. 3. Everyone who works has the right to just and favourable remuneration and ensuring for himself and his family an existence worthy of human dignity, and supplemented, if necessary, by other means of social protection. 4. Everyone has the right to form and to join trade unions for the protection of his interests."

58. What follows is my summary of Sarah White's "Voices of Victims" presentation at the UN World Conference Against Racism, Racial Discrimination, Xenophobia and

Related Intolerance in Durban, South Africa, August 31–September 7, 2001. I attended that presentation in Durban, so this summary includes my own impressions of her speech.

59. "Sarah White's Voice," transcript of UN Voices, April 20, 2009, 1.

60. Ibid., 1–2.

61. Ibid., 2.

62. Ibid.

63. Ibid., 3.

64. Lee Ann Banaszak, *The US Women's Movement in Global Perspective* (Lanham, MD: Rowman & Littlefield, 2006), 320.

Chapter 5. Weaving Together Global Tapestries

1. Ushered in by *The Black Woman: An Anthology*, edited by Toni Cade, a small sampling of that robust literature includes other important anthologies such as *This Bridge Called My Back: Writings by Radical Women of Color*, ed. Cherríe Moraga and Gloria Anzaldúa (Watertown, MA: Persephone Press, 1981); *All the Women Are White, All the Blacks Are Men, but Some of Us Are Brave: Black Women's Studies*, ed. Gloria T. Hull, Patricia Bell Scott, and Barbara Smith (New York: Feminist Press, 1982); and *Home Girls: A Black Feminist Anthology*, ed. Barbara Smith (New York: Kitchen Table Press, 1983).

2. Each government was allotted two passes for their country's nongovernmental representatives. Most countries had several nongovernmental organizations attending the NGO forums, so they had to rotate their two passes through those organizations. The result was that few people who were not representatives of their governments were able to attend more than one session.

3. Unless otherwise indicated, the information included here on Filomina Chioma Steady is from our interview on August 20, 2002, in Madison, Wisconsin.

4. Steady described the sixth form as similar to American junior (community) college but more academically oriented. After primary school, education in Sierra Leone, which is modeled on the British system, guides students from the age of eleven or so into either an academic or vocational stream. Students take a school certificate exam after completing the fifth form to attain the equivalent of a high school diploma. Students with good scores continue into two years of the sixth form, which prepares them to sit for the Higher School Certificate Examination. If successful, students proceed on to college.

5. AAWORD aims to promote the multidimensional development of African people (political, economic, social, cultural, and psychological dimensions). They would engage in "decolonizing research," developing lines of communication between women researchers and with others concerned with Africa's problems around development. They are also committed to promoting action-oriented research and evolving methodologies and research priorities. See UIA Open Yearbook, accessed August 24, 2018, uia .org/s/or/en/1100067689.

6. A/RES/2730I0, United Nations General Assembly, December 18, 1972.

7. See "Introduction: World Conferences," accessed July 19, 2017, www.un.org/geninfo/bp/intro.html.

8. The UN secretariat is the bureaucratic arm of the organization. Under the leadership of the secretary-general, it is the organization that is "on the ground" doing its work, including collecting the statistics and other information to develop reports and to provide background information for world conferences, among other things.

9. Although the Decade for Women ended in 1985, it was felt that there was a need to hold another conference on women five years later to monitor and report on the "Forward-Looking Strategies" that had been produced at the Nairobi conference.

10. Unless otherwise indicated, quotations and additional information about Barbara Phillips were obtained in our interview at the Ford Foundation on May 24, 2004, and during a phone update interview on June 29, 2017.

11. Barbara Phillips, "How I Became a Civil Rights Lawyer," in *Voices of Civil Rights Lawyers: Reflections of the Deep South, 1964–1980*, ed. Kent Springs (Gainesville: University Press of Florida, 2017), 17–27.

12. Ibid., 21.

13. Charles Evers was the elder brother of Medgar Evers, who was assassinated for his work as the field director of the Mississippi NAACP. Evers returned to Mississippi in 1993 after his brother was killed to take over his position with the NAACP. He was elected mayor of Fayette, Mississippi, in 1973, serving until 1981 and then again from 1985 to 1989. He also mounted unsuccessful bids for the governorship in 1971 and the US Senate in 1978.

14. Phillips, "How I Became a Civil Rights Lawyer," 21.

15. Ibid., 22.

16. "Who We Are," Industrial Areas Foundation, accessed January 25, 2021, https://www.industrialareasfoundation.org/.

17. The Loyalist Democratic Party in Mississippi was the successor to the Mississippi Freedom Democratic Party, which had organized and attended the 1968 Democratic Convention to unseat the Mississippi Democratic Party on the basis that it was undemocratic, since Black people had been unable to vote for the representatives. It was at that convention that Fannie Lou Hamer provided riveting testimony before the rules committee about the state of terror that Black people were experiencing living in Mississippi.

18. Phillips, "How I Became a Civil Rights Lawyer," 22.

19. Ibid.

20. The Emergency Land Fund, which also operated in Mississippi, Alabama, and Georgia, sought to educate people to write their wills in a manner so that upon their death the land would not simply be dispersed to all their children. They also tried to help farmers develop methods that would help them earn more income from the land they did own (e.g., pig farming or growing tomatoes, etc.).

21. Phillips, "How I Became a Civil Rights Lawyer," 24.

22. Ibid., 25–26. (One wonders if he, too, was proficient in shorthand!)

23. Ibid., 27.

24. James Loewen and Charles Sallis, *Mississippi: Conflict and Change* (New York: Pantheon Books, 1974; revised 1980). Renowned historian Eric Foner once dubbed Loewen "a one-man historical truth squad" for his impressive body of work focused on setting the historical record straight.

25. Charles Eagles, *Civil Rights, Culture Wars: The Fight over a Mississippi Textbook* (Chapel Hill: University of North Carolina Press, 2017).

26. See *Color of Violence: The INCITE! Anthology*, ed. INCITE! Women of Color against Violence (Durham, NC: Duke University Press, 2016).

27. For more information, see the CREA website, accessed January 25, 2021, https://creaworld.org/.

Chapter 6. Bringing International Human Rights Home

1. Unless otherwise indicated, information on Gay McDougall was obtained from an interview on June 13, 2002, in Washington, DC.

2. At that time, the Atlanta University Center was composed of Atlanta University, Clark College, Morehouse College, Morris Brown College, Spelman College, and the Interdenominational Theology Seminary.

3. "Atlanta Students Sit-in for US Civil Rights, 1960–61," Global Nonviolent Action Database, a project of Swarthmore College, accessed January 25, 2021, nvdatabase.swarthmore.edu/content/atlanta-students-sit-us-civil-rights-1960-1961.

4. Jeva Lange, (PRO)FiLES, "Behind the Struggle to Free South Africa," *Bennington Magazine*, July 6, 2017.

5. Reagan Morris, "The Life and Career of Gay McDougall, Executive Director Global Rights, Partners for Justice," accessed December 16, 2020, https://www.lawcrossing.com/article/442/Gay-McDougall-Executive-Director-Global-Rights-Partners-for-Justice/.

6. Ibid.

7. Ibid.

8. Ibid.

9. Lange, "Behind the Struggle." See also James E. Coleman Jr., "Human Rights Hero: Gay J. McDougall," *ABA Human Rights* 41, no. 2 (2015): 26.

10. Lange, "Behind the Struggle."

11. Lange, "Behind the Struggle."

12. Lange, "Behind the Struggle."

13. Lange, "Behind the Struggle."

14. "Gay J. McDougall" (biography), International Human Rights Law Group, accessed January 25, 2021, hrlawgroup.org/about_ihrlg/bios/gay_mcdougall.asp.

15. "Gay J. McDougall."

16. "About IHRLG," International Human Rights Law Group, accessed November 23, 2018, http://www.hrlawgroup.org/about_ihrlg/letter.asp.

17. Human Rights Watch developed out of the 1978 Helsinki Watch, which was created to monitor the governmental compliance of countries in the Soviet bloc with the Helsinki Accords. Adopting a policy of "naming and shaming," other watches were

developed, including an Americas Watch, Africa Watch, Asia Watch, and Middle Eastern Watch. The organization became formally known as Human Rights Watch.

18. Gay J. McDougall, "Shame in Our Own House," *The American Prospect*, September 20, 2004, prospect.org/article/shame-our-own-home.

19. Ibid.

20. Ibid.

21. Phone interview with Gay McDougall, November 12, 2018.

22. Committee on the Elimination of Racial Discrimination, General Recommendation 25: Gender-Related Dimensions of Racial Discrimination, 56th sess., 2000, UN Doc. A/55/18, annex V (2000), 152, para. 1.

23. Gay McDougall, *The First United Nations Mandate on Minority Issues* (Leiden: Brill Nijhoff, 2016), 3.

24. See Declaration on the Rights of Persons Belonging to National or Ethnic, Religious and Linguistic Minorities, GA Res. 47/135, annex, UN GAOR, 47th sess., supp. no. 49 (vol. 1), UN Doc. 47/49 (vol. 1), December 18, 1992.

25. McDougall, *The First United Nations Mandate*, 12, 4.

26. Ibid., 4.

27. Ibid.

28. International Covenant on Civil and Political Rights, Adopted by the UN General Assembly, December 19, 1966, entry into force March 28, 1976.

29. McDougall, *The First United Nations Mandate*, 8.

30. Ibid., 10.

31. Ibid.

32. Ibid.

33. In 2013 the OAS adopted the Inter-American Convention Against Racism, Racial Discrimination and Related Intolerance and the Inter-American Convention Against All Forms of Discrimination and Intolerance.

34. McDougall, *The First United Nations Mandate*, 10.

35. Ibid., 11.

36. "Leitner Scholar Receives Highest Honor in South Africa for Work against Apartheid," *Fordham Law News*, December 4, 2015.

37. Regan Morris, "The Life and Career of Gay McDougall, Executive Director Global Human Rights, Partners for Justice," accessed January 25, 2021, https://www.lawcrossing.com/article/442/Gay-McDougall-Executive-Director-Global-Rights-Partners-for-Justice/.

Conclusion

1. See Danielle L. McGuire's award-winning book *At the Dark End of the Street: Black Women, Rape and Resistance—a New History of the Civil Rights Movement from Rosa Parks to the Rise of Black Power* (New York: Alfred A. Knopf, 2010).

Index

146–50; and the work of Linda Burnham, 122–29; and the work of Lisa Crooms, 33–36; and the work of Loretta Ross, 77–81, 100–103, 106–14; and the work of Mary McLeod Bethune, 4–5; and the work of Patricia Viseur Sellers, 68–71. *See also* feminism; intersectionality; sexuality

generations of rights, 51–52, 55, 106, 112, 208n1. *See also* civil rights; human rights

Geneva Conventions, 53–54, 58, 62

genocide, 59, 64–69, 195–96

Giddings, Paula, 101

global critical race feminism, 14, 19, 29–31. *See also* critical race feminism; critical race theory (CRT)

Global Critical Race Feminism (Wing), 30

globalization, 9, 32, 127

Global North, 160–62

Global South, 84, 111, 121–22, 136, 160–64

grassroots organizing, 42, 48–49, 81, 117–51, 176, 192

Greenwood, Christopher, 60

Groth, Lauren, 69

Guinier, Lani, 26, 205n13

Hall, David, 37, 206n30

Hamer, Fannie Lou, 142, 168–71, 176, 199, 218n17

Hamilton, Charles, 55

Haradinaj, Ramush, 70

Harper, Conrad, 58

Harris, Angela, 29

Harris, Cheryl, 18

Harris, Elihu, 32–33

Harvard University, 15, 36, 205n13

Hasties, William H., 6

"Haunting Mirrors" (Hill), 150

Hayden, Casey, 119

Helie Lucas, Marieme, 89

Henkin, Louis, 45

Henry, Aaron, 170–71

Herenton, Willie, 168

Heritage Foundation, 110

heterosexism, 35–36, 122, 133. *See also* gender; homophobia; sexuality

Highet, Keith, 23

Hill, Anita, 29

Hill, Jaribu, 11, 117–18, 139–51, 164

Hirohito (emperor), 72

historically Black colleges and universities (HBCUs), 12, 99–100, 139, 167–69, 174, 180–81, 212n35, 214n24, 219n2. *See also* Howard University; *specific institutions*

Hitler, Adolf, 103

HIV/AIDS, 130–36, 139

homophobia, 122, 133. *See also* heterosexism; sexuality

hooks, bell, 31, 79, 101

Howard University, 6–7, 16, 25, 31, 55, 99–100, 204n3, 209n14

How Long? How Long? African-American Women in the Struggle for Civil Rights (Robnett), 118

HRE. *See* human rights

humanitarian law, 51–76. *See also* human rights

human rights: about, 6–12, 83, 208n1; Adrien Wing and, 18–31, 50, 183; Ayesha Imam and, 77–99, 112–16; Barbara Phillips and, 166–78; Black women and, 200–202; Catherine Powell and, 19, 42–50; and critical race feminism, 14, 18–19, 29–41; Dazon Dixon Diallo and, 117–18, 129–38, 151, 176; education, 48–49, 77–80, 99, 106–16, 125; Filomina Steady and, 152–66; Gabrielle Kirk McDonald and, 51, 55–66, 70–76; Gay McDougall and, 106–8, 179–98; generations of, 51–52, 55, 106, 112,

Native Americans. *See* Indigenous
groups
NATO Stabilisation Force (SFOR),
61–63
NBWHP, 33, 102, 130, 134
NCBL, 20–23, 67, 183
NCNW, 4–5
neo-Nazis, 102–5, 110
New York City Human Rights Initiative,
37, 48, 50
Niebuhr, Reinhold, 203n7
Nigeria, 82–87, 91–92, 95–97,
212nn22–23
Nightingale, Florence, 52–53
Nikolić, Dragan, 70
Nimeiry, Gaafar, 23
Northeastern University School of Law,
37, 206n29
NOW, 101–2

OAS, 189, 220n33
Obasanjo, Olugegun, 212n22
Office of the High Commissioner for
Human Rights, 80, 159, 165, 196
Operation Rescue, 131, 215n28
Orangeburg Massacre, 139–40
Organization of American States (OAS),
189, 220n33
Orić, Naser, 70
Our Bodies, Ourselves (Boston Women's
Health Book Collective), 171

Palestinian Liberation Organization
(PLO), 21–25
Parks, Rosa, 199
patriarchy, 16–18, 34–35, 54, 77–79, 88
Patterson, Eva, 32
Patton, Gwen, 120
Pavlovna, Elena, 52
Perdue, Beverly, 206n22
"the personal is political" slogan, 30–31,
99, 113
Phillips, Barbara, 11, 152, 166–78, 183

Phillips, Stephanie, 17
PLO, 21–25
police brutality, 68, 110, 141
polygamy, 28, 205n18
polygyny, 85–86, 97, 205n18
"Position Paper" (King, Hayden), 119
Powell, Catherine, 11, 19, 30–31, 37,
41–50
Powell, Colin, 147
"Problems, Obstacles, and Achievements
of the ICTY" (McDonald), 60
"The Prosecution of Sexual Violence in
Conflict" (Sellers), 71

race: and apartheid, 7, 36, 129, 184–85,
198; and the Black identity, 38–41,
119–20; Black women and civil and
human rights and, 5–13, 50, 120–21,
199–202, 203n5; and critical theory,
14–19, 27–41; and segregation, 4–5,
140, 144, 148–49, 167–68, 179–83;
and voting rights, 56, 107, 169–71,
174, 182; and the work of Adrien
Wing, 19–22, 27–30; and the work of
Barbara Phillips, 167–78; and the
work of Catherine Powell, 44; and the
work of Dixon Diallo, 130–39, 215n42;
and the work of Filomina Steady, 153,
157, 163–65; and the work of Gabrielle
Kirk McDonald, 56–58, 65; and the
work of Gay McDougall, 188–98;
and the work of Goler Teal Butcher,
6–9; and the work of Hope Lewis,
37–41; and the work of Jaribu Hill,
140–50; and the work of Linda
Burnham, 122–29; and the work of
Lisa Crooms, 33–36; and the work of
Loretta Ross, 78–79, 100–113, 137–38,
215n42; and the work of Mary McLeod
Bethune, 3–9. *See also* class; gender;
intersectionality; white supremacy
Race, Racism and American Law (Bell),
16, 26

STANLIE M. JAMES is a professor emerita of African and African American studies and women and gender studies in the School of Social Transformation at Arizona State University. She recently completed a four-year term as the Vice Provost for Inclusion and Community Engagement at ASU. She is also a professor emerita at the University of Wisconsin–Madison in the Department of Afro American Studies and the Women's Studies Program. Her coedited volumes include *Still Brave: The Evolution of Black Women's Studies* (with Frances Smith Foster and Beverly Guy-Sheftall), *Genital Cutting and Transnational Sisterhood: Disputing U.S. Polemics* (with Claire C. Robertson), and *Theorizing Black Feminisms: The Visionary Pragmatism of Black Women* (with Abena P. A. Busia).

Critical Human Rights

www.ingramcontent.com/pod-product-compliance
Lightning Source LLC
Chambersburg PA
CBHW071737270326
41928CB00013B/2711